P9-APM-451

Education and Emancipation

Theory and Practice in a New Constellation

Education and Emancipation

Theory and Practice in a New Constellation

Scott Fletcher

WITHDRAWN

MONTGOMERY COUNTY PUBLIC SCHOOLS
PROFESSIONAL LIBRARY
850 HUNGERFORD DRIVE
ROCKVILLE, MARYLAND 20850

SEP 24 2001

TEACHERS COLLEGE PRESS

Teachers College
Columbia University
New York and London

Published by Teachers College Press, 1234 Amsterdam Avenue, New York, NY 10027

Copyright © 2000 by Teachers College, Columbia University

All rights reserved. No part of this publication may be reproduced or transmitted in any form or by any means, electronic or mechanical, including photocopy, or any information storage and retrieval system, without permission from the publisher.

Chapter 4 contains an edited passage from "Turning in(to) Stories: A Critique of the Postmodern Turn" (Liston & Fletcher, 1992), originally published in *The Review of Education, 14* (1992): 215–222, and used here with the permission of Gordon and Breach Science Publishers (copyright ©1992 by Overseas Publishers Association B.V.).

Library of Congress Cataloging-in-Publication Data

Fletcher, Scott, 1959–
    Education and emancipation : theory and practice in a new constellation / Scott Fletcher : foreword by Ann Diller.
        p.   cm.
    Includes bibliographical references (p.) and index.
    ISBN 0-8077-3927-8 (pbk.)—ISBN 0-8077-3928-6 (cloth)
    1. Educational sociology—United States.   2. Critical pedagogy—United States.   3. Education—United States—Philosophy.   I. Title.

LC191.4.F54 2000
371.11′5—dc21   99-058995

ISBN 0-8077-3927-8 (paper)
ISBN 0-8077-3928-6 (cloth)

Printed on acid-free paper

Manufactured in the United States of America

07 06 05 04 03 02 01 00   8 7 6 5 4 3 2 1

This book is dedicated to my son, Galen,
for his kind heart and generous spirit.

Contents

Foreword

When, in 1966, Nat Hentoff's book *Our Children Are Dying* was published, followed a year later by Jonathan Kozol's *Death at an Early Age: The Destruction of the Hearts and Minds of Negro Children in the Boston Public Schools*, the situations that they described often went ignored, and the issues they raised were just beginning to be acknowledged. Now, decades later, concerns similar to theirs have become the foci for political and theoretical battles throughout the nation. Whatever their ancestral roots, the educational theories that make up the heart of this book have taken their present form in response to these seemingly intractable crises over schooling and the ensuing conflicts over what should be done.

More recently, Nel Noddings posed what she called "an extensive thought experiment." She wrote:

> We will pretend that we have a large heterogeneous family to raise and educate. Our children have different ethnic heritages, widely different intellectual capacities, different physical strengths, and different interests. We want to respect their legitimate differences. At the same time, we think there are some things they all should learn and some other things they should all be exposed to so that they can make well-informed choices. How shall we educate them? (Noddings, 1992, p. xiii)

The pretending is over, and Noddings' question has now moved into an urgent front-and-center position in our national quest for direction in education. In this brilliant and timely book, Scott Fletcher sheds new light on Noddings' question and on some of the most promising competing efforts to come up with a satisfying answer. Here at last is a book for all of us who are troubled both by the trends toward a neo-conservative takeover of public schooling in the United States and also by the seeming inability of other voices to reach beyond the confines of their own constituencies. Fletcher's impressive study rescues us by showing how it is possible for emancipatory educational theories to align themselves so as to present a strong, clear, and practical alternative to the neo-conservative view of schooling. The book makes at least two much-needed contributions to contemporary social and educational thought. First, *Education*

and Emancipation: Theory and Practice in a New Constellation gives us a fasci-
nating, richly informative guided tour across the perplexing skies of current theoretical controversies over schooling in this country. Second,
through astute analysis, constructive critique, and creative realignments,
Fletcher maps out a new vision of complementarity among four contemporary theories: (1) liberalism, (2) critical theory, (3) postmodernism, and
(4) care-based theories. Fletcher makes a persuasive case that no one of
these theories can be a sufficient guide to educational practice if it stands
alone, yet each plays a necessary crucial role as part of Fletcher's "new
constellation."

In a series of in-depth analyses, Fletcher exposes the major fault lines
that lie within each theory and also locates the solid ground needed for
constructing supportive interconnections. In every case Fletcher's analyses are remarkably fair-minded, whether his own position is one of advocacy or of opposition. Both for the reader who comes as a novice to
this territory and for the expert already weary from familiarity with the
details of theoretical controversies over schooling, Fletcher provides lucid
accounts and accessible lines of rigorous reasoning. Those new to these
subjects will find a reliable, easy-to-follow guidebook. Those familiar
with the territory will encounter fresh insights.

Scott Fletcher is well qualified for the tasks he has taken on in this
search for a new constellation to guide education. Not only an astute
social philosopher, Fletcher is also an experienced teacher. He had taught
students from seventh grade through graduate school and his current
position as a teacher educator gives him ample opportunities to practice
navigating by his new constellation as he works with teachers and students in public school classrooms and hallways.

Nat Hentoff's book *Our Children Are Dying* had a true educational
hero, Dr. Elliott Shapiro, the principal of P.S. 119 in central Harlem; the
principal whose words gave Hentoff his title. In his "Author's Note"
Hentoff said that "Elliott Shapiro's way of educating is relevant to all
schools, not only schools in the ghettos." I would say the same of Scott
Fletcher's new constellation. In this book, Fletcher shows us a way of
educating that is relevant to all schools today, a way of educating that can
be "emancipatory" for all students tomorrow.

Ann Diller

Acknowledgments

Special thanks to Ken Howe, a friend and mentor, for his support, encouragement, and advice. I have benefited in many ways from his wise and generous counsel. Special thanks also to Barbara Houston, who read various drafts of this work with great care, patience, and attention to the nuance of philosophical argument. Her support for my work has been unwavering and matched only by the warmth of her friendship. And, finally, special thanks to Ann Diller, who always gave me the added perspective I needed (on everything).

Thanks to other friends and colleagues who provided insightful feedback on various drafts of this work. They are responsible for much that is good and right in it, and they deserve no blame for the errors and infelicities that remain: Margaret Eisenhart, Liza Finkel, Ernie House, Alison Jaggar, Dan Liston, Patrick McQuillan, and Aaron Schutz. Thanks to the anonymous reviewers at Teachers College Press for their suggestions and encouragement, and thanks to Wendy Schwartz for her editorial advice. Thanks to Brian Ellerbeck at Teachers College Press for the considerable expertise he lent in bringing this work to publication. Thanks to Tareth Mitch for handling the production of the book, and thanks to Maureen Marshall and Lisa Canfield, who provided secretarial support.

I especially want to acknowledge the many friends, relatives, and colleagues who contributed to the completion of this project. I crossed a good deal of the country during the course of my writing, from the University of Colorado, to the University of Michigan, and, finally, to my current home at the University of New Hampshire. In all of these travels, I never found myself far from a kind word or warm shoulder. To these people, I give my heartfelt thanks and deepest gratitude: Eleanor Abrams, Mike Andrew, Martha Cohen Barrett, Larry Berlin, Barbara Bleyaert, Grant Cioffi, Ardra Cole, Ellen Corcoran, Katharine Dougherty, Rosebud Elijah, Donald and Connie Finkel, Kate Fletcher, Margaret Fletcher, Maurene Flory, Susan Franzosa, Matthew Goldwasser, Rick Gordon, J. Gary Knowles, Nancy Lawrence, Ron Marx, Joe Onosko, Jean McPhail, Paul Michalec, Andi O'Conor, Annemarie Palinscar, Colleen Presswood, Tom Schram, Aaron Schutz, Bill Wansart, and Janet Wise.

My greatest appreciation goes to Liza Finkel, who never missed a beautiful moonrise, or an opportunity to express her faith in my work. It often made the difference.

1

Introduction

To improve schools, we need educational theories that take seriously the social context in which change takes place (or fails to) and recommendations for classroom practice that make political conflicts over the goals of education explicit. The purpose of this work is to offer a new framework for understanding emancipatory theories of education and their implications for the classroom. There are two specific reasons for my decision to focus on emancipatory theories here: First is the success of recent neo-conservative views on curriculum and pedagogy that constrain the capacity of large groups of students to engage in meaningful decision making about their identities and life-plans; second is the persistent and debilitating fractiousness that exists among emancipatory theorists themselves, a circumstance that is in part responsible for their relative lack of success in formulating effective proposals for educational reform.

Designing a new framework for emancipatory theories is a complex task, and it will take most of this volume to fill in the details of the picture. It may be useful, therefore, to define some of the central terms in the argument, and indicate where each is developed more fully in the chapters that follow.

SOME COMMENTS ON METHOD AND DEFINITIONS OF KEY TERMS

Projects like this one must confront the twin dangers of searching for common bonds among competing theories, only to find some kind of haphazard eclecticism or, perhaps worse, some tendentious reductionism. These are two results I want to avoid. I consider myself a critical theorist, albeit significantly influenced by developing theories of care, and I believe that the neo-Marxist tradition from which critical theory grows is the most adequate conceptual framework of the four I consider. However, this is not the thesis that I wish to argue in this book. Rather, I argue that the differences among emancipatory theories have been overemphasized and have received too much attention among philosophers of education. This divisiveness has diverted energy that might have been better spent overcoming the barriers between theory and practice that continue to represent a significant weakness among emancipatory perspectives. In relation to the educational agenda that has been successfully promoted by neo-conservatives, much more unites emancipatory theories than divides them.

What this situation requires is philosophical analysis that helps us better understand the assumptions and arguments underlying the conflict among emancipatory theories, and a better understanding of how these different views might develop in ways that make them more effective in opposing the neo-conservatives. Because such theorizing can easily become abstract and detached from the actual circumstances of schooling, I focus on issues of curriculum and pedagogy throughout the analysis. This strategy helps ground my arguments in educational practice and circumscribes the analysis of conceptual issues within and among the theories themselves. It is at this intermediate level of theoretical complexity and practical application that I see my attempt to create a more inclusive conception of emancipatory educational theory to have the most value.

Creating a New Constellation of Emancipatory Educational Theories

Richard Bernstein's *The New Constellation: The Ethical-Political Horizons of Modernity/Postmodernity* (1992) is a work that I have found helpful in formulating the general strategy I use in this analysis, a point I acknowledge in the subtitle of this volume. While Bernstein's text is at once both more ambitious in its philosophical goals and more detailed in its analysis of a handful of contemporary philosophers, his assessment of the relationship between modernity and postmodernity is reflected in two important features of the extended argument I present here.

First, much of the current debate among emancipatory educational theorists is based on the same kind of "grand Either/Or" thinking that Bernstein uses to describe partisans in the controversy over modernity and postmodernity. For Bernstein, this opposition is based on extreme renderings, sometimes to the point of parody, of the limits of each position. By exploring the nature of the opposition between a thoroughgoing commitment to foundationalism and postmodernity's apparent (but contested) rejection of any basis for critique in rationality or principled argument, Bernstein pursues the possibility of finding a "third" alternative or intermediate position.

> We seem then to be drawn into a grand Either/Or: *either* there is a rational grounding of the norms of critique *or* the conviction that there is such a rational grounding is itself a self-deceptive illusion. But . . . both of these

extreme alternatives have themselves been subject to sharp criticism. So the question arises, can we avoid these extremes? Is there some third way of understanding critique that avoids—passes between—the Scylla of "groundless critique" and the Charybdis of rationally grounded critique that "rests" upon illusory foundations? (Bernstein, 1992, p. 8, emphasis in original)

This is not unlike the situation that currently exists among emancipatory educational theorists, in both the tone and substance of their engagement. Although there have been some useful attempts to engage advocates of other positions in productive dialogue, many of the same conflicts that Bernstein tries to mediate in his analysis underlie a set of fundamental and unproductive oppositions among emancipatory theories in education. What we need is a way to look beyond the current impasse, a way to frame the central issues of the debate that encourages dialogue rather than entrenched opposition. But more still needs to be said about the nature of these conflicts and about how the analysis will proceed.

The second aspect of Bernstein's work that I want to emulate here is the general strategy he takes up in response to the either/or dilemma(s) presented in the debate over modernity and postmodernity. The strategy he pursues, drawing on the work of Martin Jay, aims at creating a "new constellation" or framework for understanding the relationship of moral and political theories that currently exist in opposition to one another in this debate. Quoting Jay, Bernstein (1992) describes the concept of a constellation as "a juxtaposed rather than integrated cluster of changing elements that resist reduction to a common denominator, essential core, or generative first principle" (p. 8). One proceeds with such an analysis through sympathetic but careful critique of each position, with a ready eye for points of possible interconnection or mutual support. It is crucial to see that the goal of this process is "to do justice to both elements, without succumbing to the illusion that they can finally be integrated" (Bernstein, 1992, p. 309). Similarly, the goal of my analysis is *not* to reduce or integrate all emancipatory theories into one all-encompassing perspective. Aside from the unwieldiness (to put it mildly) of such an endeavor, it would quite likely fall prey to the eclecticism or tendentiousness I warned against earlier.

Instead, my goal is to draw a systematic picture of the relationships that exist among emancipatory theories, for the purpose of demonstrating their undeveloped potential as mutually reinforcing and complementary approaches to educational practice. This calls for a selective, rather than comprehensive, treatment of current emancipatory perspectives, emphasizing scholarship that rests firmly within the boundaries of each approach (without, of course, ignoring new and exploratory ventures). I make no claim that the scholars I include here represent *all* proponents of their general orientations, nor is such a claim necessary (indeed, I doubt it is even possible). I do argue, however, that *all* emancipatory perspectives can benefit in *some* way from the conceptual tools provided in the new constellation. The potential of this work rests in the potential for shared insights it develops and the guidance it provides for implementing emancipatory school practices.

Autonomy and the New Constellation

The new constellation I propose revolves around an expanded notion of autonomy as central to the goals of emancipatory theory and practice. From this start, it is important to acknowledge that no singular or consistent interpretation of autonomy exists across the disparate approaches to political and educational philosophy discussed in this work; indeed, significant disagreements exist even within the philosophical traditions represented here. While it no doubt would be useful to sort and categorize these different uses of autonomy for other reasons, it is not necessary to take up such an ambitious project here. As in my description of the new constellation above, I make no claims to offer a comprehensive account of autonomy to which all emancipatory theories owe their allegiance. Rather, what I have in mind here is to use a suitably elaborated concept of autonomy as a common resource on which emancipatory theories may draw, albeit in different ways, to establish connections that are both complementary and reinforcing.

As a starting point, the traditional interpretation of autonomy as self-governance, self-legislation, or the capacity to make and carry out decisions unencumbered by arbitrary external constraints, is not without appeal or utility. For political philosophers who have explored this view, obstacles to autonomy can take many forms, from prison bars to laws that limit or curtail self-expression. The common result of these constraints is that they prevent individuals from achieving desired outcomes or enacting their plans for the future. Thus, understanding the nature of oppression as a limitation on meaningful choice requires a theoretical account of how choice is enabled and constrained in society, or, put another way, it requires an account of the relation between individual agency and social context.

While the traditional view of autonomy as self-governance, rooted in the uncoerced expression and pursuit of individual preferences, is certainly present among the theories represented in the new constellation, this view is only a first step in understanding how autonomy might be used as a basis for elaborating emancipatory approaches and the connections among them; there is much more to say about the qualities of our collective association and how social relations affect the capacity of individuals to make choices and pursue particular ends. Without elaborating the influence of social context on autonomy, the way social affiliation shapes thought and action, the concept of autonomy is too thin and fails to help guide emancipatory movements (in and outside of education). As Benjamin Barber suggests, what we need is a more socially contextualized way of understanding what it means to choose freely, an account that is embedded in the context of history and community. Such a view would go well beyond the kind of noninterference that has often been associated with autonomy.

> Metaphysically, freedom may appear as abstract indeterminism: My actions are not caused by anything external to me, and hence, because undetermined, are free. No one has a gun to my head; no manacles shackle my hands. . . . Yet psychologically and politically, freedom is relational and depends on a nexus of social linkages, and when it comes to the rest of our behavior, we assume richer meanings for freedom. My actions are chosen by me in response to a communal world of values and life plans that I share with others, and in whose determination I may ideally participate. . . . When liberty is contextualized as a feature of identity and history, it no longer appears as synonymous with deracination. (Barber, 1992, p. 26)

This is not, of course, a new notion. We might just as well have appealed to John Dewey in this context, especially to *The Public and Its Problems* (1980/1927). In this well-known work, Dewey argues for the merits of a community that places its highest value on the capacity of individuals to learn, grow, and pursue their interests in the company of others. Dewey (1980/1927) writes, "Liberty is that secure release and fulfillment of personal potentialities which take place only in rich and manifold association with others: the power to be an individualized self making a distinctive contribution and enjoying in its own way the fruits of association" (p. 150). The recognition that individual choices and life-plans depend for their meaning on the social context in which they are pursued suggests a central starting point for exploring the relationships of emancipatory theories of education in the new constellation. What we need is an interpretation of autonomy that can support and sustain our understanding of how schools work in a social context where the actions of individuals are always conditioned by a complex network of conflicts involving power, status, and identity.

My account of autonomy and the role it plays in the new constellation is based on the insights I draw from each of the four emancipatory theories considered here: liberalism, critical theory, postmodernism, and caring. This argument turns on my elaboration of *critical consciousness* and *authenticity* as complementary aspects of autonomy and, thus, of an education for autonomy. My strategy for creating a new constellation of emancipatory theories involves demonstrating the complementarity of critical consciousness and authenticity, even their mutual dependence, in spite of their sources in putatively oppositional emancipatory approaches. I say a bit more below about how I use autonomy as a foundation for the new constellation, with the understanding that these points are developed in much greater detail in the chapters that follow.

Autonomy as Critical Consciousness and Authenticity

In creating the new constellation, I argue that critical consciousness can be used to identify and elaborate an important common ground between liberalism and critical theory, which I group together under the heading of "universalist" emancipatory perspectives. It can be argued that the historical and conceptual roots of universalist theories lie in the Enlightenment, because these views tend to share an emphasis on abstract, rational, and generalizable accounts of the individual in society. These approaches frequently rely on universal moral principles to guide or assess human conduct, and the explanations they offer of human behavior and the nature of society are held to be applicable across time and culture. Prominent historical examples of this tradition include Rousseau's general will, Kant's categorical imperative, Mill's utilitarianism, and Marx's historical materialism.

Autonomy as critical consciousness represents a capacity for decision making that draws on the strengths of universalist perspectives by taking into account how social structures (like race, class, gender, and sexual orientation, for example) enable and constrain the kinds of choices individuals can exercise in society. The extent to which individuals can act autonomously in this sense will depend in part on the scope, quality, and potential outcomes of choices available in a particular social context, which is to say that it will depend on how prevailing social structures affect (mediate) the choices individuals can make in a particular time and place. This is crucial for emancipatory educational theorists because schools are often places that restrict rather than expand the meaningful choices available to students.

Schools inhibit or constrain the development of critical consciousness when, for example, their organizational patterns and instructional practices reinforce deeply embedded forms of exclusion or stereotyping (based on racism, classism, sexism, and heterosexism, for example), thus disempowering students by constraining the decisions they can make about their identities and life-plans. To explain and, ultimately, to change these conditions requires a conception of autonomy that helps us understand how schools enable and constrain the capacity of students to make healthy and productive decisions about their lives, and how changes in the way schools work might expand this capacity for *all* students. Critical consciousness helps identify a common commitment to autonomy among universalist approaches like liberalism and critical theory.

I appeal to authenticity in my analysis of postmodernism and caring, as a way of showing how these "particularist" emancipatory perspectives can be connected in a more complementary and mutually reinforcing manner. Particularist theories reject the abstract, rational, and generalizable, in favor of a focus on the personal, local, and relational. Particularist approaches are relatively new compared with universalist theories and often find their starting point in a critique of the universalist perspective. Particularist theories draw on qualities of individual experience to describe the implications of choices made within relationships, communities, and institutions. Advocates of such views tend to be especially interested in how individuals respond to others, how these responses are shaped by the concrete circumstances of relationships, and how social or institutional norms shape (regulate) behavior in a specific social context. Particularist theorists generally place high value on the irreducible diversity of human experience and thus on the need to acknowledge multiple forms of identity, relationship, and community.

I use autonomy as authenticity to establish some common ground among particularist theories like postmodernism and caring. Authenticity is a form of autonomy rooted in our experience of uniqueness and originality; it is expressed through efforts to create a sense of self in the "local" context of our relationships with others or, put another way, in communities where individuals find genuine recognition and reciprocity. Recognition and reciprocity suggest both an awareness of what it is that makes individuals who they are and a constructive form of engagement with the needs and desires that follow from this awareness. The success of this process depends on the extent to which individuals can develop plans and projects that meet their own needs, as well as the extent to which these individual projects can be shared and collaboratively pursued with others. On this view, it is essential for schools to develop autonomy as authenticity because it helps students to create and explore a wider range of meaningful choices in their lives, especially as these choices emerge in and through relations with others.

The implications of strengthening the connection between critical consciousness and authenticity are important for emancipatory educational theories. As the relationship between these two aspects of autonomy is more clearly articulated, the once formidable boundary between universalist and particularist perspectives will become more permeable. Looking for this common direction gives us a better chance of overcoming differences that have in the past inspired more polemics than productive dialogue. What we have to gain from this analysis is a more coherent and consistent set of strategies for guiding emancipatory school reform.

HOW THE ARGUMENT IS ORGANIZED

In Chapter 2, I situate neo-conservative and emancipatory perspectives in their conflict over the direction and goals of public schooling. In describing the neo-conservative approach to educational policy and practice, I focus on two issues: the primacy of disciplinary knowledge and the role of culture in the curriculum. In the section on emancipatory theories, I offer a brief overview of the four traditions treated in this analysis, for readers who might benefit from a quick reminder about the central concepts and contemporary representatives of these views. I then survey a number of arguments, common among emancipatory theorists, made against the neo-conservative position. This effort to situate some of the most common critiques made by emancipatory theorists aims at establishing a preliminary sense of their potential for a more coherent and consistent opposition to the neo-conservatives than exists at present. This general introduction to emancipatory theories gives way, in subsequent chapters, to a much closer analysis of the arguments offered by each view and their relation to the two aspects of autonomy described above.

Chapters 3 and 4 are similar in their purpose and organization. I analyze universalist perspectives in Chapter 3 and particularist perspectives in Chapter 4, focusing on the strengths and weaknesses of each as a philosophical foundation for emancipatory theories of education. The chapters themselves are divided into sections according to the representative approaches considered: liberalism and critical theory in Chapter 3, postmodernism and caring in Chapter 4. I look at the general relationship between moral/political theories and the educational theories that have applied their insights, noting how each holds out certain problems and promises for the development of emancipatory educational theory. I am measured in the criticisms I offer of all four competing theories, but argue nonetheless that no one of these approaches, by itself, provides a satisfactory basis for emancipatory schooling. At the end of each chapter, I use the appropriate aspect of autonomy (critical consciousness for universalist theories, authenticity for particularists) to articulate the common strengths of the perspectives considered, showing how critical consciousness and authenticity function as the twin polestars of the new constellation.

In Chapter 5, I begin to fill in the details of the new constellation. Although significant differences persist between universalist and particularist perspectives, assessing their contributions in relation to critical consciousness and authenticity provides a basis for identifying a mutually reinforcing pattern in both theory and practice. Using examples of educational problems that confront emancipatory educators, I argue that regardless of our initial starting point in the new constellation (i.e., with a universalist or particularist approach), we are drawn back into a consideration of the complementary quality of autonomy. To emphasize this point, the first two sections of the chapter mirror each other in their structure: The first begins with universalist perspectives and demonstrates the necessity of including particularist perspectives (i.e., it begins with critical consciousness and demonstrates the need for authenticity); the second section reverses the direction of the analysis, moving from particularist to universalist perspectives (i.e., it begins with authenticity and demonstrates the need for critical consciousness). In the final section of Chapter 5, I consider the role of social structure and community as two concepts that are essential for emancipatory education and are profitably elaborated in the new constellation.

Chapter 6 focuses on the relationship between classroom teaching and autonomy. In the first section, I describe and critique the constraining effects schools often have on the capacity of students to develop and exercise autonomy. This assessment follows, in part, from a return to the narrow and exclusionary approach to curriculum exemplified in the neoconservative agenda and the disempowering pedagogical approaches associated with it. I then focus on the development of instructional practices that nurture the capacity for autonomy in students. I argue that treating autonomy as a primary goal of emancipatory schools requires a more constructivist, participatory, community-oriented, and socially conscious approach to the decisions we make about what and how to teach in public schools. I consider three pedagogical approaches that support emancipatory practice in the classroom. These examples include the reconstruction of subject matter in the social context of experience, culturally relevant teaching, and the pedagogical potential of narrative. Throughout the chapter, I draw on the insights of educational researchers, school reformers, and classroom teachers to fuel the development of emancipatory approaches to instruction.

In Chapter 7, the conclusion, I review the new constellation as a

framework for understanding, developing, and implementing emancipatory theories of education. I reconsider the general argument mapped
out in the analysis and reassert two of its central claims: first, that the
new constellation provides a more effective basis for opposing the neo-
conservative agenda that constrains the capacity for autonomy in a vast
number of public school students; and second, that the new constellation
makes significant progress in reorienting the current pattern of conflict
and contradiction among emancipatory theories, offering in its place
a more complementary and mutually supportive set of relationships
among these perspectives.

2

Situating the Conflict Between Neo-Conservative and Emancipatory Educational Theories

The position taken by neo-conservatives is especially important to consider at the beginning of this analysis because of the powerful influence it has had on contemporary educational policy and practice. Advocates of this view have influenced the way schools operate on an institutional level, through legislated curriculum content and standardized assessment procedures, and they have affected classroom instruction more indirectly, but just as profoundly, through the rationalization of instructional norms that serve these goals (Apple, 1993, 1996; Beyer & Liston, 1996; Shor, 1992). While diversity exists among neo-conservative theorists, as among advocates of any view, their collective capacity to direct educational policies and practice in the direction described below has been striking.

THE NEO-CONSERVATIVE APPROACH TO EDUCATIONAL POLICY AND PRACTICE

From the perspective of emancipatory theorists, what distinguishes neo-conservative views on education is their promotion of falsely objectified and depoliticized disciplinary knowledge at the expense of diverse student experience, and a monolithic set of exclusionary cultural values at the expense of critical reflection. Emancipatory theorists are especially concerned about the damaging forms of pedagogy that go along with these educational commitments, including instructional practices that aim, often quite explicitly, at diminishing or excluding key dimensions of student identity, social experience, and political critique from the classroom. These two key aspects of the neo-conservative approach will serve as focal points of the analysis, because in them lie educational policies and practices that radically constrain the development of autonomy in students and give emancipatory theorists good reason to search for common grounds of opposition.

The Neo-Conservative Critique of Experience and the Primacy of Disciplinary Knowledge

A wide variety of neo-conservatives have traced the shortcomings of our present schools to the progressive movement in education, and often to John Dewey in particular. While these criticisms are sometimes presented as if progressive reforms were substantively the same as whatever happened during "the 1960s" in American education, and in the broader society as well, there are a number of specific arguments that come to be repeated in a variety of texts. A key aspect of the arguments made against the progressive education movement concerns the role of experience and the claim, commonly made by progressives, that teachers should recognize, honor, and integrate the diverse experiences of students into the everyday practices of teaching and learning in the classroom. Another way of making this claim is to say that progressives support the view that decisions about curriculum and pedagogy must take place in relation to the experiences that help define the identity and life-plans of students in any given educational context.

Attention to experience and interest in schools is an obstacle to learning valuable content. An important attempt to repudiate the role that experience might play in education has come in response to the efforts of progressive educators to alter the relationship between the student and the school curriculum. Neo-conservatives have criticized progressive education by claiming that it encourages teachers to rely on "spontaneous expressions" of interest by students, and that this reliance limits the pursuit of challenging intellectual questions and diverts instruction away from substantive academic content. Chester Finn (1991), a policy analyst and director of the Educational Excellence Network, suggests that the weakness of this approach lies in the "adversarial" relationship that exists between student experience in and outside the classroom.

> If we settle for spontaneous interest and intrinsic enjoyment as motivators for children to learn more in school, we'll find ourselves competing with some potent adversaries. For how many youngsters do we really think we can make algebra more seductive than television, chemistry more beguiling than rock music, and literature more alluring than romping with their pals? (p. 126)

William Bennett, Secretary of Education under Ronald Reagan, makes a similar argument based on his observation of historical changes in American schooling. For Bennett, the "cultural deconstruction of our schools" is rooted in the "confusion and diffidence" Americans experienced during the 1960s. In response to this cultural crisis, Bennett argues, schools moved away from curricula organized around traditional subject-matter definitions, experimenting instead with approaches that emphasized thematic, interdisciplinary, or experiential structures. Bennett's (1992) contempt for these approaches is evident in the following passage, especially in the examples he provides as self-evident parody:

> English, history, math, and science gave way to a curriculum lacking substance, coherence, or consistent structure; it was replaced by faddish, trivial, and intellectually shallow courses. If you give the average fifteen-year-old the choice of trigonometry or, say, "Rock and Roll as Poetry" and "Baja Whale Watch," many will opt to take the latter—not because they're stupid or bad kids, but simply because they're teenagers. (p. 53)

These arguments reflect a distinction that neo-conservatives often make between the experiences of students outside of school and what the proper "substance" of instruction ought to be. Finn and Bennett worry that the things students are *really* interested in are not relevant or conducive to education, and both emphasize the distance of student experience from the true subject matter of school, which, for them, is constituted by the traditional academic subject areas.

From these judgments about the distance between the legitimate concerns of schools and the experience and interests that students bring with them to the classroom, neo-conservatives draw the conclusion that education necessarily involves a form of external imposition, an imposition that originates in, and is legitimated by, the disciplinary (i.e., subject-matter) authority of teachers. Finn, for instance, suggests that we "refrain from pressing children to learn" at the risk of leaving them unprepared for life's challenges (Finn, 1991, p. 126). He believes that the most worthy goals of education are likely to be met by more direct, or teacher-centered, forms of instruction.

Thus, a key proposition defended by neo-conservatives is that disciplinary knowledge, which rests in teachers and texts, should be the fundamental organizing principle of curriculum. Bennett's *James Madison High School* (1987), for example, is dominated by diagrams of a "four-year plan," with course descriptions and vignettes of schools and teachers whose programs serve as examples. Course titles reflect standard disciplinary divisions between content areas (American Literature, Western

Civilization, Art History, etc.), and the descriptions offered are basically lists of the texts and concepts to be covered. E. D. Hirsch's contribution in *Cultural Literacy* (1987a) is similar: an alphabetical appendix (over 60 pages long, with a book-length version published separately) entitled "What Literate Americans Know." Hirsch subsequently published a series, beginning with *What Your First-Grader Needs to Know: Fundamentals of a Good First-Grade Education* (1993), the logical progression of which is apparent. Bennett and Hirsch offer these documents as if they are based on more or less easily agreed-upon selection criteria, and leave it to schools to put on whatever final touches they require to "adapt to local circumstances" (Bennett, 1987, p. 3).

Attention to experience and interest in schools is an obstacle to sound moral development. Allan Bloom takes the critique of experience in education a step further when he considers the implications of progressivism not just for the intellectual or cognitive growth of students, but for their moral reasoning and moral development as well. He argues that the liberal/progressive focus on human diversity, or the sense in which experience provides multiple starting points for social endeavors like education (and politics as well, one might add), has led us away from a concern for "natural rights" as the "fundamental basis of unity and sameness" (Bloom, 1987, p. 27) and toward an insidious form of moral relativism. The political and educational emphasis on what he calls "openness" (to other forms of experience) leaves no place for "fundamental principles" or "moral virtues."

> Liberalism without natural rights, the kind that we knew from John Stuart Mill and John Dewey, taught us that the only danger confronting us is being closed to the emergent, the new, the manifestations of progress. No attention had to be paid to the fundamental principles or the moral virtues that inclined men to live according to them. To use language now popular, civic culture was neglected. And this turn in liberalism is what prepared us for cultural relativism. (Bloom, 1987, pp. 29–30)

Bloom's critique suggests that the experience of individuals must be understood and assessed relative to fundamental principles or virtues, which do not vary from one circumstance to the next, and that we miseducate students when we encourage them (and their teachers) to think of individual experience as constituting legitimate (and multiple) educational starting points.

Bennett, in his essay "Moral Literacy and the Formation of Character" (1988), describes an instructional approach that fits nicely with

Bloom's critique. Here Bennett (1988) appropriates Hirsch's concept of cultural literacy for the purpose of describing moral education.

> As Professor E. D. Hirsch has pointed out, being literate entails more than recognizing the forms and sounds of words. It is also a matter of building up a body of knowledge enabling us to make sense of the facts, names, and allusions cited by an author. . . . So it is with "moral literacy." If we want our young people to possess the traits of character we most admire, we must teach them what those traits are. They must learn to identify the forms and content of those traits. (p. 30)

Bennett (1988) argues that instead of discussing the "great, difficult, controversial disputes of the day" (including "nuclear war, abortion, creationism, or euthanasia"), we would be better off providing "familiar accounts of virtue and vice with which our young people should be familiar" (pp. 32–33). Bennett's examples are generally historical anecdotes or plainly moralistic fables aimed at "preserving the principles, the ideals, and the notions of greatness we hold dear" (p. 33). As he says in a later essay,

> If we want our children to know about honesty, we should teach them about Abe Lincoln walking three miles to return six cents and, conversely, about Aesop's shepherd boy who cried wolf. If we want them to know about courage, we should teach them about Joan of Arc, Horatius at the bridge, and Harriet Tubman and the Underground Railroad. If we want them to know about persistence in the face of adversity, they should know about the voyages of Columbus, and the character of Washington during the Revolution and Lincoln during the Civil War. And our youngest should be told about the Little Engine That Could. (Bennett, 1992, pp. 59–60)

Bennett's point is not that, pedagogically, it would be more effective to avoid intractable moral dilemmas in favor of more pragmatic examples in order to instruct students in the process of moral reasoning. Rather, the primary goal of this effort is to achieve a rather straightforward form of cultural transmission in which students grasp values by imitating (memorizing?) famous historical examples.

Displacing interest and experience with a common curriculum. One way of summarizing this aspect of neo-conservative educational policy is to point out that for each of these theorists and policy makers, individual experience is an obstacle to be overcome through schooling, rather than a starting point or resource for instruction: Finn and Bennett argue that one cannot begin with student experience and get to appropriate educational substance; Bloom and Bennett argue that one cannot begin with experience and get to a place where moral judgments that extend beyond individual taste or preference can be made.

Issues of experience, especially as they help define a student's (or any individual's) identity, figure prominently in the accounts offered by emancipatory theorists. As we will see, emancipatory theorists aim at exposing the ways schools constrain the capacity of students to envision alternatives for themselves and society that lie outside the dominant forms and patterns promoted by existing social structures. This critical dimension is present in each of the theories considered here. Emancipatory educational theorists also support the idea that paying attention to individual experience, in a variety of ways, is crucial for positive educational outcomes. These positive outcomes involve growth through a combination of self-reflection, socially contextualized content, and collaborative inquiry with others. Before going on to look at some of these common characteristics of emancipatory theories, however, it is important to consider another aspect of the neo-conservative agenda that is central to the conflict with emancipatory theorists.

Neo-Conservatives and the Role of Cultural Identity in Education

The debate over multicultural education has been joined by many scholars from across the academic spectrum, and the conversation over its meaning and significance has been heated. For the purposes of this analysis, I focus on four arguments that have been made by neo-conservatives with respect to multicultural education. Together, these arguments have been used to diminish or exclude issues of cultural diversity from the public school curriculum, thereby marginalizing important issues of identity for minority students. It is important to note that, while I do not pursue it in this chapter, arguments similar to the ones described below have been used by neo-conservatives in response to challenges made by feminists regarding the patriarchal assumptions and practices that exist in schools. I pursue these parallels more explicitly in Chapters 3 and 4.

The curriculum of American schools should be based on American culture. Neo-conservatives widely agree on the proposition that the curriculum of American schools should be rooted in a clear sense of American culture and history. The advantages they claim for this curriculum orientation vary, from providing essential background knowledge for all citizens, to establishing a coherent social and moral fabric for the nation. E. D. Hirsch (1987a), for example, argues that curricular content is justified first and foremost as a matter of competence in communication.

Cultural literacy [is] the network of information that all competent readers possess. It is the background information, stored in their minds, that enables them to take up a newspaper and read it with an adequate level of comprehension, getting the main point, grasping the implications, relating what they read to the unstated context which alone gives meaning to what they read. (p. 2)

Others, like William Bennett (1992), hold that the purpose of a curriculum rooted firmly in American culture and history is to bind our nation together or, to use one of his more startling metaphors, to defend the body politic from infection by foreign "values and attitudes."

One of the things that has kept America from fragmentation (as is happening in Canada), dissolution (as is happening in the Soviet Union), and even breaking up into warring nationalities (as has happened in Lebanon and Yugoslavia) is that we share a common culture. It is our civic glue. Our common culture serves as a kind of immunological system, destroying the values and attitudes promulgated by an adversary culture that can infect our body politic. . . . One vital instrument for the transmission of the common culture is our educational system, and we need to ensure that our schools meet that responsibility. (p. 195)

Despite their various starting points and the special emphasis they give to particular points, neo-conservatives stand together in their conviction that a coherent sense of American culture exists and that it can guide (indeed, they propose that it should determine) the choices we make about what schools should teach.

But even while such confidence pervades neo-conservative writing, there is also an uneasiness about the nature and implications of pluralism (of various sorts) for education. While virtually all of those who support the primacy of American culture in education argue that it begins with a pluralist conception of democracy, a number of neo-conservatives respond with a surprising kind of *real politik* to the criticisms expressed by minority groups who object that they have been marginalized from this mainstream. Arthur Schlesinger (1992), for example, who is a firm believer in making the evils of racism and slavery clear to all history students, nonetheless offers the following defense of history textbooks that clearly reflect an Anglocentric perspective:

The Anglocentric domination of schoolbooks was based in part on unassailable fact. For better or for worse, American history has been shaped more than anything else by British tradition and culture. Like it or not, as Andrew Hacker, the Queens political scientist, puts it, "For almost all this nation's history, the major decisions have been made by white Christian men." To deny this perhaps lamentable but hardly disputable fact would be to falsify history. (p. 53)

E. D. Hirsch (1987a) provides a similar, albeit more global, justification.

> Although nationalism may be regrettable in some of its worldwide political effects, a mastery of national culture is essential to mastery of the standard language in every modern nation. This point is important for educational policy, because educators often stress the virtues of multicultural education. Such study is indeed valuable in itself; it inculcates tolerance and provides a perspective on our own traditions and values. But however laudable it is, it should not be the primary focus of national education. It should not be allowed to supplant or interfere with our schools' responsibility to ensure our children's mastery of American literate culture. The acculturative responsibility of the schools is primary and fundamental. (p. 18)

These apologies for an emphasis on American culture will be important to consider from the point of view of what Gloria Ladson-Billings (1994) calls "culturally relevant teaching," a pedagogy and curriculum orientation that aims at challenging the goals and advantages of a curriculum based on an Anglo- or Eurocentric interpretation of American culture.

Multicultural education is based on an attempt to politicize the curriculum. Based in part on the preceding account of American culture and its role in defining the curriculum, neo-conservatives argue that advocates of multicultural education illegitimately "politicize" teachers' efforts to prepare students for a successful future in society. The efforts neo-conservatives are most concerned about here are those that aim at helping students identify, analyze, and resist systematic forms of oppression (like racism), by making explicit connections between individual identity and the structural inequalities that exist in society. The position that neo-conservatives frequently defend in this regard suggests that, while teachers are responsible for presenting American history "objectively" (e.g., recognizing that slavery existed in this country), they must *not* emphasize race as a central aspect of identity or as a structural factor in the distribution of power, status, or opportunity in society. William Bennett (1992), for example, argues that, while we should consider American history in its "totality," this process excludes giving any special recognition to the role played by race in the construction of identity and prohibits the kind of radical social critiques that often are dismissed by neo-conservatives as "distortion[s] of American history."

> We should insist on honesty in telling about this country and its history. . . .
> But for many other advocates of a multicultural—or more precisely, "Afro-
> centric"—curriculum, the purpose is the politicization of the curriculum, the
> promulgation of cultural myths, the distortion of American history, and the
> primacy of ethnic and racial thinking (the "new tribalism" as it's been
> called). In this version, identity is reduced to ethnicity; identity is deter-
> mined by race. (p. 194)

Neo-conservatives are concerned that schools will (or have) become
"political" in the sense that students are allowed (indeed, encouraged)
to critically assess the forms of knowledge traditionally dispensed in
schools and to question whether this "official knowledge" (Apple, 1993)
truly represents the interests of all groups in society. The prospect of such
inquiry seems especially repugnant to neo-conservatives when they consider that existing forms of curriculum might be contested by whole
groups of students who experience American culture very differently
from their teachers and from the authors of their textbooks. As Diane
Ravitch (1990), an educational historian and former Assistant Secretary
of Education under George Bush, points out, a successful policy of multicultural education might open up the question of what common purposes our public schools are really meant to serve.

> Demands for "culturally relevant" studies, for ethnostudies of all kinds, will
> open the classroom to unending battles over whose version is taught, who
> gets credit for what, and which ethno-interpretation is appropriate. . . . The
> spread of particularism throws into question the very idea of American pub-
> lic education. (p. 351)

In response to this perceived attempt at politicization, neo-
conservatives have offered counterproposals that share a common thread:
Virtually all represent some kind of return to a technical-professional approach to determining what should be taught in our schools. Neo-
conservatives often suggest that questions about the curriculum should
be answered by panels of "experts" who lay claim to their educational
authority through strong disciplinary qualifications. While Bennett often
writes as though competent educators could hardly disagree about the
broad contours of a sound educational program, Hirsch is more explicit
in his writings. His idea is that a group of culturally qualified experts (the
most "literate" of our society) should rule on these matters of educational
policy. He writes:

> There can be no substitute for informed judgments by educated adults re-
> garding the most important contents to be taught to children. If we as a

nation decide that we want our children to possess mature literacy, there is no substitute for asking literate persons collectively to decide upon the contents required for mature literacy. After we make that determination, we need to develop an effective sequence of those core contents and effectively present them during the 13 years of schooling. (Hirsch, 1987b, pp. 69–70)

The remedies suggested by Hirsch and other neo-conservatives deflect or suppress disputes over curricular content by assuming the cultural agreement on which their prescriptions rest. As we will see, emancipatory theorists argue that this strategy obscures and mystifies the role played by members of the dominant culture in defining what knowledge should be taught in schools and gives the neo-conservative agenda a false sense of commonsense restoration or "depoliticization" of the curriculum.

Multicultural education is an obstacle to integrating minority students into society. In response to calls that more attention be paid to issues of cultural diversity, neo-conservatives have become more explicit in their support for educational practices aimed at assimilating minority students into what they perceive as the mainstream of American culture. Consider Arthur Schlesinger's (1992) summary of, and response to, a widely contested multicultural education initiative in New York.

Students, the report recommended, should be "continually" encouraged to ask themselves what their cultural heritage is, why they should be proud of it, "why should I develop an understanding of and respect for my own culture(s), language(s), religion, and national origin(s)." But would it not be more appropriate for students to be "continually" encouraged to understand the American culture in which they are growing up and to prepare for an active role in shaping that culture? Should public education strengthen and perpetuate separate ethnic and racial subcultures? Or should it not seek to make our young boys and girls contributors to a common American culture? (pp. 89–90)

Schlesinger's suggestion that students think about the nature of American culture and their place in it is not, at first glance, inconsistent with the broad aims espoused by emancipatory theorists. The broader implications of Schlesinger's analysis, however, suggest that assimilation is the goal of this effort, and the process necessary to achieve it turns out to look quite different from the critical and self-reflective pedagogies offered by advocates of emancipatory schooling. In fact, Schlesinger ends the section from which the preceding excerpt is taken by implying that any culture possessing "genuine vitality" would not have to depend on schools for acknowledgment or support, even if this were a legitimate function of the public schools (which it is not).

> One senses a certain inauthenticity in saddling public schools with the mission of convincing children of the beauties of their particular ethnic origins. The ethnic subcultures, if they had genuine vitality, would be sufficiently instilled in children by family, church and community. It is surely not the office of the public school to promote artificial ethnic chauvinism. (p. 90)

Given such views on both the power and desirability of the dominant culture in American society, it comes as little surprise that neo-conservatives translate difference into deficit, and resistance into moral recalcitrance. Based on the twin assumptions that everyone wants access to the kinds of societal benefits to which members of the dominant class have relatively ready access, and that success in the classroom translates more or less directly into access to these benefits, neo-conservatives argue that American schools should concentrate on raising educational attainment by reproducing the central values and beliefs of mainstream American culture. For rich and poor, Black and White, girl and boy, neo-conservatives argue for a common school experience that overcomes or transcends difference as the most efficient path to a quality education and, in virtue of this, an equitable share in society's benefits. As Bennett (1987) argues:

> Every American child has an equal claim to a common future under common laws, enjoying common rights and charged with common responsibilities. There follows the need for common education. In the past, American schools have proved that all children can learn and that scholastic excellence can transcend differences of race, religion, gender, and income. (p. 6)

On this account, schools serve an important gatekeeping role in what neo-conservatives see as a properly functioning meritocracy; schools help distribute the values and dispositions on which success in society is legitimately based (e.g., hard work), as well as the actual resources (e.g., the credentials necessary for good jobs) on which success depends. Multicultural education mis-educates students, its critics claim, in a way that prevents them from obtaining either of these benefits. William Bennett's (1992) reference to the success of Asian American students in school is a striking example of how the model-minority approach is used by neo-conservatives to explain the motivation and performance of other minority and immigrant students as the result of free choices made by individuals within the context of family life.

> All Americans can learn from the successes of the Asian-American commu-
> nity. There is ample evidence of the success of Asian-American children,
> many of whom are children of immigrants, in American schools. Studies
> show that they outperform all other major population groups in education
> attainment. The "secret" of their success is the high value Asian parents put
> on educational achievement, homework, an ethic of hard work, and strong
> family ties. Asian-American children are taught that schools are not repres-
> sive institutions, but places to learn; America is not a racist society, but the
> land of golden opportunity. (pp. 195–196)

Thus, neo-conservatives make difference both a private matter (one for
the "family, church, and community," as Schlesinger argues) and an obstacle to be overcome through the common curriculum of our public
schools. In this public sphere, racial, linguistic, religious, and ethnic differences give way to a common culture that offers successful students a
"land of golden opportunity."

Multicultural education breeds divisiveness and separatism. The last
claim made by neo-conservatives that I examine here is their accusation that multicultural education breeds divisiveness within society by
encouraging minorities to separate themselves from the majority culture
and create "ethnic enclaves," expressing deep resentment and antagonism in the process. Schlesinger, whose book is instructively titled *The
Disuniting of America: Reflections on a Multicultural Society* (1992), is one of
the clearest proponents of this view.

> The historic idea of a unifying American identity is now in peril in many
> arenas—in our politics, our voluntary associations, our churches, our lan-
> guage. And in no arena is the rejection of an overriding national identity
> more crucial than in our system of education. . . . The militants of ethnicity
> now contend that a main objective of public education should be the protec-
> tion, strengthening, celebration, and perpetuation of ethnic origins and iden-
> tities. Separatism, however, nourishes prejudices, magnifies differences and
> stirs antagonisms. The consequent increase in ethnic and racial conflict lies
> behind the hullabaloo over "multiculturalism" and "political correctness,"
> over the iniquities of the "Eurocentric" curriculum, and over the notion that
> history and literature should be taught not as intellectual disciplines but as
> therapies whose function is to raise minority self-esteem. (p. 17)

While Schlesinger's work is concerned mostly with the negative effects
of multicultural education on our civic life, he often seems more piqued
by the way that disciplines like history and literature have been used,
or in his view misused, by people whose political agenda includes the

reinterpretation or reconstruction of academic practice within the university. This emphasis is understandable given that Schlesinger is a noted academic historian, and many of his arguments reflect this in their emphasis on historical documentation as a means of arguing for the untenability of multicultural theorists' views (e.g., the debate over whether the Egyptians were really Black). Nonetheless, he argues that the lasting harm of efforts to implement multicultural education is to be found in the way that they undercut the positive vitality of our civic life and, ultimately, the civic virtues on which a pluralistic democracy is based.

Schlesinger is not alone, however, in raising the alarm over social divisiveness and laying responsibility for it at the feet of multicultural education's proponents. Diane Ravitch, for instance, argues that blame for the growing movement toward separatism in society lies with educators who are more concerned about the self-esteem of minority students than they are about curricular content that reinforces a common cultural heritage. Ravitch argues that the unfortunate tendency of these proponents of multicultural education has been to promote the false or overblown achievements of non-European ancestors at the expense of an education that focuses on what students share in common, which in her view is their shared commitment to American social values and institutions. She argues that a "particularist" view of multiculturalism foregrounds questions of cultural identity/diversity, reducing questions of self and self-worth to ethnicity and undercutting the common bond students share as citizens of the same nation.

> The particularist version of multiculturalism . . . teaches children that their identity is determined by their "cultural genes." That something in their blood or their race memory or their cultural DNA defines who they are and what they may achieve. That the culture in which they live is not their own culture, even though they were born here. That American culture is "Eurocentric," and therefore hostile to anyone whose ancestors are not European. Perhaps the most invidious implication of particularism is that racial and ethnic minorities are not and should not try to be part of American culture; it implies that American culture belongs only to those who are white and European; it implies that those who are neither white nor European are alienated from American culture by virtue of their race or ethnicity; it implies that the only culture they do belong to or can ever belong to is the culture of their ancestors, even if their families have lived in this country for generations. (Ravitch, 1990, p. 341)

The mistake that advocates of multiculturalism make, according to Ravitch, lies in searching for and cultivating a sense of identity outside of the symbolic and other resources provided by American culture. Indeed,

Ravitch argues that schools already pursue a pluralistic form of multiculturalism that reflects an open and inclusive American society. To go further than this, according to Ravitch, panders to the misconceived agenda
of the particularists and encourages the kind of divisiveness or separateness that Schlesinger warns against.

The paradox of the political. The neo-conservative educational goals
described above, articulated as they are in terms of subject-matter competence and cultural assimilation, must be seen in relation to the larger
political battles that people like Bennett, Hirsch, and Ravitch are committed to winning. Ironically, while neo-conservatives frequently decry and
dismiss the reforms I associate with emancipatory theories as "political,"
and therefore illegitimate in the debate over public schooling, there is
often a striking clarity in the call to arms neo-conservatives issue in what
everybody seems to agree (at times) is a battle over cultural values. Bennett, for instance, is quite frank in his appraisal of the motivation neo-
conservatives must rally to "win the battle" occurring in our society over
the beliefs and values on which our public institutions are based. Pro-
jecting the image of a stalwart and practically minded citizen advocate,
Bennett (1992) argues that

> Those whose beliefs govern our institutions will in large measure win the
> battle for the culture. And whoever wins the battle for the culture gets to
> teach the children. This cultural and institutional reclamation project will
> not be easy. . . . So be it. Reclaiming our institutions is less a political oppor-
> tunity than a civic obligation. It involves hard work. But it is work of
> immense importance. At the end of the day, *somebody's* values will prevail.
> (p. 258, emphasis in original)

The battle that Bennett describes here pits good citizens like himself,
those who "roll up their sleeves and work to ensure that their institutions
and government reflect their sentiments, their good sense, their sense
of right and wrong," against others who, by implication, oppose "what
democracy—a government of, by, and for the people—is all about" (Bennett, 1992, p. 258).

Bennett is quite right, on the one hand, to describe this battle as a
cultural and political one, as scholars on the left have for a long time (e.g.,
Apple, 1993; Bastian, Fruchter, Gittell, Greer, & Haskins, 1986; Giroux,
1992; Shor, 1986). Emancipatory theorists, however, enter this debate on
very different terms, with a very different image of what democratic values might entail for our schools (and society). Emancipatory theorists
argue that the position neo-conservatives have taken concerning the role

of individual experience and the role of cultural diversity in schooling is deeply destructive of an education for autonomy; it excludes or diminishes aspects of identity that are essential for developing the capacity to make informed, uncoerced choices about present interests and future plans. These issues are explored and elaborated in the emancipatory theories of education to which I now turn.

EMANCIPATORY THEORIES OF EDUCATION

Emancipatory educational theorists are united in their desire to provide an alternative to schools that limit, constrain, and deform the capacities of individuals to lead rich and fulfilling lives. At the root of their response to the neo-conservatives is the belief that schools must not ignore issues of power and privilege, and they must not fail to concern themselves adequately with the growth and flourishing of their students, who possess a diverse range of experiences, interests, and goals. Although the remainder of this work treats emancipatory theories in significant detail, it may be useful to situate the analysis in ways that make it more accessible to a variety of readers. Two strategies suggest themselves in this regard: first, to describe the four theories I place within the emancipatory tradition; and second, to provide an overview of the conflict between these emancipatory theories and the neo-conservative agenda described above.

Four Theories in the Emancipatory Tradition

For readers who are relatively new to this material, I offer a brief summary of each emancipatory theory considered here, noting some of the central tenets and contemporary proponents of each view. More experienced readers may benefit from this reminder, but some may also feel inclined to dispute what is said or not said in these brief summaries; my advice in this regard is to suspend judgment until the initial response is confirmed or resolved in subsequent chapters, where some of the nuances within theories are considered and some alternative perspectives are compared.

Liberalism. Liberal theorists most often appeal to justice, equality, and democracy as guides to educational policy and practice (Gutmann, 1987; Howe, 1997; Strike, 1982). While variously interpreted, liberal perspectives generally aim at assessing the distribution of educational opportunities or outcomes, giving special attention to the effect of schooling on individuals' pursuit of their life-plans. The capacity individuals possess to exercise freedom or autonomy is legitimately constrained by the state in relation to the needs of others to pursue their own notions of the good in a common public sphere. Under these circumstances, the positive effects of schooling are often measured against a lower limit or threshold that schools must help all students meet (e.g., all students should possess the skills and knowledge necessary to participate in a democratic society). Conversely, the negative consequences of schooling are often described in terms of practices that unfairly limit or constrain the potential of students to grow and succeed in society (e.g., tracking limits the economic choices and life-plans available to some students).

Liberal theories also create and protect a private sphere, or a realm of decision making that relies strictly on individual choice and preference. This sphere is excluded from what the state may legitimately require or prohibit, and is therefore also protected from what schools may consider justifiable components of the (mandatory) curriculum. The distinction between what may and may not be taught is often articulated in terms of content (e.g., religious values, sex education, controversial social issues like domestic violence and incest, etc.), but may also be defined in terms of pedagogy or instructional method (e.g., discussions based on personal beliefs and values, activities aimed at encouraging specific social behaviors like tolerance for diversity, etc.).

Recent work in liberal theory has attempted to refine the approach in response to challenges offered by critics (especially feminist theorists and communitarians) who find it inadequate, at least without further elaboration, to account for much that is central to the goods we actually pursue in life. These critics have been especially concerned with the proposition that "the good" is best thought of not in terms of individual desires or preferences, but rather as embedded in a complex web of social relationships; in this account, the good emerges from, and is dependent for its meaning on, our relationships with others. The attempt to reconstruct liberalism in light of this critique is consistent with a central argument of this work, namely, that individual goods cannot be easily defined and separated from the collective circumstances under which they are formulated and pursued. Liberal theorists have wrestled with empirical cases that raise this question, including recent political movements to grant special rights to indigenous peoples whose way of life is threatened by the influence of a dominant cultural group (Kymlicka, 1991, 1995).

Critical theory. Critical theorists in education are concerned with the role schools play in societies that are deeply divided by issues of power and status (Apple, 1979, 1993, 1996; Bowles & Gintis, 1976; Carnoy & Levin, 1985). Critical theorists generally draw on Marxist theories of class and exploitation, emphasizing the structural nature of oppression and thus its roots in the fundamental organization of society. Oppressive social relations are built upon forms of exploitation that benefit a dominant group, illegitimately providing economic and other benefits at the expense of those who are less powerful. Under these circumstances, many individuals in society are constrained from participating in the kind of activities necessary for human fulfillment or self-realization; exploitation limits the capacity for self-expression and the pursuit of diverse life-plans.

Critical theorists argue that the social and economic structures underlying differences in power and status are produced/reproduced by institutions within society. Schools are especially important in this process because of the significant role they play in the socialization of youth. The production/reproduction of social hierarchies is achieved, according to critical theorists, through the habits and dispositions that social institutions encourage, the patterns of interaction among individuals that they enforce, and the differential access to resources they regulate. On this latter account, resources may be of a material sort, as in the ownership of factories and farms, or they may take a less tangible form, as in the distribution of educational credentials. Social institutions obscure or mask the process of social production/reproduction on which exploitation depends by offering "ideologies" or legitimizing myths that make these arrangements seem acceptable on the surface, often by promoting the view that these arrangements are based on "commonsense" beliefs about the way the world works. The methodology of critical theorists, therefore, involves demystifying the false assumptions and hidden political interests that underlie ideological justifications of inequality, and exposing groups who benefit from the perpetuation of existing social hierarchies.

In their analyses of schooling, critical theorists often focus on practices that sort and channel students according to particular social attributes (e.g., the vocational tracking of working-class students; the overrepresentation of students of color in lower-track classes, disciplinary referrals, and dropout statistics; the underrepresentation of girls in advanced science and technology classes, etc.) as a way of connecting educational policies and practices with broader social outcomes. The direction taken by recent advocates of this perspective clearly reflects the influence of feminists and others who have argued that critical theory must go beyond an emphasis on class in their accounts of the crosscutting social structures (gender, race, sexual orientation, etc.) on which oppression and exploitation depend (Jaggar, 1983; McRobbie, 1991; Weis, 1990). This movement away from reductive, class-based analyses has led to an increasing emphasis on how these various aspects of identity might be taken into account in a more broadly conceived critical agenda (Beyer & Liston, 1996; McCarthy & Apple, 1988).

Postmodernism. Postmodernism is a diverse intellectual movement, spanning a variety of academic fields and interdisciplinary areas of research. For the purpose of describing postmodernism as an emancipatory educational perspective, it is useful to look at it as made of up of theories that are unified in their rejection of the universal or structural in favor of a conceptual and methodological emphasis on difference, multiplicity, and the fragmented nature of experience (Cherryholmes, 1988; Ellsworth, 1992; Popkewitz, 1991). In place of the epistemologically suspect approaches left to us by modernity (including liberalism and Marxism), postmodernists call on us to accept the inescapable partiality of what we know about the world, what we understand about others, and even our perceptions of self. Postmodern theorists have problematized the notion of identity, in particular, arguing that it never comes in an easily defined package and it can never be adequately expressed through tidy categories of essentialist attributes (Butler, 1990). For postmodernists, the nexus of individual identity and social experience is almost intransigently complex, and they encourage us to be suspicious of any theory that promises to deliver us from these circumstances through the use of abstract principles or hypothetical models.

This approach has led postmodern theorists to develop a linguistically sensitive, historically embedded, and textually oriented methodology for social scientific research (Foucault, 1972; Lyotard, 1979). Postmodern accounts focus on social control and self-regulation (Foucault, 1978, 1979), emphasizing the manner in which these goals are achieved through social norms that are taken for granted, and through the exclusion of critical or competing forms of understanding. Concepts like voice and discourse figure prominently in these accounts, and an emphasis on the local circumstances in which social regulation and self-control are practiced (or enforced) is also characteristic. Despite their rejection of modernist approaches like critical theory, postmodernists often promote a methodology that shares some similar goals; most important in this regard are their efforts to disclose and resist institutional circumstances that diminish the capacity for self-expression and self-exploration. The presumption here, as earlier, is that by understanding how action and identity are shaped by social position, arguably in a more local sense for most postmodernists, we can better understand alternatives that would empower or free individuals from existing constraints.

Postmodern theorists in education have taken a number of paths in applying this form of analysis to schooling (Cherryholmes, 1988; Ellsworth, 1992; Popkewitz, 1991). They generally argue that schools operate in ways that emphasize social control and self-regulation as part of both the explicit and implicit (critical theorists would say "hidden") curriculum. What many of these accounts share is the sense that what we need, and what postmodernism can provide, is a way of transgressing the oppressive or constraining norms that are treated as given in schools, or a way of crossing over the "borders" that separate a false sense of normality and acceptability from the liberating possibilities of resistance and reconstruction (Giroux, 1992). The point of these critiques is that schools should reject their commonly accepted goal of socialization, which rewards compliance and punishes resistance to the prevailing discourse, substituting in its place an emancipatory approach (or diversity of approaches) that free(s) students to explore and pursue a more diverse range of life-plans (McLaren, 1995).

Caring. Caring is a moral theory that grew, in part, from research on the distinctive qualities associated with women's moral reasoning (Gilligan, 1982). The general idea that women's experience might represent an approach to resolving moral dilemmas, which was largely unexamined (indeed, excluded) from prior inquiry, led scholars in a variety of fields to consider seriously the implications of this "new" perspective on questions of value and relation. Among philosophers, Nel Noddings' *Caring: A Feminine Approach to Ethics and Moral Education* (1984) was a groundbreaking text. It was followed by a variety of research that sought to elaborate caring as a moral theory, applying it to specific issues and problems in philosophy, as well as responding to critics (Held, 1995; Tronto, 1993). It was not long before educational philosophers began to work out the implications of caring for framing educational goals and guiding classroom practice. In this case, it was Noddings (again) and Jane Roland Martin who offered especially influential work on the nature of caring in education, and the kinds of changes this approach might suggest for the way schools are organized and the way students are taught (Martin, 1992; Noddings, 1992).

As a moral and educational theory, caring is rooted in the particularity of our relationships with others; it focuses our attention on the commitments we hold to specific others and our responsiveness to their needs and desires as particular persons. Like postmodernism, care theorists reject abstract moral principles and hypothetical models of moral reasoning as inadequate explanations of what happens when we are called upon by a child, a parent, or a friend. Caring seeks to explain a central aspect of the commitment we feel to these others based on the concrete particularity of their lives, plans, and hopes; these others become the focus of our concern because of the relationship we have entered into with them. The caring relationship requires a form of attention Noddings calls "engrossment," in which we focus on the other's needs and desires in a way that, in turn, inspires what she calls "motivational displacement," whereby we are moved to assist the other. The extent and nature of our caring depends on the circumstances of our relationships and the potential for this relation to be sustained through reciprocation. How to develop and promote caring among young people is a central goal of education, according to advocates of this view, and thus we are led to consider how schools might do this.

Among care theorists, answers to this question are likely to involve changes in both the content of the curriculum and the environment in which teaching and learning take place. With respect to curriculum content, care theorists often advocate dislocating the current emphasis on traditional subject-matter definitions of curriculum and replacing it with opportunities for students to engage in collaborative, interdisciplinary forms of inquiry, often based on activities that have a plausible connection to the lives children actually lead (or could lead, if given the opportunity) outside of school. Students are encouraged to pursue these activities in a classroom environment characterized by an eagerness to explore difference and a commitment to mutual success in learning. Educational theories based on caring thus aim at creating conditions under which students can explore issues of self-identity and self-expression through the projects they pursue in a collaborative and supportive environment.

Defining Emancipatory Theories of Education in Opposition to the Neo-Conservative Agenda

Liberal, critical, postmodern, and care-based educational theories share important commitments that place them in opposition to the dominant, neo-conservative discourse in American public education. One way of summarizing the critical agenda of emancipatory theories is in terms of their analysis of the many and complex ways that school policies and practices can have a limiting or constraining effect on individuals, especially insofar as they thwart the efforts of individuals to understand and pursue diverse identities and life-plans. Each emancipatory theory recognizes some means by which relations between differentially situated groups (e.g., women and men, cultural minority and majority members, homosexuals and heterosexuals, etc.) can (and have) become hierarchically organized in society according to how power and status are attached to membership in one group or another. The response of emancipatory educational theorists has been to promote the role of schools (among

other institutions) in resisting the various forms of oppression and exploitation that grow out of these hierarchies.

In elaborating some of the arguments that underlie this common
ground, I weave together examples from all four emancipatory approaches considered here. In fact, I am more concerned at the moment
with this common starting point for emancipatory theories than with offering my own critique of the neo-conservative position; Chapters 5 and
6 will take up this latter goal in a more focused manner, after the new
constellation has been further developed. The fact that the arguments
presented below can be juxtaposed, even in this rough-and-ready manner, is part of the point that I will be trying to make in a more formal and
systematic way throughout this work, namely, that emancipatory theories
share an important sense of consistency in their opposition to the neo-
conservative discourse in education, as well as in their potential to help
create a viable alternative vision. Some small success at this preliminary
stage in the analysis only begins to suggest the basis for a new framework
for understanding the parallels and convergences on which I try to capi-
talize in later chapters.

*Disputing the meritocracy of public schooling and the value neutrality
of a curriculum based on the Western canon.* A common and important
position taken by emancipatory theorists is that neo-conservatives assume or advocate a dubious educational meritocracy, where schools appear to fulfill their public responsibilities by offering all students an equal
opportunity to compete for the resources society has to offer, based
on acquiring a culturally specified body of knowledge and skills necessary for social success. Emancipatory theorists have criticized neo-
conservatives for misconstruing the nature and availability of these
"opportunities," and for falsely equating the acquisition of formally
sanctioned knowledge with success in the adult world. According to
emancipatory theorists, there are a number of problems with these claims.

First, emancipatory theorists have questioned the very possibility of
a value-neutral curriculum, while strongly denying that what is currently
identified by neo-conservatives as the Western canon (defined loosely,
say, by the "great books" tradition) is in any way an "objective" representation of American history or society. The opposition of emancipatory
theorists to this position often begins in an argument for the curriculum
as (necessarily) socially constructed, that is, as created through a long
(but observable and recordable) history of negotiation with, and accommodation to, powerful social interests. As critical theorist Michael Apple
(1993) points out, "What counts as legitimate knowledge is the result
of complex power relations and struggles among identifiable class, race,

gender, and religious groups. Thus, education and power are terms of an indissoluble couplet" (p. 46). Indeed, one might argue, as postmodernists like Henry Giroux have, that the current debate over the canon is itself proof enough for the point made by emancipatory theorists; the struggle over what counts as a liberal education is a manifestation of the political and moral struggle over what knowledge we hold to be most valuable and thus what is worth learning in school.

> What is being protested as the intrusion of politics into academic life is nothing less than a refusal to recognize that the canon and the struggle over the purpose and meaning of the liberal arts has displayed a political struggle from its inception. There are no disciplines, pedagogies, institutional structures, or forms of scholarship that are untainted by the messy relations of worldly values and interests. (Giroux, 1992, p. 89)

We can, in one sense, see neo-conservatives and emancipatory theorists in agreement here; both seem to acknowledge that this conflict is really all about who will define the cultural norm (or canon) and thus decide what values will be transmitted through our public institutions, schools perhaps most important among them. The significance of framing the question in this way, however, as emancipatory theorists have argued, suggests that what is at stake here is power rather than knowledge or, perhaps better, power masquerading as knowledge. In either case, the battle shifts to terrain more commonly tread by emancipatory theorists, giving up considerable ground to approaches that can identify and explain the connections between schooling, knowledge, and power.

A second kind of argument made by emancipatory theorists against the neo-conservative view of schools as meritocratic institutions dispensing politically neutral but culturally useful knowledge to all who work for it, focuses on how students outside the "culture of power" (Delpit, 1986) experience this process and its assimilationist trajectory (it is useful here to recall the model-minority account of Asian American educational success cited earlier from William Bennett). Critical theorists and liberals have both focused on the unexamined challenges that students of color face when they confront the assimilationist pressure that the common curriculum brings to bear, as well as the transmission-oriented instructional practices that are very often used in classrooms to convey it. Students whose experience and self-identity are not rooted in the dominant culture face the almost unbearable dilemma of trading their cultural identity for the distant promise of success in a society that has so far denied it to them. For these students, the culture they bring to school is at best secondary, and at worst an obstacle to be suppressed and overcome through diligent study.

Critical theorists and liberals have both argued that neo-conservatives have expressed little understanding of, or concern for, the potential risks and costs that an education into mainstream values and forms of knowledge involves for minority students (Fordham & Ogbu, 1986; Howe, 1997; Nieto, 1996), and this argument may apply equally well to the double bind women face in the home and workplace (Martin, 1981). There is a growing literature on the psychic cost of assimilation, the "burden of acting White" in school, and the destructive feelings of anger and self-hatred that students of color often experience when their educational "success" is achieved through the adoption of norms associated with the majority culture (Fordham & Ogbu, 1986; Nieto, 1996; Ogbu, 1988; Rodriguez, 1982). With the persistence (even resurgence) of racism in society and the continued obstacles to full employment (and satisfactory promotion) for people of color and women, emancipatory theorists conclude that the meritocratic promise of the common curriculum may well be empty and, in the end, a tool of exploitation.

A third and final argument against this aspect of neo-conservative educational thought comes from care theorists who argue that we should give up on the idea that curriculum is best defined as a matter of content knowledge in the first place. In its place, according to care theorists, we should focus our attention on helping students learn how to build constructive and caring relationships with others as a central aspect of schools' educational mission, selecting and exploring specific content as it becomes relevant in the context of authentic questions and projects collaboratively pursued by students. Jane Roland Martin (1992), for example, argues that schools should be thought of as the "moral equivalent" of home and the virtues of the curriculum represented in the "three Cs" of "care, concern, and connection" (p. 34).

Thus, instead of trying to agree ahead of time on a common curriculum that reflects some mythical cultural unity, Martin's approach emphasizes each student's commitment to, and involvement in, the projects of others as the primary goal of the school's physical and pedagogical organization. This is distant enough from the neo-conservative conception of curriculum that Martin (1992) points to so-called "extra-curricular" activities, like drama and the school newspaper, to model the way students might interact with each other, and teachers with them, to promote this alternative vision of school practice. According to Martin, a school community built on these, the three Cs, would emphasize: "learn[ing] to work and live with people from diverse backgrounds," "an experimental stance toward questions of school organization as well as curriculum and instruction," "an affectionate climate," and, finally, the simple quality of "joy" (pp. 37–39).

Rejecting economic productivity as the central goal of public school-ing, and the marketplace as a metaphor for education. Another neo-conservative view that emancipatory theorists commonly critique in-volves the proposition that the goal of public schooling is first and foremost to promote national economic productivity, a view that often is closely intertwined with the neo-conservatives' desire that schools help the nation return to a broad consensus on social values. Here, neo-conservatives often appeal to a kind of civic and economic restoration, one that recalls a mythical "golden age" in American education and soci-ety. An especially important aspect of this view is the belief that schools, through their failure to equip students with the appropriate knowledge and skills, have threatened America's once proud standing in the global community and, what is actually the same point, have made the Ameri-can economy vulnerable to the depredations of international competition.

Based on this concern, neo-conservatives have held the improvement of national economic productivity and the return of America to a position of global preeminence to be defining objectives of American educational reform. It has been common for major federal reports and programs to highlight the relationship between educational policy and economic pro-ductivity, and few documents of this kind received greater public or pro-fessional attention than *A Nation at Risk* (National Commission on Excel-lence in Education, 1983). Describing the situation in schools as "an act of unthinking, unilateral education disarmament," the authors of the report describe "the risk" to our nation in this way:

> History is not kind to idlers. The time is long past when America's destiny was assured simply by an abundance of natural resources and inexhaustible human enthusiasm, and by our relative isolation from the malignant prob-lems of older civilizations. The world is indeed one global village. We live among determined, well-educated, and strongly motivated competitors. We compete with them for international standing and markets, not only with products but also with the ideas of our laboratories and neighborhood work-shops. America's position in the world may once have been reasonably se-cure with only a few exceptionally well-trained men and women. It is no longer. (National Commission on Excellence in Education, 1983, p. 6)

Critical theorists have long rejected this characterization of educational goals (e.g., Bowles & Gintis, 1976), arguing that it helps justify a system of schooling that sorts students according to their socioeconomic class and reproduces social inequalities among adults (in income, wealth, opportunity, etc.) based on these divisions. Other critical theorists, as I described above, look carefully at the way knowledge is constructed in school and the way this process privileges some students, equipping them for success in the dominant culture, while it excludes others, preparing them to assume positions where they are likely to be exploited in the workplace (Apple, 1979, 1993). What we have in the end, according to critical theorists, is an educational system that neo-conservatives have pressed increasingly into the form and functioning of a "marketplace," where individuals (students, parents, teachers, administrators) figure primarily as components in the broader calculation of profit and loss.

> Behind the rhetoric of economic recovery and sustainable, wide-spread economic growth is another reality. This is the reality of crisis, of an economy that increases the gap between rich and poor, between black and brown and red and yellow and white. It is driven by a set of policies in which the real lives of millions of people count less than "competitiveness," "efficiency," and above all profit maximization. (Apple & Zenk, 1996, p. 71)

Liberal theorists have raised similar concerns, as arguments in the preceding section suggest, based on the false promise of America's educational meritocracy. For example, in 1986 Ann Bastian and her colleagues urged educational policy makers to look carefully at the disturbing disparity between increasing educational achievement and increasing inequality of economic success (measured by average income). The paradox she points to reflects the entrenched hierarchy of social class in America:

> What labor markets tell us is that a long-standing paradox of schooling will become a more intense contradiction in coming years: education will mean more for a few and less for many. Access to rewarding jobs will require greater educational attainment and proficiency, but there will be fewer chances of success even with the fullest schooling. For the great majority, job destinies will not utilize intellectual skills beyond basic literacy, although years of schooling may still count in arbitrarily sorting out who gets hired and who gets rejected. . . . Given the disjuncture between economic and educational rewards, the effort to link school reform to the market value of education threatens to abandon large segments of American youth. (Bastian et al., 1986, pp. 54–55)

The decade that followed this prediction has shown it to be prescient: Wages have decreased at the lowest income levels, previously secure white-collar employees have suffered decreased job security, and "downsizing" has left many workers unable to find positions of similar status or compensation (Schultze, 1996). These circumstances have led to a dramatically increasing disparity, as reflected in income statistics, between rich and poor (Schultze, 1996). It is worth noting that, as these disparities began again to receive some public scrutiny, social scientists Richard Herrnstein and Charles Murray, authors of *The Bell Curve* (1994), resurrected arguments that purport to explain how low achievement among minorities, and the social inequalities that follow from it, are the inevitable result of genetic differences.

Displacing the primacy of subject matter in the curriculum and recognizing the role of experience. A third common critique of the neo-conservative position that emancipatory approaches share lies in their rejection of traditional definitions of subject matter as the sole foundation for curriculum, and a common commitment to recognizing and nurturing the variety of interests, capacities, and concepts of individual identity that students possess (and bring with them into school each day). Because education, for neo-conservatives, consists primarily in the distribution of specialized forms of socially sanctioned knowledge, and because instruction tends to be organized around traditional content-area divisions and related in a more or less didactic fashion, emancipatory theorists argue that there is little room or respect for what students themselves bring to the educational experience. For neo-conservatives, students are immature, naive, or empty vessels into which the requisite knowledge is to be deposited.

This is especially troublesome for emancipatory theorists who are interested in the relational or developmental qualities of students' educational experience. This has been a focus of concern for many critics of neo-conservative educational policies, but perhaps most of all for care theorists like Nel Noddings and Jane Roland Martin. Both offer critiques of disciplinary definitions of curriculum and the radical separation of the curriculum from student experience. Noddings argues, on the one hand, that modest revisions in the standard curriculum hold little hope for genuine school reform because the engagement of students in their education is not rooted, in the first place, in the *content* of the curriculum. As in my brief summary of Martin's work above, the kind of reform Noddings has in mind here calls on schools to help students learn to be healthy and caring adults. In the following passage, Noddings (1992) turns the "nostalgic dreams" of the neo-conservatives on their head, arguing that their focus on decontextualized subject matter is likely to deflect school reform from the relational issues on which success may actually depend.

It is natural to feel nostalgic about our own school days if they were happy ones. But we cannot build our children's future on nostalgic dreams. . . . What is important is to recognize and admit that curriculum content—in the form of traditional subjects—was not a big contributor to satisfaction with schooling. Periodically, curriculum is touted as the key to educational reform and huge amounts of money are spent on its revision, but astute observers have commented more than once that a focus on curriculum revision is "not the answer" (Bruner, 1971). . . . The emphasis on revision of the standard curriculum, far from contributing to school reform, may actually have induced greater alienation and unhappiness in students. (pp. 2–3)

Noddings goes on to argue for a curriculum based on "centers of care," which she identifies by the different potential objects of caring (e.g., self; intimate acquaintances, strangers, and distant others; animals, plants, and the earth; the human-made world; and ideas). I consider her arguments in more detail (and more critically) in later chapters. I also consider Jane Roland Martin's challenge to subject-matter definitions of curriculum, which I find even more damaging for the neo-conservative perspective.

Critical theorists have also engaged neo-conservatives on issues concerning the centrality of subject matter and its potential for marginalizing and excluding student experience from the classroom. Critical theorists argue that the transmission-oriented pedagogies associated with neo-conservatives' emphasis on traditional subject-matter definitions of curriculum deflect the potential for a student-centered curriculum that aims at empowering students by recognizing the diversity of their experience and the inseparability of this experience from the actual content of instruction. Of particular concern in this regard are forms of experience and social identities that may be sources of social critique and insight into the oppressive assumptions of the dominant culture. According to critical theorists, by organizing instruction in a way that ignores or attempts to overcome diversity among learners, neo-conservatives actively pursue practices that harm individuals and perpetuate the marginalization of whole groups of students who fall outside of "mainstream" American culture. Ira Shor (1992) provides a good example of the contrasting view critical theorists hold on the nature of student experience and its role in schooling.

Empowering education, as I define it here, is a critical-democratic pedagogy for self and social change. It is a student-centered program for multicultural democracy in school and society. It approaches individual growth as an active, cooperative, and social process, because the self and society create each other. Human beings do not invent themselves in a vacuum, and society cannot be made unless people create it together. The goals of this pedagogy are to relate personal growth to public life, by developing strong skills, academic knowledge, habits of inquiry, and critical curiosity about society, power, inequality, and change. (p. 15)

Emancipatory theories oppose the homogeneous interpretation of human needs that neo-conservatives assume in their characterization of educational practice. Because of the close connection between experience and identity, any view of curriculum that does not recognize the nature and importance of student experience (including how this experience can be represented in the shared interests of particular groups of students) is inadequate for the purposes of promoting individual growth and social justice.

Notwithstanding these important points of agreement in their opposition to the neo-conservative agenda, there are still many important differences in the way liberals, critical theorists, postmodernists, and care theorists have argued for educational change. Indeed, emancipatory theorists of education remain deeply divided on fundamental philosophical issues, and this has significantly reduced their effectiveness in opposing neo-conservative educational policies. By exploring these differences in greater detail, I propose to offer a more effective basis for developing both the critical and constructive powers of emancipatory theories. The new constellation will help us reconstruct some of the most fundamental divisions among emancipatory theories in a way that leads these approaches into a more complementary relation, a relation that allows them to inform each other more effectively at various levels of theory and practice. Like any meaningful negotiation, however, this one requires us to navigate some thorny disagreements.

3

Universalist Approaches to Emancipatory Educational Theory

Liberalism and critical theory represent a universalist approach to emancipatory educational theory. By that I mean that what connects these two perspectives, despite important differences, is their shared commitment to the view that universal moral principles and abstract models of human conduct provide the primary foundation upon which to understand social relations and institutions. For liberals, moral assessment is frequently rooted in the concept of justice or, since the work of John Rawls (1971), "justice as fairness." For critical theorists, following the tradition of Marxist social analysis, the struggle to overcome economic exploitation and other "structural" forms of oppression constitutes the conceptual foundation for social critique and reconstruction. In educational analyses, liberalism and critical theory have been adopted for the critique of existing school policies and practices, and for establishing new ways to define the goals of education.

The persuasiveness of universalist accounts derives in part from the power of the normative principles they promote and their broad application across differences in individual experience and social context. The accounts of persons and social relations offered by such theories are thus rooted in "universal" human qualities. For liberals, this has meant an emphasis on rationality and the common desire of all humans to maximize the degree to which their desires (or, more commonly in this literature, their preferences) are satisfied. Critical theorists, on the other hand, see these universal human qualities growing from the material/economic conditions of production (broadly construed) and the labor required to sustain life and achieve self-realization.

Starting from these shared human qualities, universalist approaches derive generalizable principles or normative frameworks that can be used to redress the moral shortcomings of society. For liberals, these shortcomings generally involve some kind of inequity or injustice in the distribution of resources, such that individuals are unfairly constrained in pursuing their different conceptions of the good. Critical theorists, on the other hand, are concerned with structural forms of domination that result from illegitimate and exploitative social hierarchies; these hierarchies (e.g., class society) privilege the interests of one group over another, thereby constraining many individuals from realizing their full potential as humans. These concepts are persuasive and powerful in proportion to their success as models for understanding the widest range of human experience, and to the extent that they justify normative assessments that are applicable across the most diverse forms of social relation and institutional organization.

In the end, I argue that liberalism and critical theory best inform the new constellation through their advocacy of autonomy understood as critical consciousness. Both perspectives provide rich ways of elaborating critical consciousness as a central goal of emancipatory education and both provide essential insights concerning how schools might develop this capacity in their students.

LIBERALISM

It would not be unfair to begin, as Judith Shklar does in her essay, "The Liberalism of Fear" (1989), with this powerfully simple definition: "Liberalism has only one overriding aim: to secure the political conditions that are necessary for the exercise of personal freedom" (p. 21). While spirited debate continues among liberals about the nature, purpose, and limits of personal freedom, liberal moral theory has been dominated in recent times by the legacy of John Rawls and his extraordinarily influential defense of liberal egalitarianism, *A Theory of Justice* (1971).

Liberal egalitarianism gives special attention to the relative distribution of goods in society and is often associated with the social contract tradition in moral and political philosophy. In "rationally reconstructing" the basis for civil government, liberal egalitarians frequently utilize complex, hypothetical decision-making models to derive and justify normative principles. Rawls, for example, sets out to discover the moral principles that individuals would find most rational to adopt in governing themselves, under circumstances that encourage impartiality and limit irrelevant background knowledge. He describes an extended thought experiment in which participants adopt a hypothetical "veil of ignorance" (removing knowledge of one's place in society) and reason from a hypothetical "original position" (a discussion among equals over the basic structure of society) to determine the principles that would fairly govern the actions of all citizens. As in most hypothetical choice situations, Rawls' conception of the original position is based on a few assumptions about human nature that liberals believe are relatively uncontentious and therefore useful as starting points in the process of establishing agreement on fundamental moral principles. These assumptions include the possession of instrumental rationality (as a reasonably uncontentious, universal capacity in human beings) and the desire of individuals to satisfy their preferences to the greatest extent possible (as a reasonably uncontentious view of human motivation).

While a detailed assessment of the liberal egalitarian tradition is well beyond the scope and requirements of this project, I use Rawls' work as a touchstone for this approach. The following passage may be useful in keeping the language of *A Theory of Justice* before us and in laying an appropriate bit of groundwork for critics and defenders alike:

> My aim is to present a conception of justice which generalizes and carries to a higher level of abstraction the familiar theory of the social contract as found, say, in Locke, Rousseau, and Kant. In order to do this we are not to think of the original contract as one to enter a particular society or to set up a particular form of government. Rather, the guiding idea is that the principles of justice for the basic structure of society are the object of the original agreement. They are the principles that free and rational persons concerned to further their own interests would accept in an initial position of equality as defining the fundamental terms of their association. These principles are to regulate all further agreements; they specify the kinds of social cooperation that can be entered into and the forms of government that can be established. This way of regarding the principles of justice I shall call justice as fairness. (Rawls, 1971, p. 11)

The Feminist Critique of Liberal Egalitarianism

The strategy taken by many critics in disputing the liberal egalitarian conception of justice involves challenging the putatively uncontentious assumptions on which it is based. A number of related arguments have been made in this regard, many by feminist theorists. One such line of argument focuses on the assumptions liberals make about the role of rationality and impartiality in defining the hypothetical circumstances in which deliberation over first principles takes place. Some feminists, for instance, have argued that, instead of being "neutral" with respect to their effect on the normative principles derived, these assumptions actually diminish the likelihood that liberal theories will provide the kind of tools needed to analyze and oppose women's oppression (Held, 1987; Pateman, 1979). In particular, socialist feminists have argued that liberals' appeal to abstract models of human rationality, practiced by impartial, disembodied knowers, actually obscures the kinds of oppressive power relations that obtain in patriarchal societies like our own (Jaggar, 1983).

These arguments call into question the initial circumstances of deliberation that liberal egalitarians use to determine the basic structure of society, and challenge their conception of the rational and autonomous moral agent.

A stronger version of this critique goes beyond challenging the usefulness of rationality and impartiality in the struggle against patriarchy, by suggesting that these assumptions actually represent a specific, and prototypically male, orientation to questions about how to resolve social conflicts and moral dilemmas. Liberals, these critics contend, have taken a worldview identified with the experience of men and used it as the foundation from which subsequent (hypothetical) agreements about first principles can be made on behalf of all rational and impartial subjects. Virginia Held (1987) argues that taking this starting point already excludes the experiences and intuitions that many women would bring to the fundamental questions of social affiliation.

> To see contractual relations between self-interested or mutually disinterested individuals as constituting a paradigm of human relations is to take a certain historically specific conception of "economic man" as representative of humanity. And it is, many feminists are beginning to agree, to overlook or to discount in very fundamental ways the experience of women. (p. 113)

This kind of critique challenges the place where liberal theories begin and questions whether principles derived from this starting point will serve the needs of all members of society, especially those who would (if they could) bring a fundamentally different set of experiences and assumptions to the "original position."

A second strand in the critique offered by feminist theorists challenges the capacity of abstract models to account for the forms of oppression that actually exist in society, the historical development of these forms, and the culturally specific ways they are experienced. Such critics argue that hypothetical models like those offered by liberal egalitarians have limited value in their explanation of the oppression women experience in patriarchal societies, for example, because these models are not sufficiently sensitive to the social context in which relations of dominance and subordination actually occur; that is, these theories fail to embed moral subjects in the conditions under which individuals actually plan and carry out their projects. Held (1987) advances this critique as well, noting:

> When subjected to examination, the assumptions and conceptions of contractual thinking seem highly questionable. As descriptions of reality they

can be seriously misleading. Actual societies are the results of war, exploitation, racism, and patriarchy far more than of social contracts. Economic and political realities are the outcomes of economic strength triumphing over economic weakness more than of a free market. And rather than a free market of ideas, we have a culture in which the loudspeakers that are the mass media drown out the soft voices of free expression. (p. 113)

Held argues that we must attend to the social and historical processes that underlie the oppression some groups face in society in order to make useful judgments about what harms have been done and what to do about them. The capacity to make such contextualized judgments is an essential aspect of emancipatory theories, and to the extent that such reasoning is diminished or fails to play a role in the elucidation of liberal principles, these principles will be of limited value to those who need them most.

As in the previous example, this critique also has a stronger version, one that questions whether a principle like justice as fairness, even if it could be justified in the way liberals describe, would help us create the kind of society in which we would actually want to live. Annette Baier is a feminist theorist who is especially concerned about how moral subjects are constructed in a society where individuals are guaranteed certain formal rights, but where they still face circumstances that are not conducive to finding meaning and purpose in their lives. In such societies, as one might describe those constituted by capitalism and/or patriarchy, large groups of individuals are constrained in the capacity they possess to make choices and act in ways that make their lives fulfilling.

Baier holds, as do other critics of traditional liberal egalitarianism, that we should not settle for "justice as the first virtue of social institutions" (Rawls, 1971, p. 3), where this assumes the customarily self-interested, and instrumentally rational, citizen of these models. She argues that we must replace the effort to "distance" one individual from another in our moral theories, as she believes talk about rights inevitably leads us to do, with a more collectivist view of society based on mutual interdependence. We need to understand the nature and organization of societies, she argues, in terms of how they promote or inhibit meaningful social relations, and this should be the basis on which we morally assess particular communities.

The main complaint about the Kantian version of a society with its first virtue justice, construed as respect for equal rights to formal goods . . . is that none of these goods do much to ensure that the people who have and mutually respect such rights will have any other relationships to one another than the minimal relationship needed to keep such a "civil society" going. They may well be lonely, driven to suicide, apathetic about their work and about participation in political processes, find their lives meaningless and have no wish to leave offspring to face the same meaningless existence. Their rights, and respect for rights, are quite compatible with very great misery, and misery whose causes are not just individual misfortunes and psychic sickness, but social and moral impoverishment. (Baier, 1987, p. 47)

Baier's analysis reminds us that the circumstances under which individuals make choices and decisions about their lives are fundamentally social and collective. Based on this socially contextualized view of the individual, she rejects liberalism's vision of society as an aggregation of individuals whose beliefs, desires, and preferences can be easily isolated from one another and regulated by abstract principles of justice. This kind of individualist social ontology fails to address the roots of oppression and exploitation and is thus limited in the tools it offers to challenge existing social hierarchies. Conceptions of the good life cannot exclude this kind of analysis without losing an essential piece of what explains who we are, and the capacity we have for being and doing something different in the future.

If these criticisms are in any measure on the right track, as I believe they are, they significantly undermine the appeal of liberalism, as represented in the work of John Rawls, for emancipatory educational theory. In the past several years, however, liberal theorists in political philosophy (Kymlicka, 1991, 1995), as well as in educational philosophy (Howe, 1997), have suggested what I believe are fundamental and productive revisions in the liberal egalitarian framework. These contemporary liberal theorists, as I will call them here, emphasize the participatory nature of liberal democracies, and they worry, as I do, about the obstacles that oppressed groups face in finding what Ken Howe (borrowing a similar phrase from philosopher Daniel Dennett) calls "opportunities worth wanting."

New Perspectives in Liberalism

Two issues are especially relevant in considering the educational significance of work done by contemporary liberal theorists: The first is their recognition that liberal theory must offer a more contextualized understanding of the good than it has (or perhaps has appeared to) in the past; the second is their promotion of a new participatory paradigm for explaining the nature and moral implications of justice in societies built upon fundamental structures of inequality.

One of the most interesting and sustained efforts to address recent critics of liberalism is presented in the work of Will Kymlicka (1991, 1995). The arguments Kymlicka makes are rooted in the belief that liberalism has been unfairly criticized as overly individualistic and that the resources necessary to answer many objections (including those offered above) can be mined from a more sympathetically interpreted liberal egalitarian tradition or at least reconstructed from reasoning that does not violate its most central tenets. I use Kymlicka's work here as a springboard for considering what I find to be the most plausible foundation for liberalism's evolution as an emancipatory educational theory.

One of the most important strategies in the evolution of contemporary liberal theory has been its move away from the individualism that is generally foregrounded in assessments of how goods are distributed in society, toward a focus on the social context in which individual goods are constructed and understood in relation to group identity. Will Kymlicka (1991) describes this challenge in relation to one of the most important applications of this trend, the defense of minority rights in a liberal democracy.

> How can we defend minority rights within liberalism, given that its moral ontology recognizes only individuals, each of whom is to be treated with equal consideration? We need to be able to show two things: (1) that cultural membership has a more important status in liberal thought than is explicitly recognized—that is, that the individuals who are an unquestionable part of the liberal moral ontology are viewed as individual members of a particular cultural community, for whom cultural membership is an important good; and (2) that the members of minority cultural communities may face particular kinds of disadvantages with respect to the good of cultural membership, disadvantages whose rectification requires and justifies the provision of minority rights. That is, we need to show that membership in a cultural community may be a relevant criterion for distributing the benefits and burdens which are the concern of a liberal theory of justice. (p. 162)

For Kymlicka, this means moving away from liberal proposals concerned with equalizing resources (e.g., progressive tax policies that effectively transfer wealth from those who have more to those who have less) as the only or even the primary means by which to achieve justice, although such transfers may still be necessary and helpful. Instead, Kymlicka works within the liberal egalitarian tradition to show how its central principles can account for the way power and status are regulated in societies built around systematic relationships of dominance and subordination. By following this strategy, Kymlicka is forced to confront in a more profound sense the degree to which all goods are socially constructed, and the fact that some of the most potent obstacles faced by individuals in their pursuit of the good are woven into the fundamental fabric or basic structures of society.

Instead of beginning, as Rawls and other liberal egalitarians do, with as "thin" a set of assumptions as possible about the nature of individual goods and the context within which they are pursued, Kymlicka acknowledges that membership in a group or class fundamentally conditions the selection and pursuit of individual goods, and that liberals cannot avoid this in the process whereby first principles are determined. Kymlicka thus treats culture as a crucial aspect of the "context of choice," recognizing that it is inextricably bound up with issues of power, identity, and human flourishing. What liberal egalitarians need in this situation is a way to treat cultural membership as something that can be assessed in terms of its relative distribution in society, and "cultural structure" as a context within which this good is pursued. Kymlicka pursues this strategy by adding cultural membership to Rawls' list of "primary goods," which Rawls (1971) defines as goods that "have a use whatever a person's rational plan of life" (p. 62). For Kymlicka (1991),

> It is of sovereign importance to this argument that the cultural structure is being recognized *as a context of choice*. If we view cultural membership as a primary good within Rawls's scheme of justice, then it is important to remember that it is a good in its capacity of providing meaningful options for us, and aiding our ability to judge for ourselves the value of our life-plans. (p. 166, emphasis in original)

The difference between this view and other interpretations of liberal egalitarianism, Kymlicka's defense of Rawls aside, is extremely important. By allowing culture to enter into and help organize the context of choice, contemporary liberal theorists no longer defend so thin a conception of the good or so uncontentious a set of initial assumptions about human nature and motivation. Kymlicka fundamentally redefines the circumstances under which individuals make judgments about the good, and thus the relationship between self-identity and social context. While talking about the distribution or redistribution of cultural membership may still require some fairly abstract thinking about the way some groups are oppressed or exploited in society, this strategy nonetheless opens up some interesting new possibilities for liberals who are interested in distancing themselves from the kind of ontological individualism that appears characteristic of their predecessors.

Perhaps most important for this analysis is the point that Kymlicka's consideration of the context of choice commits contemporary liberal theorists to a more structural conception of power and oppression in society, and probably a more interventionist role for the state, than previous liberal egalitarian thought would have sanctioned. For Kymlicka, the current social circumstances faced by women and members of the working class, for example, provide ample evidence to suppose that something has gone drastically (systematically) wrong in the context of choice that these two groups face, and thus that some fundamental aspect of this context must be altered. With respect to gender, Kymlicka argues that Rawls and Dworkin are wrong to give the impression that their conceptions of justice would be best served by transferring resources (e.g., income) from one group to another. Instead, Kymlicka argues that justice requires examining, in a more fundamental sense, the relative distribution of power and status associated with the positions held by members of different groups in society (e.g., women and men, workers and capitalists). It is worth quoting Kymlicka at some length on the implications of justice in both of these cases. With respect to gender inequality, Kymlicka (1991) writes:

> These are predominantly matters not of the material rewards for a given job, but of the power relations entailed by the job. People would not choose to enter social relations that deny these opportunities, that put them in a position of subjection or degradation, if they were able to choose from a position of equality. From a position of equality, women wouldn't have agreed to a system of social roles that defines "male" jobs as superior to, and dominating over, "female" jobs. We have every reason to believe this, since those gender roles were created not only without the consent of women, but in fact required the legal and political suppression of women. (p. 93)

With respect to social class exploitation, Kymlicka (1991) offers a similar argument, focusing on differences in power and status instead of the (mal)distribution of income.

> The same sort of injustice is present in the exaggerated distinction between "mental" and "manual" labour in our society. We have every reason to believe that people in a position of initial equality would not have created such a system, since the implementation of the "scientific management" system, for example, was opposed by the workers, and would have been stopped if workers had the same power as capitalists (Braverman). Dworkin says that increased transfer payments are justified because we can assume that the poor would be willing to do the work in higher-paying jobs, if they entered the market on equal footing. But we can also assume that if the poor entered the market on an equal footing, they wouldn't accept relations of unequal power and domination. We have as good evidence for the latter as the for-

mer. Liberals, therefore, should seek not only to redistribute money from doctors to nurses, or from capitalists to workers, but also ensure that doctors and capitalists don't have the power to define relationships of power and domination. Justice requires that people's circumstances be evaluated, not only in terms of income, but also in terms of power relations. (pp. 94–95)

Despite Kymlicka's intention to revive Rawls and Dworkin on these points, the form his argument takes is quite unlike that of traditional liberal egalitarians, and it provides a good deal more room for contemporary liberal theorists to extend their social and political analyses in emancipatory directions. The importance of Kymlicka's analysis for this project lies most significantly in the distance he moves away from liberal egalitarian proposals that focus on plans for redistributing goods held by individuals, toward advocating changes in the fundamental social circumstances that shape the choices and life-plans of individuals. It is, in fact, just this kind of evolution in liberal theory that I believe is required to pursue the most promising possibilities of contemporary liberal theories for emancipatory education.

New Perspectives in Liberal Educational Theory

One educational theorist who has attempted to look at liberal educational theory through this newly evolving lens is Ken Howe (1997). Howe is specifically interested in clarifying and working out the implications of the concept of equal educational opportunity, and he uses Kymlicka's work, among others, to do this. Howe gives equal educational opportunity a broad treatment, conceptually and empirically, with applications to specific issues such as gender equity, multiculturalism, tracking, testing, and school choice. I want to focus here on Howe's analysis of equal opportunity as defined, at least in part, by "opportunities worth wanting." What is particularly relevant for this project is the way Howe's self-avowedly "radical liberal theory" confronts Kymlicka's challenge to acknowledge the context of choice as essential to understanding and assessing the effects of social relations on individual choice.

Howe uses Kymlicka's notion of the context of choice to help explain the nature of the circumstances under which individuals can be said to have a genuine chance to achieve a particular goal or to follow a particular plan. After rejecting, for their obvious counterintuitiveness, the propositions that a meaningful opportunity must guarantee success, or that real opportunities can exist in the face of easily predictable failure, Howe (1997) argues that:

> The existence of a (real) opportunity . . . requires a favorable *context of choice*, in which the thwarting of the desired results of individuals' choices is reduced as far as possible to the kind of uncertainty that gives *deliberation* and *choice* their meanings. (p. 19, emphasis in original)

These conditions, at a minimum, constitute the basis for an opportunity worth wanting. But what counts as *illegitimately* thwarting the efforts of individuals to carry through successfully with their plans is the question that emancipatory educational theories must help answer, as Howe points out, since it is this form of constraint that emancipatory schools must help overcome.

One of the most important contributions Howe (1997) makes to the discussion of liberal educational theory is his characterization of the context of choice as an interaction between "the formal features of educational institutions" and "the characteristics that individuals bring to educational institutions" (p. 28). In place of an empty formalism that does little to address the complex forms of inequality that exist in society, and that are reproduced in schools, Howe's analysis of opportunities worth wanting attempts to answer liberalism's critics by pursuing school-based arguments similar to the ones that Kymlicka made at a broader social level. While it takes little imagination to see the importance of schools as a context in which students' identities are significantly shaped, the particular way we characterize schools as a context of choice is important for understanding the potential contribution of contemporary liberal theorists in confronting the systematic inequalities that have been built around race, class, gender, and sexual orientation. I consider gender inequality in schools here as a test case for this framework.

For girls and women, the process of constructing a sense of self-identity has been described, often and from various theoretical perspectives, as dependent on the views held by others, especially by men. In fact, even when the analysis of women's educational experience focuses on the role played by female peers, at least one study has found that the most important criterion of assessment among women (of each other) remains their attractiveness to men (Holland & Eisenhart, 1990). Myra Sadker and David Sadker (1994), well known for their work on issues of gender equity, take up the common metaphor of the mirror to describe how the reflected views of others dominate the experience of identity construction among adolescent girls.

> In the central drama of adolescence, high school is when girls begin their quest to develop an adult identity. . . . As girls struggle to reconcile different aspects of their personalities, they look to parents, teachers, classmates, and

friends for reactions. Girls use these reactions as a yardstick to measure themselves, pooling and reflecting them in a process Charles Horton Cooley called "the looking-glass self." (p. 100)

To sort out and assess the various ways that this "looking-glass self" is constructed in schools would take this analysis too far from its central objective. Looking at one or two examples of how this happens, however, will help illuminate the way contemporary liberal theorists have put the idea of a context of choice into practice. Howe's consideration of the experience of girls and women in math and science classrooms, and Amy Gutmann's discussion of school leadership hierarchies, are both good examples of this kind of analysis.

Early in his consideration of the debate over gender equity, Howe directs his readers' attention to an explanation of the observed differences between girls and boys that is of particular importance to this analysis. This explanation holds that differences between girls and boys are largely the result of "free choices" made by members of each group. Howe (1997) associates the "suggestion that girls and women have chosen the present arrangements" with "the kind of justification characteristic of libertarianism and its formalist interpretation of the principle of equal opportunity" (p. 37). The research that he considers (especially Oakes, 1990) involves studies that look at the process by which girls are gradually "winnowed" from advanced coursework in science and math, until their underrepresentation in careers associated with these disciplines is virtually guaranteed. As part of the empirical case to be made on this point, Sadker and Sadker (1994) note that "almost 70 percent of today's students who major in physics, chemistry, and computer science are male [and] engineering tops all of these . . . with 85 percent of bachelor degrees going to men" (p. 165).

The fact that there are no *formal* barriers preventing girls and women from pursuing advanced studies, and then careers, in science and math obscures the real reasons for these decisions and thus fails to provide an adequate account of the "choices" that girls and women make. What is missing from this explanation is a more contextual account of how meaningful choices are systematically denied to girls and women in school (including an analysis of the complicit role played by key actors within these institutions) and how the opportunities open to girls and women are conditioned by the gendered social meanings associated with them. This information about the context of choice in schools is essential to understanding the decisions that girls and women make about their academic interests and talents.

Howe cites recent work by Jeannie Oakes (1990), among others, to describe the influence of gender on the context of choice that girls and women face in most public schools. His summary of this work focuses on the role that adults in schools play in limiting the meaningful opportunities that girls and women have to reach advanced levels of instruction in math and science, and the obstacles they face in planning to undertake the kind of postsecondary education that is required for jobs in these fields.

> Oakes identifies three general features of schools that squeeze girls out of the pipeline. First, teachers hold expectations and employ teaching strategies and activities that systematically favor boys over girls. In particular, teachers have higher expectations for boys in math and science, interact with them more, and use predominantly competitive/whole-group instructional methods. Second, girls receive less encouragement to pursue careers in math and science and less advice about how to go about it. This happens directly, through the words and deeds of teachers and counselors, and indirectly, through role modeling. As a consequence, girls have less access to math and science experiences than do boys, because girls receive less constructive attention within math and science courses and ultimately choose fewer overall. (Howe, 1997, p. 38)

These experiences have a dramatic effect on the context of choice that girls and women face in school. From implicit practices that reinforce gender stereotypes to more explicit forms of institutional tracking, girls and women are subject to pressures that constrain their capacity to develop particular areas of interest and to pursue educational experiences associated with these interests. Like the patriarchal structures in society they reflect, these schools represent a context of choice that is hostile to girls and women. As Howe (1997) concludes, we must include this understanding in any account we offer of the "choices" girls and women have made: "In the end, girls do *choose* to leave the pipeline. But these choices must be viewed in terms of the larger context of choice, the cumulative effects of which are quite powerful in the direction of encouraging them to leave" (p. 38, emphasis in original).

The argument that schools create a context of choice in which girls and women are discouraged from exploring new roles or opportunities is also supported by the work of liberal educational theorist Amy Gutmann (1987). She addresses an issue related to the situation that girls and women face in science class when she considers the implications of school organization for the "structure of gender preferences" (Gutmann, 1987, p. 114). She argues that, instead of reflecting the (morally) arbitrary vocational preferences of men and women in society, schools reflect and help reproduce a hierarchical division of labor based on stereotypical gender attributes. Schools reify and enforce this division through the positions that women and men occupy in relation to each other. Women are considered more qualified to be teachers than administrators, and more often elementary than secondary teachers. The explanation that Gutmann gives for the relative distribution of these roles depends, in part, on elaborating the context of choice that women face in making decisions about work and family. As Gutmann (1987) points out:

> Elementary-school teaching is a career more attractive to adults who see themselves as nurturers of children, who place a high premium on being at home with their children after school and during the summer, who do not assume that they must be the primary breadwinners in their families, and who do not depend for their self-esteem on moving steadily up a career ladder or exercising authority over other adults. (p. 113)

This, of course, describes a set of characteristics that commonly are associated with women in American society, and it accurately predicts the lopsided picture of gender and power in our schools: According to the National Center for Education Statistics (NCES), while 73% of all public school teachers are female, only 35% of principals at all levels are female (NCES, 1996).

The relevance of Gutmann's argument for considering the context of choice that women face in schools is that she, like Howe, is interested in assessing the consequences of institutional patterns that constrain the opportunities that are genuinely open to women within these institutions. As Gutmann (1987) says:

> The problem is roughly the following: as long as women are hired as elementary-school teachers in far greater proportions than men, and men are hired as school administrators in far greater proportions than women, schools will teach children that "men rule women and women rule children" (Pogrebin, 1980). Why shouldn't schools teach this lesson, someone might ask, if it reflects the social reality of gender preferences rather than discriminatory hiring practices? A preliminary answer is that schools do not simply reflect, they perpetuate the social reality of gender preferences when they educate children in a system in which men rule women and women rule children. The authority structure within schools serves as an additional lesson in the nature of "normal" gender relations. Girls learn that it is normal for them to rule children, but abnormal for them to rule men. Boys learn the opposite lesson. The democratic problem lies not in the content of either lesson per se, but in its repressive nature: the lessons reinforce uncritical acceptance of an established set of sex stereotypes and unreflective rejection of reasonable (and otherwise available) alternatives. (pp. 113–114)

Gutmann's position here is consistent with the view I have attributed to Kymlicka and Howe, namely, that understanding individual preferences (and the extent to which they have been constrained or distorted) requires careful scrutiny of the circumstances surrounding their formation. Gutmann's analysis is also consistent with the claim that conclusions about the circumstances under which preferences have been constructed may justify forms of intervention by the state that exceed those sanctioned by previous liberal egalitarian accounts. As Kymlicka (1991) warns, "Just as favouring the elimination of class-based inequalities may bring liberals closer to the traditional socialist programme, so favouring the elimination of gender-based inequalities may bring liberals closer to the radical feminist programme" (p. 93).

The Liberal Agenda for Reform: A Participatory Paradigm

Based on this characterization of the context of choice, we now need to look more closely at what might be included in the kind of expanded program of liberal reform suggested by Kymlicka. The answer, I believe, brings us to one of the most important features of the contemporary liberal perspective, which is the advocacy of a profoundly participatory paradigm for understanding and reconstructing social institutions. This approach is "profoundly participatory" in the sense that it assumes from the start that inequities in the context of choice have left us with "opportunities" that cannot be trusted (they are "not worth wanting," according to Howe) and social roles that already reflect the exercise of power by one group over another. Issues of power and identity must therefore be placed in the foreground of discussions about social (and educational) reform, leaving open, for the moment anyway, the question of what progress might look like to the participants involved in these discussions.

The oppression of girls and women remains a good example on which to focus here, because it illuminates so well the complexity of the dilemmas liberals face in elaborating this kind of solution. The systematic way that patriarchy has influenced Western societies makes reform a far more complicated issue than simply redistributing resources from men to women, or creating access for women to roles currently held by men (although, to invoke the customary qualification of these compensatory reforms, they may still be necessary and they may still considerably improve the material status of women in patriarchal societies). Kymlicka (1991) has noted this difficulty, for instance, and again reminds his liberal colleagues that the necessary reforms may well fall outside the boundaries that once distinguished them from their more radical critics.

> While liberals from Locke through Mill to Rawls have officially proclaimed
> that their theories are based on the natural equality of individuals, they have
> in fact taken the male-headed family as the essential unit of political analy-
> sis; women's interests are defined by, and submerged in, the family, which is
> taken to be their "natural" position. . . . The assumptions of women's inferi-
> ority are deeply embedded in many of society's institutions, from the teach-
> ing of sex roles to children to the public devaluation of domestic labour.
> Removing them will require changes not only in the access women have to
> social positions, but also in their ability to shape and define those positions.
> These reforms have not on the whole been endorsed by liberals, even by
> liberal feminists. (p. 92)

Kymlicka's conclusion here is, again, quite different from the kind offered
by the liberal egalitarians who preceded him. He argues that individuals
must have the capacity to "shape and define" the positions available in
society, by altering the context of choice that situates all choices and life-
plans. This conclusion moves contemporary liberal theory an important
step closer to the position held by feminist and Marxist critics: that
oppression and exploitation are firmly rooted in the basic structure of
society and therefore cannot be adequately addressed through traditional forms of liberal regulation (of individuals' pursuit of the good) or
through the compensatory redistribution of resources like money or access to jobs.

On this account, liberal theorists must be especially concerned with
institutions, like schools, that play a powerful role in mediating the capacity of individuals to deliberate over their life-plans and to pursue a conception of the good consistent with this deliberation. Howe recognizes
the danger of focusing only on increasing access to existing structures of
meaning and identity and, in place of this formalist interpretation of
equal educational opportunity, argues for a more participatory vision of
what it means for oppressed or exploited groups to be meaningfully included in a dialogue over the needs and interests that schools should
attempt to meet. What he is in fact describing is an educational context
in which all participants have a say in creating opportunities for self-
expression, recognizing that this sense of "self" depends, in part, on
group membership and social position.

> The participatory interpretation seeks to overcome the defect in the compen-
> satory interpretation by building into the principle of equality of educational
> opportunity the requirement of including the needs, interests, and perspec-
> tives of all groups—especially groups that have been historically excluded—

in determining what educational opportunities are indeed worth wanting. (Howe, 1997, p. 4)

In response to circumstances that have excluded or marginalized women from the educational process, for example, Howe concludes that adopting the "participatory educational ideal" will "require broad—and deep—change of a kind that disrupts and transforms traditional gender assumptions and relationships in schools" (Howe, 1997, p. 50).

A variety of educational reforms have been proposed that are consistent with this approach and that might, in some combination, help schools make concrete progress toward Howe's participatory ideal. At the level of curriculum and pedagogy, more collaborative forms of instruction and less competitive systems of assessment may help create a classroom atmosphere that girls and women find more congenial and in which they are more likely to become active participants (Sadker & Sadker, 1994). Girls and women may also benefit from curriculum that is more explicitly "connected" to the concerns of others or that have some clear purpose in meeting the needs of others (Belenky, Clinchy, Goldberger, & Tarule, 1986). Some educational philosophers have argued that the customary academic disciplines themselves should take a backseat to a more contextualized, student-centered curriculum that would be more open to the interests and needs that girls and women bring to their education (Noddings, 1992; Martin, 1992). Feminist educational philosophers have also argued in favor of a "gender-sensitive" approach to school policy and classroom practice (Martin, 1992; Houston, 1996), believing that such an orientation may contribute to the emancipation of women and help to disrupt the customary valorization of "reproductive" over "productive" labor in schools and society (Martin, 1981).

At the level of school or institutional organization, the growth of women's studies departments and courses that focus on issues of power and exclusion in society have provided a context for critical discussions and activism around issues of inequality (Fiol-Matta & Chamberlain, 1994; Maher & Tetreault, 1994). New outlets (e.g., school clubs, professional organizations, support groups) where women can find peer support for high academic achievement may also be important in deflecting the pressure that women feel to opt out of rigorous educational programs or to reject traditionally male occupational goals (Holland & Eisenhart, 1990). Single-sex schooling, either in specific disciplines or across the curriculum at particular ages, may help girls and women gain a greater sense of ownership in their work and make them less vulnerable to the constraints placed on them by male peers (Sadker & Sadker, 1994). Affirmative action plans based on the gender role modeling that takes place throughout all levels of educational leadership would require that women assume more visible positions of authority (in number and kind) and that schools consciously disrupt the unspoken expectation that men should have power over women (Gutmann, 1987).

It is not the case that *all* of these reforms are justified *only* (or even best) by the type of liberal theory that philosophers like Kymlicka, Howe, and Gutmann have described. In fact, it should be clear from the citations given above that educational philosophers and policy advocates of various sorts have recommended these changes. The importance of the analysis presented here is that it makes more plausible the contention that liberal educational theory can make legitimate and persuasive claims about the social context within which educational goods and opportunities are situated. Liberal educational philosophers like Howe have argued that the participatory ideal requires more inclusive deliberation over educational goals and that this process should be especially open to claims made by those who have been excluded, not just from access to existing opportunities, but from participating in their very constitution. If liberals can successfully defend this point, and I think they are well on their way to doing so, it will give us an even better set of reasons for seeing their insights as potentially consistent with, and mutually supportive of, the central arguments about schooling made by critical theorists, to whom I now turn as a second example of the universalist emancipatory perspective.

CRITICAL THEORY

Like liberalism, critical theory also offers a generalizable descriptive and normative framework, based on universal qualities of human experience, for understanding social relations and institutions. Critical theorists try to show how school practices help reproduce patterns of oppression and exploitation that exist in society, based on structural differences in power and status. While social class has historically been at the heart of these radical critiques, contemporary critical theorists have expanded their interpretation of the structures on which social relations are based to include other features of experience that powerfully organize meaning and therefore identity in individuals' lives, including gender, race, and sexual orientation. This development is central to using critical theory as a guide for emancipatory educational practice, especially in promoting schools as sites for exploring the connection between individual experience and social reconstruction. These accounts put a premium on students developing an awareness of oppressive social structures and their capacity to participate meaningfully in resistance and reform.

Michael Apple's *Ideology and Curriculum* (1979) was a groundbreaking text in this tradition, and the following excerpt serves as an appropriate touchstone and summary of the central features of this approach:

> The intent of . . . critical scholarship in general, then, is two fold. First, it aims at illuminating the tendencies for unwarranted and often unconscious domination, alienation, and repression within certain existing cultural, political, educational, and economic institutions. Second, through exploring the negative effects and contradictions of much that unquestioningly goes on in these institutions, it seeks to "promote conscious [individual and collective] emancipatory activity." That is, it examines what is supposed to be happening in, say, schools if one takes the language and slogans of many school people seriously; and it then shows how these things *actually* work in a manner that is destructive of ethical rationality and personal political and institutional power. Once this actual functioning is held up to scrutiny, it attempts to point to concrete activity that will lead to challenging this taken for granted activity. (p. 133, emphasis and bracketed material in original)

In what follows, I elaborate the critical tradition in education by putting two of its most powerful concepts, ideology and alienation, to use. My goal in doing this is to show how critical theory exposes oppressive conditions in schools and how it might direct emancipatory educational reforms in the future. On the basis of this analysis, I argue for a stronger and more consistent relationship between the reform agendas promoted by critical theorists and liberals.

Ideology and the Social Construction of Schooling

Ideology is a complex and contentious concept, even within Marxism (Larraine, 1983), and it is often used rather loosely in academic discourse. As a starting point for this analysis, I draw on R. G. Peffer's (1990) summary of the "defining characteristics" that have been associated with ideology in the Marxist literature.

> In the writings of Marx and Engels, as well as of later Marxists, one finds the following features of theories or sets of ideas spoken of as defining characteristics of ideology, i.e., as the necessary and sufficient conditions a theory or set of ideas must fulfill in order to be properly labeled "ideology" or "ideological:" (1) that it is generated within a class society or by a member of a class or social group that is generally sympathetic to the ruling class and/or the social status quo; that it is (2) unscientific, (3) illusory, (4) an

inverted ("upside-down" or "topsy-turvy") representation of reality, (5) a result or component of "false-consciousness," (6) systematically misleading, or (7) socially mystifying. Other suggested characteristics are that a theory or set of ideas (8) represents the interests of a ruling class as the common interest of society, (9) serves to justify the social status quo and/or interests of a ruling class, and (10) functions to maintain the social status quo and/or defends the interests of the ruling class. (pp. 236–237)

The Marxist concept of ideology is important in this analysis because it helps explain how social institutions constrain the choices and self-representations of individuals in society. To pursue this line of argument, we need an account that is particularly sensitive to the social construction of knowledge and how what we know is framed (its meaning produced) within powerful institutions like schools and outside of these institutions in the broader society.

Marxist views of ideology are based on the proposition that what we come to claim as knowledge is constituted in a social context of conflicting needs and interests. The triumph of the dominant class under these circumstances can be expressed in terms of the ascendancy of one particular set of views about the world over others. The perspective of the dominant group is gradually normalized and comes to represent the prevailing assumptions and values of social intercourse. As Alison Jaggar (1983) notes:

> At least since the inception of class society . . . societies have not been characterized by a single set of interests and values. Instead, societies have been composed of classes whose interests have been in opposition to each other and whose values have conflicted with each other. In such a situation, one cannot say that the prevailing world view or system of knowledge reflects the interests and values of society as a whole. Instead, one must specify which class's interests and values are reflected. Marxism's answer to this question is that the system of knowledge that is generally accepted within a society reflects the interests of the dominant class. (pp. 358–359)

In societies where power and status are attached to (i.e., where possessing them depends upon) membership in specific groups or classes, the views held by less powerful members of society are systematically ignored or repressed. This repression is especially intense in circumstances where these marginalized views contain some element of critique aimed at the dominant class or at any of the various aspects of the social system that support it. Understanding ideology in this way commits Marxist social theorists to analyzing not only the substance of marginalized views, as representations of competing interests and values, but also the means by which social institutions enforce or help reproduce the dominance of the ruling class ideology. Jaggar (1983) again notes:

> During times of relative stability, the dominant ideology is imposed in a number of ways. The most obvious of these ways involve the direct suppression of potentially subversive observations or theories. One effective means of doing this is by denying a voice to those classes from which such ideas are likely to emerge. Those classes are denied education and even literacy, and their ideas are labeled as superstition. By contrast, honors are heaped on those who invent theories that can be used to justify the status quo, and their ideas are popularized in the mass media. Those who do develop subversive theories are ridiculed and denied jobs or research facilities. If their ideas seem to be gaining popularity anyway, the ruling class resorts to outright censorship and persecution; for instance, subversive groups may be prohibited from access to the media or denied the right to assemble. (p. 359)

Susan Faludi's *Backlash: The Undeclared War Against American Women* (1991) provides a powerful example of how ideology has been, and continues to be, used as a political and cultural tool of oppression in the United States. Her work effectively documents how opposition to the women's movement has been carefully shaped and promoted in politics, intellectual life, and the media.

Critical theorists in education have inherited this tradition and use the concept of ideology to explain how schools regulate the production of knowledge and help reproduce the privilege of a dominant class. They urge us to look carefully at how the goals of education are framed or understood in society and to question whether these goals mask and promote the interests of a dominant group. To elaborate this view, it is appropriate to consider the neo-conservative agenda itself as an object of ideological analysis. This strategy allows us to explore the method of critical theory, while continuing to interrogate the neo-conservative position and some of the reasons for its success.

The ideological construction of an educational crisis. In Chapter 2, I described the conflict between neo-conservatives and emancipatory theorists as rooted in an ongoing battle over whose cultural values would prevail in public discourse and be promoted in social institutions like schools. As the growing sense of alarm over cultural trends and the greater proclivity for confrontation (in politics, religion, and the media) suggest, neo-conservatives are fighting hard to retain the position of cultural dominance they have occupied in American society. The increasing resistance to this domination and thus the need for an evolving neo-conservative ideology are in part due to what Tyack and Hansot (1981) have described as the "erosion of consensus."

This erosion of consensus resulted, in part, from the destabilization of an ideology that could not be sustained in the face of powerful changes in American culture, including Vietnam and Watergate; the challenges of the civil rights and women's movements; student and faculty activism on college campuses around the country, and the widespread questioning of social norms concerned with conformity, restraint, and tradition. With these historical and cultural transformations, the right's grip on American culture began to slip and the ideology supporting it began to fragment. William Bennett (1992) notes with chagrin the decline of "traditional American values" and clearly attributes the current crisis in American education to this cultural and historical process.

> In the late sixties and seventies we saw a sustained attack on traditional American values and the place where those values had long had a comfortable and congenial home—the school. . . . Academics provided much of the intellectual heavy artillery—citing how endemically corrupt and sick America is. Once the traditional teachings were discredited and then removed, the vacuum was filled by faddish nonsense, and the kids got lost. (pp. 51–52)

What critical theorists would predict in these circumstances is the emergence of a new or reconstructed conservative ideology that is more responsive to these changing historical conditions. Such an ideology would seek to establish a new consensus among members of society, reproducing the privilege of the dominant class and the hierarchy on which it depends, using the cultural resources available at the time. This is indeed what has happened, according to critical theorists, and a central concern of their work has been to explain the role of public schooling in this process.

The emergence a new (neo-) conservative ideology in education can be traced, in one respect, to a common strategy in historical struggles over public schooling: asserting the need for more direct control of schools in light of an educational crisis that threatens the very foundation of society. Concerns about such crises often involve the moral fabric of the nation, its economic productivity, and its standing in eyes of foreign competitors. I described a view very much like this one in Chapter 2, but it is worth recalling some of what neo-conservatives have said about our current educational crisis in the context of this discussion of ideology. We have seen, for instance, the rather desperate sense of alarm reflected in the accounts given by neo-conservatives and the strident martial metaphors used to describe the need for prompt and decisive action. Chester Finn's (1991) warning about "grave malfunctions throughout the society" (p. xiv) and the frightening conclusion in *A Nation at Risk* that we are "committing an act of unthinking, unilateral educational disarmament" (National Commission on Excellence in Education, 1983, p. 5) represent important pieces in the ideological puzzle that has helped convince most Americans that public education is in its worst state ever and that the cost of inaction will be a radically diminished quality of life for this and future generations.

In offering an ideological critique of this account, it is important to note from the onset that critical theorists are not forced to disagree with the claim that the American educational system is in *some* kind of crisis; indeed, this general proposition has widespread support among all the emancipatory perspectives considered here. The rub, of course, comes in saying what, exactly, constitutes the current state of crisis we are facing. Thus, critical theorists begin by acknowledging that important reasons for action exist, but they also recognize the need to inquire more deeply into the nature and causes of the problems we see. This kind of approach avoids treating the construction of ideology naively, that is, as spun from a fabric of whole cloth that has no basis in the lives of real people. As Michael Apple (1993) suggests, "The first thing to ask about an ideology is not what is false about it, but what is true. What are its connections to lived experience?" (p. 20). This is especially important in understanding how neo-conservatives have garnered enthusiastic support from some of the very groups (e.g., White, working-class males) who are significantly harmed by the educational agenda that neo-conservatives promote. To understand this better, critical theorists urge us to look carefully at how the crisis in education is "explained" by neo-conservatives and, in particular, who is blamed for causing it.

In most accounts of our current educational crisis, neo-conservatives are open and generous with their attributions of responsibility. Some of the most frequently cited culprits are lazy teachers, greedy unions, "special interest" minority groups (people of color, gays and lesbians, etc.), uncaring and incompetent (often single) parents, left-wing university professors, and educational progressives (Bennett, 1992; Finn, 1991; Hirsch, 1987a, 1996). It is also a widely held belief in the context of this neo-conservative ideology that the crisis in our schools has been exacerbated by the self-serving policies of educational bureaucrats and liberal politicians who have resisted the kinds of large-scale interventions (i.e., more effective forms of regulation and control) that would be most useful in addressing our educational problems. These interventions include the creation of a national curriculum, mandated standardized assessment procedures, changes in teacher licensing and labor policies, and extensive school choice plans (Bennett, 1992; Finn, 1991). To see how neoconservatives have promoted this agenda, we need to consider how the ideology supporting it constructs a social landscape within which disagreements over the goals of education are understood and, especially, how divergent views are interpreted. It is important to remember here that the analysis of ideology practiced by critical theorists aims at finding and exposing the hidden interests of the dominant class and demonstrating how the rationale given for particular social practices both masks (mystifies) and promotes these interests.

Critical theorists like Michael Apple (1993) have argued that the neoconservative agenda in education (and in the broader society as well) has depended to a significant extent on the success of an ideology that pits one marginalized group against another, sowing conflict where there might be solidarity and deflecting consideration of the basic structures that actually determine the distribution of power, status, and resources in society. This ideology encourages a socially sanctioned kind of victim blaming, in which one group blames another (often lower down the social hierarchy) for the dispossession they feel and the material benefits they lack. Existing social institutions are treated as fundamentally sound but working improperly or inefficiently, because less deserving members of society have somehow hijacked these institutions for their own narrow, personal gain. Accepting this ideological framework almost ensures that subsequent discussions of educational problems and what to do about them will take place in the divisive context of a dispute among already marginalized groups, who are then left to wrangle over who deserves greater access to the increasingly scarce material resources and economic opportunities available to them in society. Apple describes the evolution of this ideology as a way of rechanneling or reconstructing the insecurity of groups who already feel themselves being pushed to the margins of society. This is just the kind of demystification of ideology, the "ironic" reversal or unveiling of the rationale behind a dominant group's way of thinking about the world, that critical theorists aim to promote.

> Behind the conservative restoration is a clear sense of loss: of control, of economic and personal security, of the knowledge and values that should be passed on to children, of visions of what counts as sacred texts and authority. The binary opposition of we/they becomes very important here. "We" are law abiding, "hard working, decent, virtuous, and homogeneous." The "theys" are very different. They are "lazy, immoral, permissive, heterogeneous." These binary oppositions distance most people of color, women, gays, lesbians, and others from the community of worthy individuals. The

subjects of discrimination are now no longer those groups who have been historically oppressed, but are instead the "real Americans" who embody the idealized virtues of a romanticized past. The "theys" are undeserving. They are getting something for nothing. Policies supporting them are "sapping our way of life," most of our economic resources, and creating government control of our lives. (Apple, 1993, p. 28)

Under these divisive circumstances, neo-conservatives have mounted an effective campaign to reconstruct public schools around a new ideological construction. By equating neo-conservative educational policy with so-called "traditional" values in society, its advocates promote a "restorationist" agenda (Martin, 1992) that promises to return American society to its former greatness.

Alongside the creation of this "need" for social and educational restoration, neo-conservatives also require that this new ideology help re-establish some measure of consensus among groups in society concerning the direction and goals of public schooling. The purpose of this new coalition, it must be emphasized, is not *constructive,* that is, its purpose is not to create a vision of public schooling that incorporates the diverse views of the coalition's members. Rather, its function is *legitimating;* its purpose is to normalize the emerging restorationist view as part of a simple, "commonsense" view of education, based on values that are generally treated as self-evidently valid and, on the whole, easy to teach in school (i.e., through direct instruction). This is a central feature of the cultural war that William Bennett has described. What critical theorists have shown us is that the battle lines drawn in this conflict represent differences in power and status, that is, differences in social position and the interests that attach to them, rather than abstract differences in educational vision. The neo-conservative ideology of schooling obscures these differences, while trying to create public agreement on the terms and conditions of the debate. With the ascension of this neo-conservative ideology, Michael Apple (1993) notes:

A new hegemonic accord, then, is reached. . . . It combines dominant economic and political elites intent on "modernizing" the economy, white working-class and middle-class groups concerned with security, the family, and traditional knowledge and values, and economic and cultural conservatives. It also includes a fraction of the new middle class whose own advancement depends on the expanded use of accountability, efficiency, and management procedures which are their own cultural capital. This coalition has partly succeeded in altering the very meaning of what it means to have a social goal of equality. The citizen as "free" consumer has replaced the previously emerging citizen as situated in structurally generated relations of domination. Thus, the common good is now to be regulated exclusively by the laws of the market, free competition, private ownership, and profitability. In essence, the definitions of freedom and equality are no longer democratic, but *commercial*. This is particularly evident in the proposals for voucher and choice plans as "solutions" to massive and historically rooted relations of economic and cultural inequality. (pp. 30–31, emphasis in original)

Neo-conservatives have thus succeeded in creating a coalition of groups who believe their needs and interests will be best served by a realignment of public institutions, especially schools, around the restoration of traditional moral values. As Apple argues, this ideological transformation is taking place at a fundamental level in the public's thinking about social and educational policies, and it has opened the way for a new defense of the most persistent forms of inequality.

Redirecting schooling toward a critical pedagogy. To understand the "real" crisis in education, critical theorists urge us to consider how neo-conservatives have used this ideology to divert attention from the root causes of our most pressing problems in schools. The ideology promoted by neo-conservatives obscures the powerful effects of race, class, gender, and sexual orientation on educational outcomes, and it discourages solidarity among groups that have much to gain through collective political action. To find the roots of our worst educational failures, according to critical theorists, we should carefully examine the social structures that underlie poverty, racism, sexism, homophobia, and other forms of institutionalized oppression. These are the social dynamics that limit the capacity of individuals to pursue their life-plans, privileging a few at the expense of many. Demystifying the restorationist ideology contributes to our understanding of public schooling by helping us recognize and identify the interests embedded in the neo-conservative agenda; critical theorists show how this account is both a diversion from the real causes of our educational crisis and a politically convenient way to intensify conflict among less powerful groups.

In addition to laying bare the ideological foundations of neo-conservative proposals for educational change, critical theorists have also pursued a positive agenda of reform, based on their commitment to schools as sites for the production of emancipatory knowledge and social practice. Although this aspect of the critical tradition is somewhat more diffuse and frequently criticized for its overreliance on language that is too abstract or theoretical (and thus inaccessible to those whom it is meant to serve), there are nonetheless good examples of teacher/researchers who have written about their use of ideological critique and classroom practices that aim at demystifying oppressive social norms. Ira Shor (1992), for example, whose work I discuss in greater detail below, has reflected extensively on his own practice as a teacher of basic English in a college enrolling mostly working-class students. His teaching and scholarship are consciously motivated by emancipatory educational goals and situated in a clear understanding of the historical development of neo-conservative ideology (Shor, 1986). Like Apple, Shor (1992) sees the potential of emancipatory education to help students understand how knowledge, power, and identity are inextricably bound together in the process of schooling and thus in the (re)construction of society.

> In forming the students' conception of self and the world, teachers can pres-
> ent knowledge in several ways, as a celebration of the existing society, as a
> falsely neutral avoidance of problems rooted in the system, or as a critical
> inquiry into power and knowledge as they relate to student experience. . . .
> In sum, the subject matter, the learning process, the classroom discourse, the
> cafeteria menu, the governance structure, and the environment of school
> teach students what kind of people to be and what kind of society to build
> as they learn math, history, biology, literature, nursing, or accounting. Educa-
> tion is more than facts and skills. It is a socializing experience that helps
> make the people who make society. (pp. 14–15)

Bill Ayers is another good example of a teacher/researcher whose reflections on classroom instruction, this time at the elementary school level,
provide a clear and detailed picture of what it means to attend to issues
of knowledge construction and empowerment. In *To Teach: The Journey of
a Teacher* (1993), Ayers notes the danger of failing to recognize the dangers
inherent in becoming disconnected from the moral decision making that
inevitably guides instruction.

> Teachers, then, too often implement the initiatives of others; we pass on
> someone else's ideas of what is valuable to know or experience, and we culti-
> vate a sense of "objectivity" as the greatest good. We become passionless,
> non-thinking, uninvolved, and we hand over important considerations to
> "the experts," evading our deepest responsibility and marooning ourselves
> with the merely technical. As we separate means from ends, we begin to
> see our students as subjects for manipulation. Moral considerations become
> irrelevant; in the banal language of our time, we are each merely discharging
> our duties, following orders, simply doing our jobs. (p. 19)

Thus, a crucial starting point for this approach involves recognizing that
all teaching involves decisions about what is, and what is not, valuable

knowledge, as well as assumptions about who possesses valuable knowledge in the larger society.

Shor and Ayers both have a lot to say in their work about how their classrooms have been shaped by the recognition that knowledge is produced there and that this knowledge shapes the future of their students and society. From a curriculum rooted in student experience, to an unrelenting commitment to embedding teaching and learning in the social context that surrounds their schools, the efforts of teachers like Shor and Ayers are good examples of an emancipatory approach to curriculum and pedagogy that takes the power of ideology, and the potential for resistance to it, seriously.

Critical theorists have also focused on specific school practices that distort or limit the kind of knowledge that students learn about themselves and their communities in the classroom. Consistent with their critique of ideology, critical theorists have identified a variety of school practices that help reproduce social hierarchies in school and in society, including tracking or ability grouping (Oakes, 1985; Shor, 1992), biased forms of testing and assessment (Gould, 1996; Oakes, 1985; Sadker & Sadker, 1994), and approaches to instruction that emphasize control and inculcate acquiescence to authority (Anyon, 1980; McNeil, 1988). An especially interesting related body of literature, one that overlaps with these critiques and generally includes detailed ethnographic studies of particular sites where social production/reproduction takes place, are works that try to explain the resilience of oppressive ideologies, even in the face of "partially" successful critiques by students. Perhaps best known among these examples is Paul Willis' (1977) study of working-class students attending a school he calls "Hammertown Boys" (a pseudonym) in England, who reject the false meritocracy of schooling by "having a laugh" at their teachers' expense, but who also, in doing this, reproduce the cultural and economic constraints that push them straight into the shop floor jobs of their fathers. Related examples include Holland and Eisenhart (1990), on the implications of peer gender relations for the "culture of romance" on two American university campuses, and Foley (1990) on the role that school and community rituals play in the reproduction of gender and class identities in a small Texas town. These examples provide useful insights into the obstacles that practitioners of a critical pedagogy face in the pursuit of instructional practices that successfully connect the demystification of ideology to social and political empowerment.

It is possible (and useful) here to make a brief analogy between this analysis of ideology and the way contemporary liberals have appealed to the context of choice in their treatment of social inequality. While differences no doubt still exist concerning the precise nature of structural constraints, liberal and critical theorists are both eager to show how social circumstances shape and, in racist, sexist, classist, or heterosexist societies, distort individuals' conceptions of self and their potential to achieve future goals. Thus, in both traditions, the normative assessment of educational policies and practices depends at least in part on the extent to which these policies and practices help members of society see and understand the forces that shape them. Both traditions also promote an enlargement of the dialogue over educational goals, with the presumption that fundamental changes will result from the inclusion of members of society whose needs and interests have historically been discounted.

Before I take this analogy further, however, there is another aspect of critical theory that is useful to consider as part of the broader effort to describe the relationship between liberal and critical theories. This aspect has to do with the harm or costs of living in a society built around deeply embedded forms of structural inequality.

Alienation and the Experience of Schooling

While critical theorists in education have not used the term *alienation* in their analyses as often or as explicitly as they have ideology, it is nonetheless an important aspect of the explanations they have given for the harms that schools do to students who are not members of the dominant class in society. The Marxist concept of alienation can be used to describe and critique the various ways that social institutions constrain the capacity of individuals to grow and develop in undistorted ways. What is particularly relevant for this project is how Marxism has provided insights into the way social institutions obscure or even transform the images individuals hold of themselves and thus their sense of self-efficacy, while at the same time mystifying the oppressive circumstances that the least powerful share with others.

Marx offered several accounts of alienation, mostly in his early writings, although the concept retained some importance in the way he characterized the harms of capitalism throughout his work (Elster, 1985; Jaggar, 1983; Peffer, 1990). Two forms of alienation generally have been identified by scholars of Marx's work. Elster (1985) refers to these forms as "spiritual alienation" and "social alienation." Spiritual alienation is a separation from self, or from what it means to be fully human. For Marx, capitalism is alienating in this respect insofar as it prevents individuals from acting in accordance with their own needs and potential, that is, it precludes self-realization. The second form of alienation, social alienation, which Peffer describes as including "alienation of the product of production, alienation of the activity of production, [and] alienation of the individual from other individuals" (Peffer, 1990, p. 66), also results from capitalist economic relations. This form of alienation rests in individuals' relationships with others and the effects of the products and processes of their labor on conceptions of self. In both interpretations, alienation results in a diminished capacity for seeing and participating in activities that are essential to exercising one's full humanity.

As I pointed out earlier, it is important to see how critical theorists have expanded their treatment of oppression in ways that extend beyond social class as the only, or always the most important, dimension of social experience. Other forms of oppression are rooted in structures constituted by gender, race, ethnicity, and sexual orientation, among others. The foundation for extending the concept of alienation beyond class rests in the powerful and fundamentally different effects of these social categories on our way of thinking about and acting in the world. While class remains the central focus of Marxist political analyses, an emphasis on the broader social context of individual action by feminists, among others, has had far-reaching implications for understanding other shared aspects of human experience (Baier, 1985, 1987; Held, 1993; Jaggar, 1983). The work of these feminists has helped us to understand the profound differences that exist between the experience of women and men in society, and the implications of looking at politics and society through one of many available lenses.

The concept of alienation has been important to feminists as a way of understanding how patriarchal societies shape and distort the experience of women in such a way that makes their exploitation seem generally acceptable, even to many women. Alienation helps to mask, mystify, and legitimate differences in power, status, and social roles among women and men in society. As Alison Jaggar (1983) notes:

> A few socialist feminist authors, building on radical feminist insights, have argued that women's experience in contemporary society is a perfect example of alienation. Socialist feminist explorations reveal the ways in which women are alienated as sexual beings, as mothers, and as wives. One socialist feminist author writes that femininity itself is alienation. (p. 308)

This is just the kind of account we need in order to understand how the norms and practices of a particular context can affect the formation, development, and pursuit of individuals' life-plans, and thus their changing conception(s) of self. The concept of alienation is useful as a way of describing some of the most powerful disadvantages of living in a society built upon deeply embedded forms of structural inequality; it helps us see oppression as an experience that enforces constraints on self-identity and limits the capacity of individuals to resist domination.

Schooling and spiritual alienation. Ira Shor (1986, 1992), whose work I discussed briefly in the preceding section, is a critical theorist who has explored in some detail the connection between education and social change. Much influenced by the work of Brazilian educator and social activist Paulo Freire (1970, 1985, 1992), one of Shor's foremost concerns is helping students participate in social change through "empowering education." Although Shor does not often use the term *alienation* in his work, much of the criticism he offers of our current schools can be described and elaborated in relation to it.

For Shor, our schools fail to educate students in a number of important ways that revolve around issues of identity and power. Perhaps most important among these failures is the way schools teach students that they bring little of value to the educational process; these traditional approaches fit students with the time-worn image of an empty vessel brought to school for filling. The reliance of so many of our schools on a teacher-centered curriculum, one that depends primarily on transmission forms of instruction, draws heavily on mass-produced textbooks, and assesses students in terms of their ability to recall decontextualized bits of information taken from readings or lectures, alienates students from the true needs and interests they bring to the classroom. Shor's analysis of such approaches draws powerfully on Freire's now famous critique of the "banking model" in education. Recalling Freire's work, Shor (1992) notes:

> Because it deposits information uncritically in students, the banking model is antidemocratic. It denies the students' indigenous culture and their potential for critical thought, subordinating them to the knowledge, values, and language of the status quo. . . . In banking education, knowledge and society are assumed to be fixed and assumed to be fine the way they are. By limiting creative and critical questioning, the banking model makes education into an authoritarian transfer instead of a democratic experience. (pp. 33–34)

This banking model excludes students from meaningful participation in educational activities and teaches them that what they bring to school, the range of interests and experiences that constitute their identity, is at best irrelevant and at worst an obstacle to learning. Through the ideological process of normalization described in the preceding section, the traditional curriculum becomes an "objective" standard against which students' past and present lives are measured. The extent to which students cannot find themselves in this social construction marks the degree to which the "self" they brought into the classroom is diminished and excluded. Students learn and internalize this absence as part of their day-to-day experience of schooling and thus become alienated from their needs and desires. The false bargain of assimilation described in Chapter 2 is a particularly powerful example of this process: Students outside the dominant culture are asked to exchange their marginalized cultural identities for the dubious promise of future success among those who have been their most persistent detractors. Schools guided by this traditional model, one promoted by neo-conservatives and rationalized by their ideology of restoration, are a significant source of spiritual alienation and present significant obstacles to individuals' self-realization.

Another source of spiritual alienation identified by Shor concerns the implications of systematic or structural inequalities in the distribution of educational resources. It is important in this case to see how disempowerment depends not just on the literal absence of resources in schools, but perhaps just as importantly on the message these conditions send to students. We need look no further than schools that serve disproportionately poor and minority populations to find ample documentation of the alienating conditions these students face. As Shor (1992) notes:

> Working people did not create for themselves overcrowded and under-funded schools, subordinate tracks in education, and vocationalized community colleges. These lesser experiences were invented for them by elite policymakers. No one volunteers to become a third-class citizen. Average people don't go out looking for bad education, low paying jobs, crowded neighborhoods, and less political influence in society; they want for themselves and their children the resources and choices available in the best schools, residential areas, and jobs. But school-children from poor and working homes receive the limited learning and shabby treatment which confirm their lower status. Unequal funding, inadequate staffing and facilities, and weak curricula—all decisions made from above—dominate the socializing experiences of students from below. (p. 115)

Jonathan Kozol (1991) makes similar arguments about the demoralizing effects of the enormous inequalities that exist in school funding, and the all too visible differences in educational quality that poor and minority students often experience. Again, the language of alienation is useful in describing the effects of these differences, as it helps connect the social context in which decisions about educational policy are made (e.g., how schools are funded) to the experiences students share because of their membership in particular social groups. Students who attend bad schools know they are getting what others think they deserve; what we know about labeling and self-fulfilling prophecies in education underscores the debilitating potential of this form of spiritual alienation and gives critical theorists much to be concerned about.

The consequences of these educational policies and school practices are not limited to the classroom, of course. Recall the neo-Marxist conception of ideology I described above as a normalization of structures of meaning that serve the needs and interests of the dominant class in society. The exclusion of students from most or all forms of meaningful participation in school promotes a form of alienation that is similar to what Marxists have used to describe the harms of capitalism. Students in these circumstances are more likely to feel impotent and disaffected by the process of their education. They see little point in trying to take a more active role in it, because schooling has not provided the reasons, the tools, or the opportunities to engage in such participation. It is easy to see how the absence of these qualities would affect the participation of individuals in other settings as well.

Schooling and social alienation. This analysis has so far focused on how the concept of alienation helps explain the process by which social institutions obscure or distort the awareness individuals hold of their own needs and interests, and how this effects the capacity of individuals to see themselves as effective agents of social change. This argument turned primarily on the first interpretation of alienation identified by Elster and Peffer, "spiritual alienation" or alienation from what it means to be fully human. This analysis led me to comment on the alienation students also experience from the process of education itself, and, like the alienation of a worker from the process of production, this brings us to what Elster calls "social alienation" and Peffer calls "the alienation of individuals from individuals." I want to explore this second definition of alienation further here, as a way of explaining the obstacles schools create to collaboration between and among students, and consequently to the development of individuals' capacity for participation in other collaborative social enterprises.

Critical theorists are interested in this second conception of alienation because it helps explain some of the ways that individuals are separated from each other, or even turned against each other, through their participation in schooling. This result is especially important, given the preceding analysis, in cases where individuals are similarly situated in oppressive social circumstances and thus already marginalized as competent or successful members of that institution. In a previous section, I briefly described some of the structural components that contribute to the process of sorting and segregating of students in school (e.g., tracking, standardized testing, forms of instruction based on control), and these practices are similarly useful in the context of this argument. However, the critique I offer here is aimed more at what it would be appropriate to call the culture of schooling; it focuses on barriers that are erected between students through the values, dispositions, and forms of conduct that are rewarded at school.

Perhaps first and foremost in this critique of alienation is the notion that schools are largely places where individuals do work, individuals pass or fail, and individuals receive academic honors or the disapproval of their teachers. This commitment to individualism masks many of the social components of success and failure in school, while at the same time discouraging students from seeking any kind of collective relief. As Shor notes, the value assigned to self-sufficiency and competitive achievement in schools (and elsewhere in society) places an important constraint on the capacity of students to develop cooperative and collaborative relationships. His advocacy of critical teaching aims explicitly at the "desocialization" of this widely held and often promoted value.

> The self-reliance commonly absorbed by students develops them as isolated beings dissociated from public life and from cooperative relations with others. Of course people need to develop as self-starting, responsible, and aspiring individuals. But competitive self-reliance teaches people that win or lose we have to make it on our own. We are encouraged to build solitary careers where only our ambitions, incomes, buying power, and immediate family count. Public life, social justice, community, world peace, and the environment disappear as serious concerns. Success here is the power to make lots of money so that we can buy more than we need. This extreme individualism encourages us to blame ourselves should we fail to strike it rich by our lone efforts. It orients us to see personal initiative as the only resource people have. We do not learn that the system has been transformed in the past by organized efforts and can be changed again. The life laid out for us is to fit in one by one as winners or losers in a status quo presented as permanent and as the best of all systems. (Shor, 1992, p. 118)

Even when shared features of social experience (poverty, for instance) are used to identify the challenges students face in school, it is still the individual who ultimately bears the burden (and explanation) of success or failure. This is true not only in terms of the way grades and test scores follow students through their careers and affect the opportunities that are available to them, but also in terms of the kind of moral culpability that school officials often attribute to students who they believe could have overcome these "disadvantages" if only they had the *will* to do so. William Bennett's work, for example, relies heavily on such stories of personal triumph. We need look no further than Bennett's (1992) idolization of Joe Clark (the bullhorn and bat-wielding principal of Eastside High in Patterson, NJ, and subject of the movie *Lean on Me*) and Jaime Escalante (the East L.A. calculus teacher whose story is recounted in the movie *Stand and Deliver*) to see that, for neo-conservatives, individual discipline and motivation are the keys to success in school, and their absence, by contrast, the source of our most pressing educational problems (pp. 78–81 and pp. 84–88, respectively).

According to Shor and other critical theorists, one of the most important goals that emancipatory schools can direct themselves at achieving is the development of a context in which students learn to participate meaningfully and collaboratively in the process of their own education. As Shor argues, restoring this foundation for participation is key to carrying out the emancipatory educational agenda. He advocates a pedagogy that mirrors the democratic political process, where becoming an agent of social change depends on developing a sense of self as connected to, and able to influence, the community in which one is a member. The transformation that Shor describes depends on a fundamental change in self-identity for many students, an overcoming of the alienation that has led them to a distrust their own capabilities, to adopt a cynical view of their capacity to change the system, and to remain diffident about the potential for constructive collaboration with others. Shor's arguments draw explicitly on the notion of democratic participation as central to the goals of critical teaching. It is a language that would not be unfamiliar to the liberal educational theorists quoted earlier in this chapter.

> A learning community emerges from mutual communication, meaningful work, and empowering methods. This community can be built if I situate critical study inside student language and experience, listening carefully to students and drawing out their ideas, encouraging them to listen carefully and respond to each other, and then remembering what was said. This careful attention to the actions and words of students shifts the focus from teacher-talk to the students' learning process. By careful observation of our communication and interaction, I demonstrate to students that the curriculum is being built from them, for them, and with them. When I recall students' statements made during previous classes, they laugh, surprised that I remember them. The seriousness with which I take their remarks is a new experience of self-respect for them, and it elicits some laughter emerging from novel feelings. (Shor, 1992, p. 259)

Based on their conceptions of ideology and alienation, critical theorists have laid the groundwork for an argument that again demonstrates how our individual experience is fundamentally conditioned by our social lives; we cannot begin to account for our desires, beliefs, and preferences without giving an account of their relationship to the social circumstances under which we live and the relationships we have with others. Critical theorists have shown that structural inequalities in social relations have a limiting and distorting effect on the capacity of oppressed groups in society to realize their fullest human potential. Critical theorists have used this methodology to show how educational norms and practices enforce similar constraints on students who come from oppressed or exploited groups, and how this treatment reproduces their subordinate status in society. By making social critique and empowerment explicit goals for emancipatory education, critical theorists aim at changing schools so that they support the efforts of oppressed and exploited groups to organize and work collaboratively for social change.

AUTONOMY AS CRITICAL CONSCIOUSNESS

My analysis of liberalism and critical theory has focused on the circumstances under which individuals make choices about themselves and their life-plans. I have argued strongly for the importance of treating social context as a fundamental element in the way we understand these choices and the role schools play in shaping the nature and meaning of choice. All of these issues are bound up with the concept of autonomy, one aspect of which I interpret here as critical consciousness. The conclusions I draw about the potential for common ground among universalist theories are rooted in an argument about what liberalism and critical theory share in their insights about autonomy as a central goal of education.

Late in *A Theory of Justice,* Rawls (1971) concludes that "persons are acting autonomously [when] they are acting from principles that they would acknowledge under conditions that best express their nature as free and equal rational beings" (p. 515). Critics of liberalism have called this characterization into question, however, with arguments that challenge the hypothetical models and assumptions about the nature of moral subjects on which it is based. This general line of critique has led liberal theorists like Will Kymlicka and Ken Howe to explore the idea that fully grasping the "context of choice" that individuals face in making decisions about their life-plans actually moves liberals closer to the kinds of structural critiques and efforts at fundamental social reconstruction that Marxists and socialist feminists customarily advocate. We might recall here that Howe (1997) describes his analysis as "a radical liberal framework," and note that Kymlicka (1991) recognizes (as earlier excerpts suggest) that his argument for a liberalism more sensitive to the importance of culture may lend new support to those who see liberalism and socialism as converging on a more radical agenda of political reform.

> It might be that a full implementation of the principle of neutral concern would move us much closer to market socialism than to welfare capitalism. . . . As Hobhouse put it, liberalism "when it grapples with the facts, is driven no small distance along Socialist lines" (1964:54). The two traditions have borrowed from each other throughout history, and "in the give and take of ideas with socialism, [liberalism] has learnt, and taught, more than one lesson" (Hobhouse 1964:115; Gutmann 1980:63–68, 70–86, 145–56). I think there are still lessons to be learned and taught. (p. 91)

While neither Kymlicka nor Howe is prepared to acquiesce to the critics of liberalism (far from it, in fact), the spirit behind their arguments clearly propels them toward a form of liberalism that takes seriously the important role played by social context in defining the circumstances of meaningful choice. This evolution in liberal theory represents an important focus on the structural qualities associated with autonomy, and the need to consider these in assessing the policies and practices of schools.

For their part, critical theorists have also argued (largely as a critique of liberalism) that autonomy must represent something more than the capacity of individuals to choose and pursue particular goods in society, constrained by the rights of others to do the same. Such a narrow conception of self, critical theorists claim, is insufficient for what we need in order to understand the way humans actually grow and flourish, or fail to, in complex, class-based societies. For critical theorists, the selection of individual goods is always conditioned by a complex set of economic and other factors involving individuals' relationships to each other and to the products and processes of their labor. Critical theorists use concepts like ideology and alienation to elaborate the experience of oppression and exploitation in a way that focuses our attention on structural inequalities and their effects on conceptions of self-identity, individual agency, and the possibility of collective social action.

Taken together, the insights of liberal and critical theorists mark a territory in the new constellation where universalist theories share a crucial and compatible set of insights for advancing the cause of emancipatory schooling. The central contribution of universalist theorists to the new constellation is their combined arguments for understanding autonomy as, in part, constituted by the capacity of individuals to discern and evaluate the way their choices have been enabled and constrained by the social context in which they live. This is what I will call the capacity for autonomy as critical consciousness.

Critical consciousness is a reflective capacity that individuals possess, to one degree or another, that enables them to grasp the meaning and implications of their choices in a social context. As a condition for having an opportunity worth wanting, as Howe argued, individuals must be aware of potential alternatives *and* their meaning. Individuals need to have some sense of the long-term consequences of their choices, especially in terms of whether or not a given decision made now might forestall other opportunities in the future. This characterization resonates with the arguments given by liberal and critical theorists, for example, against tracking policies that serve as misguided and harmful sorting mechanisms in public schools. The selection of a vocational track may well appear to suit the assessed abilities or expressed desires of particular students as they enter high school but, as Oakes and others have pointed out, the process by which such decisions are made often precludes (or at least diminishes the chances for) thoughtful consideration of available alternatives and their consequences. In the end, decisions about tracking are much more likely to be associated with characteristics such as race, class, and gender than some legitimate conception of individual need or interest (Oakes, 1985, 1990; Oakes, Ormseth, Bell, & Camp, 1990).

Critical consciousness is also important as a capacity for demystifying ideologies that distort the needs and interests of less powerful members of society. Schools play a central role in constructing and distributing the forms of knowledge that are considered most worth possessing in society, and this process often hurts female and minority students in ways that perpetuate their subordinate status. Critical theorists like Michael Apple and Ira Shor argue strongly for instructional practices that demystify constraining ideologies and make this process of knowledge construction explicit in schools, while providing the tools necessary for reconstructing these forms of knowledge around more inclusive and emancipatory social goals. Liberals like Kymlicka and Howe acknowledge the importance of questioning existing roles and opportunities in schools, opening a dialogue about how these roles and opportunities might be different today if oppressed groups had been part of their constitution in the first place. In this respect, liberals and critical theorists agree that emancipatory schooling "disrupts and transforms" oppressive social structures (Howe, 1997, p. 50) through critical analysis and more inclusive forms of dialogue.

Finally, critical consciousness is a capacity that supports the collective effort of individuals to join together in the fundamental reconstruction of oppressive institutions, especially those with important "socializing" and "legitimating" functions, like schools. Emancipatory reconstruction of these institutions aims at establishing conditions under which the needs and interests of community members who have been marginalized can be expressed, and creating mechanisms that ensure that these needs and interests will be recognized. Critical consciousness requires that we listen carefully to the accounts of those who have suffered oppression and exploitation (accounts that will undoubtedly include conflicting views of this experience), and it requires that we open up the processes by which institutions regulate the construction of knowledge and shape individual identity.

4

Particularist Approaches to Emancipatory Educational Theory

Particularist theories have arisen in direct opposition to the universalist perspectives discussed in Chapter 3. These theories reject the idea that universal principles or views of universal human nature (needs, interests, etc.) can help us understand the world and reach generalizable normative judgments about our actions and institutions. In this chapter, I address some of the arguments that have been made by postmodernists and care theorists to justify the alternative approaches they advocate, and the implications of these arguments for educational theory. I take a bit more time discussing the central tenets of postmodernism and caring in the respective sections of this chapter than I did with liberalism and critical theory in Chapter 3, as these new challengers have somewhat less in the way of tradition to define their primary theoretical commitments and boundaries. As in Chapter 3, however, my strategy again aims at describing a certain kind of shared foundation for postmodernism and caring as a way of making progress in the creation of a new constellation of emancipatory educational theories.

Because of their status as challengers to "old orthodoxies," as postmodernists and care theorists might describe the universalist perspectives of Chapter 3, the critical agenda of particularists is a crucial part of both their identity and their methodology. While the arguments that postmodernists and care theorists use for rejecting universalist approaches differ, both share a fundamental distrust of the kind of principled approach to moral theory that emerged from the Enlightenment. Both argue that this approach excludes the perspectives and experiences of large groups of people and that, by privileging the voice of a particular (and powerful) minority, principled moral theorizing amounts to a form of illegitimate imposition or even "terror." What unites particularist approaches, on this account, is the rejection of "grand" or "totalizing" theories (to use the language of postmodernism), or the rejection of an abstract and instrumentally rational moral agent as the foundation for moral theory and deliberation (to use the language of care theory).

In opposition to universalist perspectives, postmodernists and care theorists offer a constructive agenda that focuses on the particular or "local" as a way of understanding the nature of social relations. Both approaches treat these socially embedded relations as the primary unit of analysis and the context within which institutions are to be understood and evaluated. Instead of championing principles that are applicable across different contexts, particularist theories focus on the implications of lived experience for understanding the texture of life in the broader society. While postmodernism and care-based theories take somewhat different views of these implications, both give clear importance to this grounded level of analysis.

What makes particularist theories persuasive is the degree to which they account for our perceptions of being in the world and how these perceptions are mediated by our relationships with others. Particularist theories provide a framework that utilizes characteristics of our individual experience, like voice and the feelings of affection we have toward loved ones, to account for the meaning of our lives and the institutions in which we participate. Postmodernism (especially) and caring (to a somewhat lesser extent) both make attempts to fix their analyses against the backdrop of a larger social context, but what matters most to them is still best described as the local. The power of particularist theories tends to exist in proportion to their ability to reflect the richness and variability of experience, and the complexity of the world in which we live our day-to-day lives.

The organization of this chapter will parallel the previous one at a general level; I dedicate a section each to postmodernism and caring, addressing central philosophical issues in the context of building the case for a new constellation of emancipatory educational theories. At a more substantive level, however, there are some key differences worth noting in this introduction. First, I do not argue here, as I did in Chapter 3, that the two approaches under consideration are in any kind of significant dialogue with each other, or that current scholarship suggests a constructive cycle of critique and response between them. The effort I make to illuminate what postmodernism and caring share depends on a more active reconstruction of their potential relationship. While this process is quite consistent with the analysis presented in Chapter 3, I require more latitude here in laying the groundwork for dialogue, and seeking the shared footing on which both views make their contribution to the new constellation.

A second important difference between this and the previous chapter concerns the reasons that justify the latitude I seek. In my attempt to reconstruct a kind of shared terrain between postmodernism and caring, I have found it necessary to be more critical of the limits, ambiguities, and even contradictions that emerge from my analysis of each view. Instead of describing a more expansive landscape in which these two perspectives converge as a result of their current trajectories, I believe a more radical reconstruction of the limits of particularist approaches is needed. This reconstruction is necessary to make particularist perspectives viable as emancipatory theories in the first place.

Based on my analysis of postmodernism and caring, I appeal to the concept of authenticity in the final section of the chapter as a foundation for my own effort to reconstruct the particularist approach in educational terms. Thinking about autonomy in terms of authenticity provides a rich conceptual terrain in which to find a place where the insights of postmodernism and caring intersect and mutually reinforce one another. Authenticity thus plays a central role in bringing together the important contributions that particularist approaches make to the new constellation.

POSTMODERNISM

The literature on postmodernism has expanded across a wide variety of disciplines beyond the point where it is possible, or at least easy, to find a clear definition. Today, the so-called "postmodern turn" represents a shifting platform from which theorists have rejected traditional views of philosophical practice and attempted to refigure the nature of power and discourse in social relations. I appeal to the work of Michel Foucault here as a dominant figure in postmodern theory and, in particular, to his arguments on truth, power, and resistance. I use Foucault as a touchstone in this section because he is generally considered one of postmodernism's most articulate and influential defenders (for a collection of commentaries, see Hoy, 1986), because of the impact he has had on educational theory (e.g., Cherryholmes, 1988; Popkewitz, 1991), and because, unlike many other postmodernists, he offers a view that is somewhat more sympathetic to the "structural" demands of the (feminist and leftist) critics whose work I consider here.

Even though, in the end, I share a good deal in common with the critics of postmodernism, I do not want to underestimate the contributions that postmodern analyses can make to the new constellation. Foucault's historical accounts of how institutions (e.g., prisons, mental asylums, hospitals) have arisen to do the work of social control and self-regulation are extremely sophisticated and insightful, and have unquestionably contributed to our contemporary understanding of how such institutions work. In addition, postmodern critiques like those offered by Foucault have successfully problematized the nature of the social subject and given us good reason to question many of our assumptions about the stability and coherence of individual identity. These insights have opened new avenues of inquiry for emancipatory theorists in education and, although they have been somewhat slow to develop, a few glimpses of what such an approach might mean for educational practice. Consistent with the broader goals of this analysis, the following treatment of postmodernism focuses to some degree on the most important obstacles that I believe must be overcome in utilizing a postmodern framework to guide emancipatory educational theory.

Framing the Postmodern Debate over Truth, Power, and Resistance

Central to most strands of postmodern thought is a rigorous denial of any rational foundation for theories that claim to provide an "objective" account of the world outside of discourse or text. The way postmodernists use concepts like discourse and text is quite complex and not limited to explicit acts (or artifacts) of speaking and writing. Instead, discourse and text are given a more public, performative aspect by postmodernists, who use them to describe the various processes by which power is codified in social or institutional norms of behavior and self-regulation (see, for example, Judith Butler, 1990, who emphasizes the performative aspect of gender relations and the emancipatory potential of "subversive bodily acts" like cross-dressing).

In epistemological terms, postmodernists use this analysis of discourse and text to deny that language provides us with any privileged access to the world it pretends to describe. Here postmodernists are not simply expressing concern about the imprecision or fallibility of language, either as a formal structure, in, say, mathematics or logic, or in ordinary speech, as a means of communication. Rather, they are denying the possibility that meaningful claims about truth or reality can be expressed through *any* systematic or principled account (i.e., explanation) of the world. Foucault uproots traditional correspondence theories of truth and transplants them firmly in the nexus of historically contingent social relations. He argues that all claims to "know" the world are necessarily embedded in a historically specific set of discursive practices that organize knowledge around existing social relations, which is to say that they are organized by and around power. This kind of "hyperskepticism" (Barber, 1992) is emblematic of the postmodern turn and reflects what critic Bryan Palmer (1990) has called "the determination of discourse" (p. 25).

Michel Foucault exemplifies this break from the modern in his "analysis of discursive formation" in *The Archeology of Knowledge* (1972). Here

Foucault describes the substitution of linguistic convention or coherence "at the level of discursive regularities" for the notion of truth (or knowledge) as correspondence with the world outside of discourse (p. 191). Foucault's general argument in this work is that power resides in and is articulated through a dominant discourse; this discourse defines the nature and conditions of knowing at any given time and place in history, and it shapes institutions and social practices in such a way that their proper functioning reinforces or reproduces relationships that are consistent with it. The function of power is thus to regulate our conception of self and relation to the world (i.e., our subjectivity), which helps explain the nature of the particular institutions and practices we have at any given time in society, as well as their effects on those who participate in them. Existing institutions and social practices valorize the skills and resources of those who grasp the dominant discourse; members of subordinate groups are forced through education, "treatment," or other means to accept the norms and practices that sustain and reproduce their subordinate position.

Foucault's methodology thus redirects our attention to discourse as a means of achieving social control and self-regulation; he treats the discursive regularities that structure institutions and social relationships as constitutive of this process. In *Discipline and Punish* (1979), for example, Foucault provides a compelling description of how "panopticism" (surveillance) came to replace the medieval "spectacle" as the dominant metaphor for social control. Foucault shows how surveillance evolved as a new way of organizing and regulating human behavior across a wide variety of social institutions, including prisons, hospitals, and schools. He describes how this process was internalized by individuals through their participation in these institutions, and thus how subjectivity (expressed as self-control) was constructed within and by the discursive practices of modern society.

The hyperskepticism of postmodernists can also be described in terms of their rejection of so-called "grand theories" or metanarratives, which are much the same as what I have described as universalist perspectives. Metanarratives such as liberalism and Marxism are defined by postmodern theorists in terms of their commitment to a comprehensive or global account of human experience (Rawls' justice as fairness, Marx's historical materialism, etc.), and thus to an explanatory framework that is generalizable across the boundaries of history and culture. Metanarratives also frequently possess some kind of teleological quality or belief in social progress as movement toward an ultimate goal or final stage of development (e.g., the historical evolution of the communist state).

Postmodernists have criticized metanarratives as based on flawed epistemological assumptions about the nature (and possibility) of truth and the role of theory in helping us to understand and act in the world. Postmodernists often dismiss such theorizing as vacuous and misguided at best. As Nancy Hartsock (1990) points out, Foucault "clearly reject[s] any form of totalizing discourse: reason, he argues, must be seen as born from chaos, truth as simply an error hardened into unalterable form in the long process of history" (pp. 164–165). At their worst, these metanarratives legitimate the efforts of socially dominant groups to define knowledge in ways that reproduce the oppression of less powerful others, in part by mystifying the control exercised by dominant groups over the criteria by which truth claims are adjudicated.

These criticisms of metanarratives notwithstanding, it would not be wrong to see a striking (and often confounding) affinity here with the Marxist concepts of ideology and alienation I discussed in Chapter 3. At one level, discursive practices seem to play a role quite like that of ideology, in terms of their capacity to regulate the actions of individuals and to normalize the constraints placed on them by the institutions in which they participate. Alienation from self and others results when these mechanisms of social control obscure and distort the needs and interests of individuals, especially through the internalization of norms for self-regulation. However, the connection between postmodernism's hyper-skepticism and the social critique it claims to offer makes the comparison with Marxist-influenced views highly problematic. This tension reflects an important ambiguity in postmodernism and suggests a vexing line of argument against the postmodern turn.

Recall that Marxist theorists and those influenced by their methodology hold that social critique is a process whereby we come to know, in the modernist or Enlightenment sense of this term, how power is used to construct and legitimate the patterns of social organization on which the exploitation of less powerful classes is founded. Marxists have "theorized" the way classes are constituted through their common needs and interests, and the way that the needs and interests of different classes come into conflict. The triumph of one class over another involves a "falsification" of the needs and interests of those outside of the dominant class. Ideology serves as part of the foundation for this process, and alienation is one of its results. To understand all of this (to one extent or another) is precisely the "truth" that Marxist theory is prepared to reveal, and the basis on which changes in society might be justified and pursued.

Foucault's commitment to explaining our experience in terms of discursive regularities appears on its face to provide a similar basis on which to understand conflict and opposition in society, as well as how power constructs patterns of social control and self-regulation. Indeed, power itself seems to have a structural dimension that becomes "crystallized" in the body of the state (Foucault, 1978, pp. 92–93). Like Marxists, Foucault and other postmodernists have tried to describe how what he calls "various social hegemonies" affect the lives of individuals in society. Under the circumstances described by postmodernists, particular groups of people are better or worse off according to the knowledge they possess and the roles they occupy in relation to the reigning discourse. This situation tends to be reproduced over time until some kind of historical transformation (revolution) takes place, and a new set of discursive regularities replaces the old one.

Critical Responses to Postmodernism

Critics of postmodernism have suggested a number of issues that are important to consider in relation to the development of a new constellation of emancipatory theories. Taken together, these sources of critique shape my response to postmodernism and my assessment of how this view has been used by educational theorists.

On "hyperskepticism" and the search for truth through social critique. One source of critique revolves around the claim that the nature and goals of social inquiry reflected in postmodern analyses are undercut by the hyperskepticism that constitutes a central element of the approach's epistemological critique. At issue here is what it is possible to know under the circumstances postmodernists have described, based on the conceptual foundations of their critical agenda. To begin, I think it is hard to disagree that, at some level of analysis, the discursive regularities Foucault explores do indeed have a profound effect on our lives and our relationships with others. The sense in which our lives are "regulated" by discursive practices (from both within and without) is a powerful tool for self-reflection and for the examination of specific institutional practices. This approach helps to make us aware of the assumptions and implicit beliefs that guide our daily lives and our frequently unreflective participation in institutional routines. Becoming more cognizant of these beliefs, assumptions, and practices is a central goal of emancipatory education.

The capacity to take up postmodern theory as a means of demystifying oppressive social relations is compromised, however, by the degree to which it has undercut the epistemological basis for such critique. The thorny question postmodernists must answer here is whether the line of argument they have offered against Enlightenment perspectives like Marxism can be sustained without having some concept of truth to play the counterpoint to their explanation of mystification and control. Put another way, can postmodernists consistently defend their position on the relationship between power and knowledge without also making the claim that these explanations are in some sense themselves true? Charles Taylor's response to postmodernism explores this general line of argument and its implications for social critique. In his essay, "Foucault on Freedom and Truth," he writes that:

> "Power".... requires "truth"—if we want to allow, as Foucault does, that we can collaborate in our own subjugation. Indeed, that is a crucial feature of the modern system of control, that it gets us to agree and concur in the name of truth, or liberation or our own nature. If we want to allow this, then "truth" is an essential notion. Because the imposition proceeds here by foisting illusion on us. It proceeds by disguises and masks. It proceeds thus by falsehood. ... Mask, falsehood makes no sense without a corresponding notion of truth. The truth here is subversive of power: it is on the side of the lifting of impositions, of what we have called liberation. The Foucaultian notion of power not only requires for its sense the correlative notions of truth and liberation but even the standard link between them, which makes truth the condition of liberation. (Taylor, 1985, pp. 176–177)

For postmodernists like Foucault, truth can be understood only in relation to the discursive regularities that give meaning and structure to social experience. Knowledge is produced in a context that reflects a particular set of power relations; all other conceptions of truth are suppressed, at best waiting in the wings to emerge as the next mystifying constructions of oppression and terror. If we accept this strident epistemological critique as characteristic of the postmodern turn, critics seem justified in asking what kind of rationale postmodernists have actually given us for accepting this view. Put more strongly, this criticism suggests that postmodern theory abandons any useful sense of epistemic justification just when its own analyses seem to require it.

On the "local" nature of social criticism and the "incommensurability" of discourse(s). Another issue that postmodernists have faced in recent critiques turns on the challenge to provide a satisfactory account of the meaning and justification of resistance. We have seen that postmodernists, motivated in part by their rejection of metanarratives, urge us to pay particular attention to the forms and regularities of discourse that govern our lives at a given historical moment and in a particular cultural and/ or institutional location. Because we have no legitimate "universal" tools (e.g., moral principles) to use in the struggle against these discursive regularities, the nature of social criticism and resistance is necessarily local and contingent (Foucault, 1980, p. 81). Recent advocates of postmodernism have continued to follow this line of argument and have considered how adopting it might change the role of the philosopher as social critic and reformer. Nancy Fraser and Linda Nicholson (1990), for instance, pursue this issue in their essay on postmodern feminism, aptly titled "Social Criticism Without Philosophy."

> No longer anchored philosophically, the very shape or character of social criticism changes; it becomes more pragmatic, ad hoc, contextual, and local. With this change comes a corresponding change in the social role and political function of intellectuals. (p. 21)

Based on the concerns that critics of postmodernism have expressed about the relationship between power and knowledge, there are a number of difficulties with this characterization of social criticism as a basis for resistance or reform, and thus with postmodernism's capacity to explain and justify efforts at emancipatory social change.

One of the most important versions of this argument holds that postmodernists have no clear basis for claiming that one set of discursive practices organizes social relations in a way that can be thought of as better than any other: On this account, discourses are "incommensurable," that is, there is no basis, in principle, for comparison or evaluation. The reasons for this can best be seen in connection with the hyperskepticism, it may even be appropriate to say nihilism here, that follows from the challenges posed in the previous section: If there can be no truth outside of the discursive regularities on which social relations are based, then no language or discourse exists that can be used to assess the adequacy of competing constructions of individual identity or social organization. This line of argument has significant implications for the capacity of postmodernism to provide a justification for opposing arrangements that advantage specific members of society over others.

Foucault's work suggests that power brings particular social relations, and thus forms of individual identity, into existence and legitimates them during a given historical moment. This way of understanding legitimation in terms of power is unlikely, by itself, to provide the basis for normative argument, however. The social relations that power constructs, whatever they happen to be at a given time, appear to be the only real options available for understanding the world. Existing social relations, and the interpretive framework on which they are based, are threatened only when power revises its grip on the institutions and practices of society, in response to fundamental changes in historical circumstance (e.g., when the modernist practice of surveillance replaced the medieval spectacle as the dominant form of social control and self-regulation) (Foucault, 1979).

Despite Foucault's (1980) argument for an "insurrection of subjugated knowledges" (p. 81), it is difficult to see how the discursive resources he describes might actually be sufficient or effective. Given that subjugated knowledges are "disqualified as inadequate to their task or insufficiently elaborated; naive knowledges, located low down on the hierarchy, beneath the required level of cognition or scienticity" (Foucault, 1980, p. 82), it seems unlikely that "it is through the re-appearance of this knowledge, of these local popular knowledges, these disqualified knowledges, that criticism performs its work" (p. 82). Foucault's analysis establishes a powerful incommensurability between these patterns of discursive regularity, and denies (in principle?) our access to tools that might allow us to make comparisons or assess one in relation to another.

Feminist theorists, among others, have pursued this line of argument against postmodernism, motivated by their desire to explain the particular forms of oppression and subordination experienced by women in patriarchal societies. In their rejection of the "view from nowhere" (e.g., moral theories that emphasize generalizability and disinterestedness as normative ideals), feminists have revealed or demystified the male-biased perspectives that often lurk behind seemingly "objective" models of normative reasoning (recall the arguments of Held and Baier from Chapter 3). For similar reasons, some feminists have voiced reservations about postmodernism's endless multiplication of perspectives and the potential for (again) losing any distinctive foundation for the oppression experienced by women. Susan Bordo (1990) cautions us, for example, against trading the Enlightenment "view from nowhere" for the postmodern "dream of everywhere."

In theory, deconstructionist postmodernism stands against the ideal of disembodied knowledge and declares that ideal to be a mystification and impossibility. There is no Archimedean viewpoint; rather, history and culture are texts, admitting an endless proliferation of readings, each of which is itself unstable. . . . The question remains, however, how the human knower is to negotiate this infinitely perspectival, destabilized world. Deconstructionism answers with constant vigilant suspicion of all determinate readings of culture and a partner aesthetic of ceaseless textual play as an alternative ideal. Here is where deconstruction may slip into its own fantasy of escape from human locatedness—by supposing that the critic can become wholly protean by adopting endlessly shifting, seemingly inexhaustible vantage points, none of which are "owned" by either the critic or the author of a text under examination. (p. 142)

While all feminists may well agree with postmodernists that patriarchy and other forms of systematic exploitation are constructed within the context of historically contingent and culturally specific social relations, many also (and rightly, I think) insist that the critique of these relations acknowledge their structural dimension. It is difficult to understand or resist patriarchy (and, by analogy, other systematic forms of oppression), without adopting a social theory that countenances the existence of such structures in the first place. These critics argue that postmodern accounts of power and truth are inconsistent with the kind of explanations we need to guide our resistance to systematic patterns of dominance and subordination, and I share this important concern.

On solidarity and resistance. The second difficulty postmodernism faces with respect to the concept of resistance involves the question of solidarity and whether postmodern theories can adequately explain efforts at reform based on the oppression individuals experience as members of a group or class. In Marxist theories, as we have seen, class membership or identity is defined by the shared needs and interests that situate individuals relative to one another and relative to a dominant group. For postmodernists, these relationships are more problematic from the start, because subjectivity rests entirely in the forms of social control and self-regulation imposed on individuals by society's dominant discursive regularities. Foucault and other postmodernists have proposed that we understand subjectivity as always constructed by power in the context of specific (i.e., local) circumstances, but also in a way that is fragmented and opaque. According to this view, the unity of subjective experience is an illusion foisted upon us by the discursive regularities that organize and direct our lives toward particular forms of "usefulness."

This line of argument has enriched emancipatory social and political theories by problematizing categorical interpretations of identity related to social attributes like gender, class, race, and sexual orientation. It has especially challenged those who apply these attributes naively, as self-evidently coherent, transparent, or generalizable representations of a particular social position or set of life experiences. Postmodern theorists have questioned what it means to speak "as" (i.e., to present for others what it means to be) a woman, a man, a homosexual, a heterosexual, and so on, and they have shown how efforts to represent the self and other(s) in this way may involve a whole range of illicit assumptions and false generalizations. Postmodernists have also critiqued this way of speaking for others through declarations about the self (e.g., as a patriotic American, a good Christian, etc.) as covert efforts to seize social, cultural, and political power. Epistemological debates notwithstanding, it is important for emancipatory theorists to preserve this critical insight and, as we will see later, to model it in emancipatory schools.

The challenge that postmodernists must face, however, is whether it is possible to maintain this view of the fragmented individual while still providing an adequate account of how a particular group's shared experience (like women's shared experience of oppression under patriarchy) can work effectively as a foundation for organized resistance and reform. Most feminists would clearly reject accounts of sexism, for instance, that construe sexual harassment, rape, and discrimination in employment as events in the lives of women that can be fully understood without some general theory that explains their common source and mutual reinforcement in patriarchal society. The degree to which postmodernists have been able to meet this challenge is a matter of both concern and contention.

It seems to me, and to many of postmodernism's critics, that the epistemological views held by Foucault and others, at the very least complicate, and may radically diminish, the potential for motivating resistance based on the common experience individuals share when they confront some systematic form of oppression. Without a conceptual framework that can explain the interrelatedness of these experiences, they may appear isolated, unconnected, or discrete, even though individuals encounter them (and their threat) as deeply interwoven into the fabric of their social experience. As Nancy Hartsock (1990) argues, Foucault's ambivalence on this point is troubling for feminists and others concerned with the domination of one social group by another.

> Much of what Foucault has to say about power stresses the systematic nature of power and its presence in multiple social relations. At the same time, however, his stress on heterogeneity and the specificity of each situation leads him to lose track of social structures and instead to focus on how individuals experience power. . . . With this move Foucault has made it very difficult to locate domination, including domination in gender relations. He has on the one hand claimed that individuals are constituted by power relations, but he has argued against their constitution by relations such as the domination of one group by another. (pp. 168–169)

While postmodern theory deals extensively with issues of power, control, and self-regulation, critics have given us good reason to question whether it provides the kind of tools that can be used to explain the systematic nature of oppression and thus effectively motivate and guide resistance.

The Problems and Promise of Postmodern Educational Theory

As might be expected from the wide-ranging application of postmodern views to social scientific inquiry, works in educational philosophy also tend to vary somewhat in their interpretation of the postmodern turn. In this section, I consider two different examples of postmodern educational analysis for what each can tell us about this evolving perspective and for the (positive and negative) lessons each holds for my own effort to build the new constellation. First, I look at a postmodern treatment of educational reform by Thomas Popkewitz (1991), which is clearly and explicitly motivated by a Foucaultian perspective (Liston & Fletcher, 1992). Second, I consider a work by Elizabeth Ellsworth (1992) that focuses more closely on the level of instructional practice and reflects her interpretation of postmodernism in the (university) classroom. I am especially interested in how these specific examples of postmodern educational theory address the general challenges posed above by critics of postmodernism.

A postmodern analysis of educational reform. What initially makes the consideration of Popkewitz's *A Political Sociology of Educational Reform: Power/Knowledge in Teaching, Teacher Education, and Research* (1991) most appropriate for this analysis is the clarity with which he takes up postmodernism's hyperskepticism and his direct application of Foucault's power/ knowledge framework to the context of educational reform. Throughout his analysis, Popkewitz (1991) adopts a typically postmodern interpretation of social scientific inquiry as an investigation into the specific cultural and historical circumstances that, at any given time, provide our only guide for understanding what constitutes knowledge and how it is used.

> I define epistemology as an exploration of the relations between the form and style of reasoning and various historical configurations and trajectories. With pragmatic philosophy, I argue that there is not a common ground on which to locate a true consensus or a permanent neutral framework by which to evaluate a rational argument. There are no universal schemes of reason and rationality but only socially constructed epistemologies that represent and embody social relations. (p. 31)

Popkewitz clearly has this framework in mind as he pursues an account of the social context in which efforts at educational reform take place and how, in the end, the meaning of these reforms came to betray their advocates. Popkewitz focuses on how his account of educational reform fits into a broader vision of the role schools play as institutions of social regulation and control. He asks, "What constitutes reform? What are its changing meanings over time? How are those meanings produced?" and answers by arguing they are "best understood as part of the process of social regulation" (Popkewitz, 1991, p. 2). Following Foucault, he concludes that "the study of contemporary school reform practices entails placing particular events in schooling within a historical formation that presupposes relations of power/knowledge" (p. 3).

One of Popkewitz's favorite targets in his analysis of educational reform, rightly chosen I think for the power that its theoretical discourse holds, is the nature and use of "cognitive science" as a mechanism for controlling teachers, schoolchildren, and parents. In a chapter he calls "Cognitive Educational Science as Knowledge and Power," Popkewitz warns against seeing science as an objective, value-free foundation for determining social policy and educational practice. To think of science in this way, he argues, permits the pseudo-objective language and classification systems offered by cognitive science to mystify their true basis in relations of power.

> Science is an abstraction of reality through the use of language; the languages of science enable us to categorize and classify events in ways that involve predispositions toward those solutions seen as appropriate. Strategies for collecting data about children's or teachers' performance, for example, create boundaries about what is important and how it should be considered. These abstractions, however, are not just linguistic. They embody power relations and are material practices. Our rules of classification contain distinctions that normalize and regulate hopes, desires, and needs. (Popkewitz, 1991, p. 189)

Throughout the text, Popkewitz analyzes forms of educational discourse that appear to support reform proposals aimed at the "empowerment" of teachers and the "professionalization" of teaching. In each case, however, he reveals an implicit agenda that belies the good intentions provided as justifications for these reforms. According to Popkewitz (1991), contemporary educational reforms have resulted in a number of contradictory and harmful outcomes, including more effective and coercive "state steering strategies," "calls for increased standardization," and a concept of "individuality . . . which is defined by the 'experts' who determine specific characteristics and abilities as universal, aggregate qualities" (p. 154).

The ironic results of these efforts at reform can be seen in their capacity to mystify coercive policies under the rubric of professional development or school restructuring and, more broadly, through the socially constructed and publicly sanctioned discourse of civic progress. Throughout the analysis, Popkewitz emphasizes two now familiar concepts, mystification and coercion, in support of his deconstructionist methodology. By uncovering or demystifying the connection between power and knowledge, Popkewitz tries to make the underlying rationale and end of these educational reforms visible, thereby opening the way for critique and resistance.

This strategy clearly represents a concern for the broadest goals of emancipatory educational theory. It seeks, for example, to make connections between social privilege and institutional policy that are often not apparent, even to well-informed citizens and thoughtful participants in educational reform efforts. It seeks to provide the kind of analytic tools necessary to understand how power and knowledge are situated in the context of specific educational initiatives aimed (ostensibly) at improving our schools. It seeks to create new ways of looking at debates over educational reform that will help redirect or reconstruct these efforts in ways that better serve those who are now oppressed, marginalized, or simply ignored by our system of public education.

To be successful in this application of postmodern theory, however, Popkewitz must still address the same set of challenges I described in the previous section; he must find a way to bridge the conceptual chasm that exists between the power/knowledge framework he borrows from Foucault and the demystifying/empowering ends he claims for his critical account of school reform. Recall, for a moment, Taylor's argument that "falsehood makes no sense without a corresponding notion of truth." Truth is necessary in Popkewitz's argument in order to make sense of schools as coercive social mechanisms and to explain the forms of self-regulation and mystification they enforce. The result of unmasking this process requires that the "truth" about educational reform stand as a way of explaining our own duplicity and subordination.

Unfortunately, Popkewitz does not do enough to meet the demands of postmodernism's critics; he says little that helps us to understand how it is that we can talk of being collectively deceived by the discourse of contemporary school reform without possessing some meaningful sense of what it would be like to have this deception removed. As preceding arguments have suggested, this makes it unclear where the various potential readers of his text (teachers, teacher educators, university researchers) will find good reasons to replace their current understanding of educational reform with the one that he has proposed. If there can be no way of comparing two historically specified and socially embedded forms of discourse, then there is no reason for us to accept the critical stance he takes at the beginning of his analysis or the demystifying explanations he offers throughout the text. We are left without an answer to the challenge, advanced by Taylor and others, that it is incoherent to offer a critique aimed at dispelling illusions, while at the same time disavowing any concern with, or conception of, the comparative value of distinct explanatory claims.

The work Popkewitz sets out to do in his text does not end with his attempt to dispel illusions about current efforts at school reform, however. His analysis also aims at justifying and motivating social and educational reconstruction. Thus far, I have focused primarily on the epistemological problems associated with his analysis, as specific examples of the challenges posed by critics of postmodernism. To push this general line of argument ahead, we must consider the justifications that Popkewitz offers for resisting and reconstructing the coercive "regimes of truth" in education.

Near the end of the text, Popkewitz offers a participatory vision of reform that is reminiscent, at least rhetorically, of the conclusions offered by liberal and critical theorists presented in Chapter 3. Popkewitz seems to recommend creating a process of reform that is more inclusive, that pays more attention to individual differences, and that sees social and educational change as an ongoing process. These qualities are quite consistent with the goals of emancipatory schooling, and I echo them later in my own comments on educational reform. The difficulty with Popkewitz's recommendations, however, is that they say too little about what these qualities actually mean within his postmodern theoretical framework and what they actually entail for educational (or social) change.

As I described earlier, critics of postmodernism have warned against undercutting the basis for resistance to systematic forms of oppression, and here Popkewitz's analysis seems to play into their hands. In fact, Popkewitz's conclusion appears to deny that we can say much of anything useful to guide efforts at resistance or reform, or about any kind of normative context in which progress might be understood or assessed. The following passage is, in its own way, typical of the unsettling conclusions that so many postmodern analyses leave us with in their withdrawal from normative argument and their silence on what a good (or even better) society might actually look like. Beyond the parenthetical reference here to unelaborated examples, Popkewitz (1991) offers little in the way of concrete advice for would-be advocates of social or educational reform, and the conclusion he takes from Cherryholmes does little to improve the situation.

> The social task of constructing more appropriate social conditions entails a broadening of specific and multiple public spheres for political thinking and

moral identity. This involves argument among particular people in specific situations, dealing with concrete cases, and with different things at stake (see, e.g., Rorty, 1988; Toulmin, 1988; and, in education, Giroux, 1990; Rizvi, 1989a; Walker, 1987). There are no final truths or fixed moral foundations that serve as guides. There are continuous interpretation and reconstruction that are, in fact, responses to the situations in which we find ourselves and "based on *visions* of what is beautiful, good, and true instead of fixed, structured, moral, or objective certainties" (Cherryholmes, 1988, p. 151; emphasis in original). (p. 243)

The problem with this and other passages like it in *A Political Sociology of Educational Reform* is in part explained by the degree to which they seem to avoid saying much about what efforts at "continuous interpretation and reconstruction" might look like. In fact, postmodernists often seem prepared to deny that further meaningful discussion about these processes is possible, except on the most local grounds of "specific situations."

The final pages of Popkewitz's work leave many of the tensions and ambivalences cited by critics of postmodernism unresolved, and his conclusion may, a more severe critic might argue, even diminish the potential for developing effective forms of resistance to oppressive social institutions and practices. If, by collapsing power and knowledge, postmodern theorists rule out any legitimate discourse of moral critique, it is unclear on what basis we might find a particular set of social circumstances/policies/institutions to be objectionable, or how the effort to reveal distorted needs and interests might result in a convincing argument for resistance. Like Foucault, Popkewitz struggles to provide a plausible justification for preferring one set of social circumstances to another, and therefore to give good reasons for struggling to create some new practice, policy, or institution. As Nancy Hartsock (1990) notes:

> In the end, Foucault appears to endorse a one-sided wholesale rejection of modernity and to do so without a conception of what is to replace it. Indeed, some have argued persuasively that because Foucault refuses both the ground of foundationalism and the "ungrounded hope" endorsed by liberals such as Rorty, he stands on no ground at all and thus fails to give any reasons for resistance. Foucault suggests that if our resistance succeeded, we would simply be changing one discursive identity for another and in the process create new oppressions. (p. 170)

My sympathy rests with postmodernism's critics here, as there seems to be no distinctively moral justification for resistance in Popkewitz's account of educational reform. The existence of multiple perspectives, as suggested by Popkewitz in the passage quoted above, guarantees nothing but disagreement. To seize on this disagreement as constitutive of a postmodern framework for emancipatory educational reform suggests little that qualifies as a moral argument, even on strictly procedural terms.

Postmodernism in the classroom. The second example of postmodern educational theory I examine here is a frequently cited (e.g., Apple, 1993; Burbules, 1993; Howe, 1997; Noddings, 1992) analysis of critical pedagogy by Elizabeth Ellsworth called "Why Doesn't This Feel Empowering? Working Through the Repressive Myths of Critical Pedagogy" (1992). As one might predict from the title, a good deal of the discussion surrounding this article has involved Ellsworth's rejection or deconstruction of critical pedagogy as an appropriate way of understanding and promoting empowerment among students. While her arguments against critical pedagogy are certainly relevant to the broader goals of my work, and I would disagree with many of her conclusions, my focus here will be on the way Ellsworth explains the nature of her own poststructural or postmodern educational practice. It is one of relatively few texts that speaks from the perspective of a postmodern theorist *and teacher.*

Two related arguments concerning Ellsworth's teaching practice in a graduate course at the University of Wisconsin called "Media and Anti-Racist Pedagogies" (renamed by the class Coalition 607) are particularly relevant to this analysis. First is the position that Ellsworth takes against the capacity of "analytic critical judgment" and "rational deliberation" to guide classroom practice in a way that reveals something (true?) about oppressive social relations. Following the postmodern tradition's rejection of metanarratives, Ellsworth (1992) argues strongly for the partiality of all discourse in understanding and motivating political action in the world.

> Educators who have constructed classroom practices dependent upon analytic critical judgment can no longer regard the enforcement of rationalism as a self-evident political act against relations of domination. Literary criticism, cultural studies, post-structuralism, feminist studies, comparative studies, and media studies have by now amassed overwhelming evidence of the extent to which the myths of the ideal rational person and the "universality" of propositions have been oppressive to those who are not European, White, male, middle-class, Christian, ablebodied, thin, and heterosexual. . . . While poststructuralism, like rationalism, is a tool that can be used to dominate, it has also facilitated a devastating critique of the violence of rationalism against Others. It has demonstrated that as a discursive practice, rationalism's regulated and systematic use of elements of language constitutes rational competence "as a series of exclusions—of women, people of color, of nature as historical agent, of the true value of art." In contrast, poststructural-

ist thought is not bound by reason, but "to discourse, literally narratives
about the world that are admittedly *partial*." (p. 96, emphasis in original)

Although it is hard to see how this ultimately helps her case, Ellsworth
seems perfectly willing to admit that the discourse of poststructuralism
is itself a partial accounting of the world and thus similarly vulnerable to
the limitations and abuses suggested by postmodern critiques of (other?)
metanarratives. She rather bluntly affirms what critics have treated as
a central conundrum of postmodernism, namely, that "like rationalism"
postmodernism is, by its own account, simply another "discursive practice" that results from a particular set of power relations and that it too
is "a tool that can be used to dominate."

The irony of this position comes at a significant epistemological cost
and leaves the foundations of Ellsworth's pedagogy vulnerable to some of
postmodernism's most obvious lines of critique. What discourses might
students take up in order to demystify deconstructionism or to empower
those who are oppressed by the discursive practice of postmodernism?
What discourse would allow students to identify and understand the experience of oppression in this case? What does it mean to be oppressed
at all on this account? Ellsworth's analysis reiterates the puzzling juxtapo-
sition of hyperskepticism and demystification that has confounded postmodernism's critics, and this should give us pause in our consideration
of postmodernism's effectiveness as a basis for emancipatory educational theory.

Ellsworth's more specific recommendations concerning instructional
practice do little to blunt the implications of this strident interpretation
of postmodernism for the classroom. For example, even though Ellsworth
argues that students' contributions to class discussions (of racism, sexism, etc.) do not go "without response," she denies that these utterances
can be challenged or compared for their capacity to help explain the
world in better or worse ways. By maintaining the radical partiality of all
knowledge, Ellsworth again rejects "rational deliberation" as a means
of understanding and assessing different accounts of social relations.
The resulting incommensurability of individual experience entails, for
Ellsworth (1992), a thoroughgoing disavowal of arguments over competing claims.

> The literature on critical pedagogy implies that the claims made by docu-
> ments, demonstrations, press conferences, and classroom discussions of stu-
> dents of color and White students against racism could rightfully be taken
> up in the classroom and subjected to rational deliberation over their truth in
> light of competing claims. But this would force students to subject them-

selves to the logics of rationalism and scientism which have been predicated on and made possible through the exclusion of socially constructed irrational Others—women, people of color, nature, aesthetics (p. 97)

The implications of this view for instructional strategies aimed at demystifying oppression and providing grounds for resistance seem quite devastating. While Ellsworth (1992) holds (and I agree with her here) that individual utterances may be critiqued "because they hold implications for other social movements and their struggles for self-definition" (p. 97), it is difficult to understand the basis on which such claims can provide legitimate reasons for action beyond the confines of individuals' "immediate, emotional, social, and psychic experiences of oppression" (p. 97) or beyond, as she concludes above, "self-analysis."

While Ellsworth clearly believes that her teaching has a better claim to empowering students than critical pedagogy, the approach to instruction she describes seems unnecessarily constrained by her postmodern commitment to the fragmented nature of identity and the incommensurability of individual experience. One of Ellsworth's greatest sources of trouble here is her apparent support for the proposition that, because *all* forms of understanding are in *some* way partial and dependent on historical context for their meaning, *no* reasonable or useful judgments about the explanatory force of competing accounts are possible. This conclusion supports the critics' view of postmodernism as nihilistic and self-defeating.

It may be possible, however, to argue that Ellsworth simply goes too far here, conceding too much ground to postmodernism's critics from the start. It may be that a more modest and constructive line of argument can be drawn from her overly strident critique of rationalism and the role of rational deliberation in emancipatory education. We might agree, for instance, that rationalism *can* be used to silence or constrain dialogue, as when it is manipulated to exclude the affective or emotional content of experience from the process of moral deliberation. Instead of rejecting rational deliberation and the assessment of competing claims altogether on the basis of this insight, however, we might instead use it to develop a greater awareness of how power subtly exerts itself in dialogue (by covertly and illegitimately raising the value of certain kinds of reasons over others, for example) and to encourage a greater sensitivity to the way that different patterns of interaction can privilege particular views or prior experiences. On this account, postmodern educational theory shows us how different forms of discourse can come into conflict in the classroom and how (subtle or obvious) imbalances in power may present significant obstacles for participants in dialogue. This would preserve some of Ellsworth's insights about the relation between power and knowledge, although it leaves a central paradox of postmodern epistemology unresolved (at best).

Ellsworth gets into more of the same kind of trouble when it comes to accounting for the possibility of resistance through affiliation with others who are similarly positioned in society (or, for that matter, anyone who wishes to struggle against the oppression experienced by "others"). She focuses again on the impartiality of knowledge here, this time our knowledge of each other, as a virtually insurmountable barrier to mutual understanding and collaboration. To pursue this point, we need to look more closely at students and teachers in the classroom, and recall the critics who argued that postmodern accounts of subjectivity obscure the relationships individuals share based on their common experience of oppression.

Ellsworth is concerned in her work to understand how various kinds of power differences, between teachers and students, and between students who occupy different social positions, operate as mechanisms for social control and self-regulation. She is especially concerned about how these differences are reflected in the capacity of dominant groups to use the classroom as a context for establishing and reproducing oppressive social relations. The cycle of domination and subordination often begins, Ellsworth rightly points out, when a person in a position of power speaks for others, or speaks as if what they say can encompass (can be generalized across) the experiences of others. This claim to knowledge/authority is common in classrooms (especially among teachers, but perhaps just as often, if we paid attention, among groups of students) and it frequently silences those students whose interests and needs are already least well understood, pushed furthest to the margins, or most readily exploited by the dominant group.

Ellsworth argues that the customary wisdom held by most progressive educators, that teachers learn from (and with) their students, is insufficient to overcome the powerful differences in status that attach to these unequal positions in the classroom. The effects of these power differences persist, according to Ellsworth (1992), not because the effort to overcome them cannot be made in good faith, but because the limits to understanding others can *never* be *completely* overcome. As with Ellsworth's wholesale rejection of rationalism and rational deliberation as a basis for emancipatory education, she argues here that the partiality of our knowledge of self and other (what we might call the opacity and incommensurability of identity) prevents us from sharing little more than a tenuous "affinity" with others. While Ellsworth's (1992) recommendations involve experimenting with forms of instruction that resist the domination of "any single voice" and re-establish the authority of personal experience in the classroom, the real obstacle to empowerment appears to be postmodernism's conception of subjectivity as fragmented, contradictory, and ultimately unknowable.

> No one affinity group could ever "know" the experiences and knowledges of other affinity groups or the social positions that were not their own. Nor can social subjects who are split between the conscious and unconscious, and cut across by multiple, intersecting, and contradictory subject positions, ever fully "know" their own experiences. As a whole, Coalition 607 could never know with certainty whether the actions it planned to take on campus would undercut the struggle of other social groups, or even that of its own affinity groups. But this situation was not a failure; it was not something to overcome. (p. 110)

As Ellsworth's analysis unfolds, the emancipatory goals she holds for her students become more and more difficult to understand outside of the inexpressible subjectivity of individual experience and thus, paradoxically, impossible to see in relation to the systematic and deeply entrenched forms of inequality that motivate her efforts. Although it is quite plausible to claim that we can never know *fully* the experiences of another, a great deal more is possible (and necessary) to say about resistance than this account appears to allow.

Ellsworth's struggle to articulate the goals of her instructional practice through the discussions and activities that took place in Coalition 607 reflects postmodernism's ambivalent theorization of resistance. Consistent with the postmodern rejection of Enlightenment metanarratives as terroristic, Ellsworth aims at disrupting all notions of truth and opposing all forms of power/knowledge as oppressive by their very nature. It is difficult to see in Ellsworth's description of her own teaching practice, however, how she will collaborate with students to construct a shared vision of oppression, resistance, or social change. The partiality of experience to which she is deeply committed stands in the way of explaining the concrete forms of oppression that individuals share and the way that this shared experience might provide a basis (in fact?) for collaborative action. As before, Ellsworth seizes an important point about the difficulty of fully grasping the differences that divide us. By overstating the radical partiality of our experience, however, she creates some very problematic barriers to mutual understanding and resistance.

The effort to name, comprehend, and struggle against oppression lies at the heart of emancipatory educational practice. And even though I share with postmodernism's critics some serious reservations about its capacity to accomplish these goals, I believe it is still quite possible, indeed essential, to identify and preserve the important contributions that postmodern educational theory can make to the new constellation. With its concern for difference and the complexity of individual identity, postmodern theory focuses our attention on the local and particular in ways that other theories have not. It warns loudly against committing ourselves naively to the generalizability of experience and against drawing conclusions about others based on commonly accepted or agreed-upon assumptions that, when examined more carefully, often turn out to be misleading at best and more likely themselves a source of misunderstanding or oppression. Without being paralyzed by this recognition of partiality, in our individual experience as well as in our knowledge of the world, we need to preserve a place in the new constellation for the important role that the local and the particular should play in guiding emancipatory educational practice.

CARING

In this section, I look at the implications of caring for emancipatory educational theories. As in the previous section on postmodernism, I describe and critically assess some of the central tenets of caring as a particularist approach. And again, like postmodernism, I find that caring seems to require the rejection of key normative concepts that limit its capacity to inform educational practice aimed at emancipation. A key difference in my analysis of postmodernism, however, rests in the fact that caring seems more amenable to (or consistent with) strategies that treat it as an important aspect of a still broader approach to moral deliberation and the normative assessment of social institutions. My strategy here is to clarify the limits I see in caring as a moral theory, and by doing so show how caring might serve as a guide for redirecting our attention to the role of community in schooling and to creating caring relationships as a goal of emancipatory educational practice.

Caring as a Moral Theory Based on Women's Experience

The concept of caring evolved out of debates in moral theory and psychology, and it is helpful to recall briefly some of this story here. After the extremely influential research of Carol Gilligan (1982) and others on women's moral reasoning, the proposition that women's experience was (at least sometimes) expressed in "a different voice" became a widespread matter of controversy and inquiry among a range of theorists and researchers. Much of this debate turned on the claim that women's experience could generally be distinguished from men's by virtue of its relational or inclusive approach to resolving moral dilemmas and social conflict. In contrast, men typically appeared to look at social relationships in individualistic or even adversarial terms, and they were more likely to be guided in their moral reasoning by abstract, generalizable principles such as justice, equality, or individual rights (i.e., noninterference).

Based on this empirical and conceptual division of moral intuitions according to gender, a new strategy became available to feminists who were at least as interested in exploring (and valorizing) the nature and content of women's lived experience as they were in seeking to expand access among women to resources and roles characteristically held by men. As a new alternative to liberal feminism, caring is grounded in a distinctively "feminine approach to ethics and moral education" (Noddings, 1984). Caring focuses attention on the commitments that individuals develop in their concrete relations with others, and on the particular circumstances in which these relationships take on meaning and significance. As a moral theory, caring questions whether the details of a particular relation could (and certainly whether they should) be excluded from decisions about the rightness or wrongness of an action, as prior moral theorizing about the role of impartiality and generalizability suggested.

It may be helpful to note that, while there may be some interesting questions here about the relationship of caring to the other theories considered in this work, given that liberalism, critical theory, and postmodernism are clearly sociopolitical theories and caring arguably is not, this distinction need not overly concern us. This is because caring, regardless of its status in relation to these other theories, is clearly shaped by the social and political circumstances in which it is practiced (Martin, 1992; Tronto, 1993), a point that I will argue in detail below and one that is crucial to our understanding of how caring might inform emancipatory educational theory.

Nel Noddings is perhaps the best known among care theorists, and she has written about caring both as an approach to moral philosophy (Noddings, 1984) and as "an alternative approach to education" (Noddings, 1992). Her perspective on caring as a moral theory is derived in part from the experiences of women, and from the experiences of mothers with their children in particular, although it is important to note at the start that the ethic of care is *for* everyone (i.e., women *and* men). Central to the foundation of caring as an alternative perspective on moral reasoning is its clear rejection of the principled approach that is characteristic of universalist theories. Like postmodernists, care theorists are critical of traditional Enlightenment concepts of moral assessment (e.g., justice), and they promote the view that local and particular circumstances provide the best foundation for understanding and assessing the actions of individuals.

For their part, care theorists are quite straightforward in rejecting what Noddings (1984) has called the "language of the father" (p. 1), which is embodied in the principled approach of Enlightenment philosophy to questions of moral theory. Despite the notion that care theorists propose a "feminine" framework for understanding moral issues, they still echo many of the "feminist" critiques of liberal moral philosophy discussed in Chapter 3. Noddings, for instance, criticizes the use of abstract rationality in trying to comprehend a human condition that she believes is better described in terms of the specific social relations in which we are constantly enmeshed. Noddings emphasizes, as do the feminist critics of liberalism, the danger of utilizing models of moral reasoning that abstract the individual from the relationships that condition such decision making. She notes that this assumption is central to most traditional moral philosophy.

> Ethics, the philosophical study of morality, has concentrated for the most part on moral reasoning. Much current work, for example, focuses on the status of moral predicates and, in education, the dominant model presents a hierarchical picture of moral reasoning. This emphasis gives ethics a contemporary, mathematical appearance, but it also moves discussion beyond the sphere of actual human activity and the feeling that pervades such activity. Even though careful philosophers have recognized the difference between "pure" or logical reason and "practical" or moral reason, ethical argumentation has frequently proceeded as if it were governed by the logical necessity characteristic of geometry. It has concentrated on the establishment of principles and that which can be logically derived from them. One might say that ethics has been discussed largely in the language of the father: in principles and propositions, in terms such as justification, fairness, justice. The mother's voice has been silent. (Noddings, 1984, p. 1)

Conceptual devices or thought experiments such as Rawls' "original position" represent the kind of models for moral reasoning that Noddings rejects as rooted in a distinctively male (and male-biased) view of moral conflict; they postulate individuals who are opposed in their struggle to obtain scarce resources, and who agree only on the basis of self-interest to be collectively constrained by moral principles adopted under conditions that guarantee impartiality.

Insofar as abstract rationality presupposes such atomistic individuals, Noddings argues, the principles derived to govern their behavior are inadequate for the purposes of understanding and evaluating what we actually experience in our social and familial relations as moral dilemmas or conflict. Enlightenment approaches yield concepts like justice, fairness, and equality, which ultimately have the effect of separating us, one from another, or putting us in opposition, one against the other. Thus, ethical principles commonly held to be at the very heart of traditional moral philosophy (e.g., impartiality and generalizability) are those that care theorists find most objectionable. This kind of principled orientation in contemporary moral theory, Noddings (1984) argues, deflects our understanding from the reality of embedded human relations and excludes them from the moral calculus.

> Everything depends upon the nature and strength of this ideal [caring], for we shall not have absolute principles to guide us. Indeed, I shall reject ethics of principles as ambiguous and unstable. Wherever there is a principle, there is implied its exception and, too often, principles function to separate us from each other. We may become dangerously self-righteous when we perceive ourselves as holding a precious principle not held by the other. The other may then be devalued and treated "differently." Our ethic of caring will not permit this to happen. (p. 5)

Because Noddings rejects abstract rationality as an unacceptable basis on which to understand or adjudicate moral claims, she is likewise compelled to reject the universal principles that issue from its application. Enlightenment views are inconsistent with the ethic of care because they fail to take into account, indeed part of their very purpose is to exclude, the personal, partial, and particularistic aspects of everyday experience.

Care theorists argue that it is imperative for us to consider the relational qualities of our lives and the obligations that follow from our commitments to particular persons in any account of moral reasoning. Marilyn Friedman describes the distinctive moral orientation of caring as a commitment to cherishing the particularity of others in our relations with them. She says:

> The "care" perspective . . . is about the nature of relationships to particular persons grasped as such. The key issue is sensitivity and responsiveness to another person's emotional states, individuating differences, specific uniqueness, and whole particularity. . . . Commitment to a specific person, such as a lover, child, or friend, takes as its primary focus the needs, wants, attitudes, judgments, behavior, and overall way of being of that particular person. It is specific to that individual and is not generalizable to others. (Friedman, 1993, pp. 268–269)

These relationships (especially the bond between mother and child) are a focal point for moral deliberation and the form these relations take is a guide for moral conduct. Citing "the tenderest feelings in most of us" and "this feeling of nurturance [that] lies at the very heart of what we assess as good" (1984, p. 87), Noddings explores the nature of these caring relationships for their capacity to guide and assess our actions. At the center of a caring relation, according to Noddings (1984), is the idea of "engrossment," an experience she describes as involving the "nonselective" adoption of the needs, goals, and judgments of the other.

> Apprehending the other's reality, feeling what he feels as nearly as possible, is the essential part of caring from the view of the one-caring. For if I take on the other's reality as possibility and begin to feel its reality, I feel, also, that I must act accordingly; that is, I am impelled to act as though in my own behalf, but in behalf of the other. (p. 16)

As a way of elaborating this contextualized notion of moral reflection and commitment, Noddings (1984) later offers two criteria to define the parameters within which caring can be operationalized.

> We should try to say clearly what governs our [moral] obligation. . . . There seem to be two criteria: the existence of or potential for present relation, and the dynamic potential for growth in relation, including the potential for increased reciprocity and, perhaps, mutuality. The first criterion establishes an absolute obligation and the second serves to put our obligations into an order of priority. (p. 86)

Noddings (1992) explores these criteria extensively in her analysis of caring and further elaborates their implications for schooling in later work. In these accounts, Noddings returns again and again to the idea of caring relationships as a foundation for understanding social relations and responsibilities, and she consistently argues that building the capacity for caring should be a central goal of social institutions like schools.

Before considering the place of caring in emancipatory educational philosophy, however, we must first consider some of the objections that have been raised against it as a moral theory based on women's experience. This analysis will tell us a good deal about the pitfalls that caring must avoid in its application to schooling, and it will help us identify the positive contribution that caring can make in the new constellation. The ultimate goal of this critique is to show how the core insights associated with caring might be retained and incorporated with other emancipatory theories of education.

Critical Responses to Caring

In considering the objections that have been made against caring, we face a series of challenges that are similar in some respects (but not in others) to those presented in my analysis of postmodernism. First among these challenges to caring as a guide for emancipatory educational theory is the question of whether it provides the descriptive and prescriptive tools necessary to address systematic forms of oppression and exploitation. In the following, I consider whether Noddings' relatively wholesale rejection of principled moral evaluation presents the same kind of problems for emancipatory theory and practice as it did in the case of postmodernism. Based on this general concern, I take up two specific arguments against the care position: The first questions the extent to which we can trust women's experience, as it is currently constructed in patriarchal societies, to describe a legitimate normative ideal; the second questions the extent to which caring, as a moral theory, can reach beyond the limits of relatively intimate or local associations to account for the responsibilities we bear (and feel) to "strangers" or "distant others."

Can caring be trusted? One of the significant questions raised by feminist critics about the caring perspective concerns its capacity to explain and resist the sexist practices that are richly embedded in patriarchal societies. This argument begins, as I have noted above, with the observation that care theorists appeal to the *present* experience of women, and frequently to that of mothers (Noddings, 1984, 1992; Ruddick, 1989), to construct a framework for describing moral reflection and decision making. Some feminists feel (at least) ambivalent about the fact that care theorists urge us to recognize and promote the qualities of relation that women have traditionally demonstrated in caring for children, husbands, and the aged and infirm. Critics argue that we should not accept uncritically the caregiving roles that women display in society as a foundation for present or future moral commitments, without determining whether the roots of these actions rest in oppressive social relations (Houston, 1987).

In patriarchal societies, one would expect to find many examples of oppressive social relations masquerading as "femininity." The fact that some men (and some women) believe that a faithful wife must bring her emotionally distant husband his slippers and serve him his favorite meal when he comes home from work each day, for instance, suggests to no one that these practices ought to be preserved or advocated more generally, and it would be ridiculous to attribute such a position to any serious care theorist. To rule out many such cases, Noddings can appeal directly and effectively to her second criterion, which supposes that caring at least must have the potential for reciprocity (and, at its best, mutuality) in order to be "completed." This result clearly fails to obtain in cases where men coerce women into subservient roles out of fear (of abandonment, for instance, or worse), or by cynically reinforcing such behavior as a cultural norm.

It is not always so easy to tell the difference between caring and co-optation, however, and the ambivalence feminists have felt in this regard is real. An even stronger version of the preceding objection holds that, because women's experience has been fundamentally shaped and exploited by men, women cannot trust *any* of these experiences to guide their intuitions about acceptable social roles and practices. On this account, we are better off starting from scratch in thinking about moral ideals (even if this is only a thought experiment) or trying to use a generalizable principle like equality to minimize the *de jure* differences between women and men. This view takes the presumption against existing social practices in patriarchal societies even more seriously and, for good reason perhaps, measures the suspicion due to caring by its general acceptance among those who benefit from it already.

This critique seems too indiscriminate, however, and the suspicion on which it is based, no matter how well earned, may come at too great a cost. A more balanced way of developing the argument might be to consider it as a challenge for care theorists to provide a more careful and specific defense of the particular norms and practices associated with women in our society. We might, for instance, urge that caring be developed and elaborated as an approach to moral reasoning even as we also pursue the critique and reconstruction of social norms (including those derived from women's experience) that support and reproduce patriarchy. Something like this strategy has in fact been suggested by Barbara Houston (1987).

> In response to Kohlberg and others who would dismiss the allegedly distinctive moral concerns of women as "personal" and secondary, I have elsewhere argued for their social importance. But more is needed than a general endorsement of the universal significance of women's concerns. We might agree that we all like, perhaps even need, caring, along with motherhood and apple pie, but particular concoctions of it may not be to our liking, or may even be harmful. Thus, many would argue that in addition to a politics of persistence we also need a feminist politics to both deconstruct the feminine and to reconstruct women's moral experience into a worthy ethics. (p. 241)

The results of such efforts would be difficult to predict, and only after such a project was well on its way might we feel confident in trying to preserve and extend the roles or relational characteristics that have been associated with the experience of women. It would still be important to retain an enduring suspicion of any moral theory that failed to discriminate between the kinds of behaviors that women *should* adopt, and those that they *have* adopted, on the way to selecting and defending the "virtues" associated with women's experience (Baier, 1985).

The problem with this defense of caring, however, is that it does little to support the idea that caring is *itself* a moral theory that women and others might support. To understand what caring entails, even on this modified account, requires that we have some other means of assessing the roles and practices associated with caring. The difficult question that advocates of caring must answer is how (on what basis) we can find a way "of assessing the values we reinforce through our interactions and a vision of how values can change" (Hoagland, 1991, p. 249). That is, how can we identify and select those characteristics in women's experience that are worth making central to moral theory or to an emancipatory theory of education? As I argue below, these questions need not go unanswered, but addressing them requires moving away from the claim that caring can be defended without the support of other emancipatory perspectives.

Can caring help us resist patriarchy? A second major concern about the adequacy of caring as a moral theory has to do with its capacity to explain and justify the nature (or even existence) of moral commitments to persons beyond the circle of those relatively close to us, or those with whom we have the potential to establish a reciprocal or mutually caring relationship. Here the question for an ethic of care is whether it is sufficient to satisfy the intuitions (often as powerful as those that support the care perspective in particular relations) that push or pull our sympathies beyond the context of the local and familiar. These intuitions include the "political" reasons we sometimes have for caring about others whom we do not know (most of whom we are likely never to know), but with whom we feel a strong solidarity of vision or purpose. This is a question about the "scope" of caring as a moral theory, or the degree to which caring as a moral theory sets useful (in this case, sufficiently broad) parameters around the possible objects of its inquiry.

Understanding moral obligation in terms of "the existence of or potential for present relation" and "the dynamic potential for growth in relation" (Noddings, 1984, p. 86) appears limiting to many critics because it restricts caring to the kinds of relationships that can be sustained only through relatively intimate acquaintance. Critics have questioned whether such a moral theory is capable of providing the tools necessary to understand fully, as well as oppose effectively, forms of oppression that are deeply rooted in structural relations of inequality. If we understand patriarchy, for example, as underlying the limited choices that women experience in society, then the concept of care will fail to provide a satisfactory basis for explaining women's oppression if it cannot account for the "relation" that women bear to those who "share" their experience (only) by virtue of the similar place in society that they occupy. By rejecting all principled views of moral inquiry, and the generalizable normative assessments they support, the care orientation risks being unable to guide us in the context of social or political, rather than interpersonal, conflict.

One way to think about this challenge is to consider how caring addresses the needs of those who live (and suffer) at some distance from us. Images of starving children in distant lands or victims of natural disasters may evoke the kind of moral sympathy or intuition on which this critique is based. We might also think, however, of the poverty that exists in our own country or the harm caused by the resurgence of racism in our streets and communities. The question I want to pursue here is not whether we can see ourselves caring for people who suffer in these different "locations," but whether caring as a moral theory gives us a way of overcoming the "distance" involved that is effective in helping us understanding the causes of this suffering and the reasons we have for taking action in response to it.

Marilyn Friedman (1991) has described this quality of moral deliberation as "global concern," and she points out that it involves a conception of the "social self" (i.e., the self in relation) that must go beyond the obligations established in relationships between individuals in order to justify moral action.

> Global moral concern raises a unique problem for the social conception of the self. A self whose identity is defined in terms of relations to certain others is capable of having immediate and direct moral concern for those others. . . . The question raised by the issue of global moral concern is whether concern for distant and unknown peoples is an immediate moral motivation of the social self. The likeliest source of such a motivation is group identity and consciousness. (p. 175)

Care theorists like Noddings struggle with this issue because "group identity and consciousness" is difficult to explain in the framework she provides for us to understand the moral dimension of human relationships. To apply Friedman's analysis to the question of political solidarity suggests that for those whose oppression or exploitation is dependent on their membership in a particular group, a theory that fails to account for the general causes that explain this treatment, or that fails to motivate action by the distant others who share it, will do little to support emancipation.

Emancipatory social practice requires global moral concern most in situations where we want to organize or raise consciousness around an issue of shared social experience; in this case, we seek to (re)affirm the identity we share with others who are similarly positioned in society. One of the most important qualities such a group can have in common is its relationship to a dominant group whose shared identity has become the norm in that society. Individuals are, in this case, likely to be divided by oppressive and mystifying social relationships rather than geographical distance, and they may have to overcome various constraints on their conceptions of self and (appropriate) social roles to effectively resist domination. Membership in this kind of group has a *political* origin and demands a kind of solidarity that cannot, for most members of the group, depend even on distant acquaintance (understood in the customary sense). We should not doubt the power of this sense of affiliation, however, as individuals have, throughout history, put themselves in great peril on behalf of others who share their social vision, but whom they have almost no hope of ever meeting. The civil rights movement and the history of labor activism in this country are examples where participants in a "global" political action sometimes paid for such solidarity with their lives.

This argument suggests another kind of limit for caring as a moral theory, although Noddings is not without resources for suggesting at least the direction from which an answer might come. Noddings argues that our obligation under the kind of circumstances described above can be fundamentally expressed as an educational one, namely, "preparing [children] to care" (Noddings, 1992, p. 117). The argument she makes here, which I consider in greater detail below, reflects a clear awareness of the need for caring to extend beyond the limits of the kinds of relationships we have with our family, friends, and closest colleagues. But it may also be that her recommendations to "encourage caring attitudes at the community, national, and international levels" (Noddings, 1992, p. 123) begin to overextend the powerful insights caring has for the particular and local aspects of our experience, and risk weakening the theory generally by this almost metaphorical usage. In the end, I think such a defense is unnecessary, but only at the cost of admitting that caring cannot do all that a moral theory must and, similarly, that emancipatory educational theories benefit greatly from, but cannot be fully expressed through, Noddings' recommendations about caring. This conclusion, however, requires looking more closely at caring as an emancipatory educational theory, as I do in the next section.

Caring as a Foundation for Educational Theory and Practice

Ann Diller (1996a) characterizes the two kinds of objections described above as concerns about caring as a "dangerous ethic" and a "domain ethic," respectively (pp. 96, 94). Caring may be "dangerous" because it reinforces stereotypical gender roles, or it may be limited in its applicability to the "domain" of familial or close interpersonal relationships. My response, as I suggested in the introduction to this section, is to worry about both possibilities, but to treat neither as definitive arguments against caring as a guide for emancipatory educational theory. These two areas of critique are most worrisome when we focus on caring as a comprehensive moral theory that eschews (or, at a minimum, finds morally inconclusive) the abstract and generalizable forms of normative argument found in universalist approaches. Noddings indeed seems to hold this general orientation but, as I argue below, it is not necessary to do so in working toward the more inclusive context of the new constellation.

But I want to be clear about one aspect of this strategy. I certainly do *not* believe that moral and educational theories can be easily uncoupled; indeed, the whole premise of this work presupposes that emancipatory educational theory cannot proceed without a clear grasp of its roots in moral and political theory. However, it seems quite defensible to argue that caring describes one, albeit extremely important, set of educational goals, without having to maintain that by itself it is definitive as either a moral or an educational theory. No doubt this would be an unattractive solution for steadfast advocates of caring like Noddings, but I argue in Chapter 5 that the new constellation is ultimately justified by the mutual dependency of *all* of its constituents; none of the four theories that I consider here provides by itself a fully satisfactory basis on which to elaborate the goals and practice of emancipatory schooling. Only taken together, in the new constellation, can these theories supply the various pieces to the puzzle whose solution we require to guide educational reform. In what follows, I examine the *educational* answers Noddings gives to the normative challenges described in the previous section. I argue that these answers *can* effectively guide emancipatory educational practice, even though they do not persuasively refute the broader criticisms that have been raised about caring as a moral theory.

Caring in schools. In *The Challenge to Care in Schools,* Noddings (1992) argues that the work of educators should be directed first and foremost to helping students develop as healthy, moral individuals, and to building school communities in which caring relationships are promoted and sustained among all members (students, teachers, parents, etc.). Although Noddings is clearly not the first to argue that caring should be an important aspect of schooling (e.g., Neill, 1960), she is the first to articulate fully an ethic of care and the first to apply it systematically to schooling. Noddings' (1992) belief in the primacy of caring is clear in her description of our most important educational goals.

> If the school has one main goal, a goal that guides the establishment and priority of all others, it should be to promote the growth of students as healthy, competent, moral people. This is a huge task to which all others are properly subordinated. We cannot ignore our children—their purposes, anxieties, and relationships—in the service of making them more competent in academic skills. My position is not anti-intellectual. It is a matter of setting priorities. Intellectual development is important, but it cannot be the first priority of schools. (p. 10)

By emphasizing the personal, and therefore the particular, Noddings displaces the priority traditionally given to subject-matter goals (based on their perceived universality) and places a renewed emphasis on individual growth. She bases the implementation of her approach on "centers of care," which serve to organize instruction around the appropriate objects of caring, including the self; the inner circle; strangers and distant others; animals, plants, and the earth; the human-made world; and ideas. Two centers of care are particularly relevant to the critiques of caring as dangerous and limited in its applicability to the familial or interpersonal domain. These are, respectively, "caring in the inner circle" (Noddings, 1992, p. 91) and "caring for strangers and distant others" (p. 110).

In discussing the ethical treatment of those closest to us, Noddings considers the nature of caring among "equal relations" (mates, lovers, friends, colleagues, and neighbors) and "unequal relations" (parents and their children, teachers and their students). With respect to the inequalities that exist between teachers and students, Noddings (1992) notes that "teachers have special responsibilities that students cannot assume" (p. 107), and here she focuses, interestingly, on differences in roles and prior experiences (e.g., teachers have a sense of what students need to learn that the students themselves cannot have), rather than differences in power that stem from the institutional dimensions of schooling (e.g., teachers have the capacity to assess, discipline, and credential students, while students have little, if any, reciprocal authority). In exploring this sense of inequality, Noddings draws on a dialogue between Martin Buber and Carl Rogers to compare a student coming to class with a patient who goes to a therapist for counseling. In the latter case, the patient comes to be "seen" by the therapist, but the patient cannot, by the nature of the situation, help or "see" the therapist. "In the same way," Noddings (1992) argues, "teachers can see students and see with them; students, by definition, cannot see in the same way with teachers" (p. 107).

Despite some of the reservations I have about this comparison (which center around the suggestion that students suffer from some metaphorical illness or deficit, an interpretation I am sure Noddings does not intend), the general responsibilities incurred by teachers in the situation described by Noddings seem well motivated by a theory of care. Noddings argues that teachers must recognize the differences that exist between themselves and their students and work toward their students' "inclusion." When this process is successful, "students are set free by their teachers' efforts at inclusion to pursue their own growth" (Noddings, 1992, p. 107).

The broad goals of setting students free and encouraging them to pursue their own growth can be pursued through a variety of educational practices. Noddings (1992) argues that one of the most important of these is "to help students learn how to be recipients of care" (p. 108). To do this requires helping teachers and students to work together to create and sustain the kind of reciprocal relationship on which caring is based. It requires a bond of trust between teacher and student that can only come from a collaborative effort.

> The contributions of teachers and students are necessarily unequal, but they are nonetheless mutual; the relationship is marked by reciprocity. Students cannot be expected to teach their teachers, but they can be expected to respond with growing sensitivity to attempts to promote their own growth. Too often—even at the collegiate level, but especially at the secondary level—students regard their teachers as enemies to be outwitted or as bumbling authorities to be suffered temporarily (Crozier, 1991). What is lost is not only academic knowledge but a relation that might yield a lifetime of friendship and wisdom. (Noddings, 1992, p. 108)

The give and take of such relationships helps create a context in which students learn to express their need for care at the same time that they increase their capacity to provide it for others. Education must emphasize and reflect the reciprocal nature of caring, which is a burden that, while shared, falls heavily on the shoulders of teachers to be involved with students as role models, guides, and mentors. As Noddings (1992) notes, this "responsibility is clearly enormous" for teachers (p. 106).

Challenges to caring in schools. There is much about this account that I find convincing and extremely important for emancipatory educational theory. Indeed, I return to Noddings' ideas about recognition and reciprocity in the next chapter as key contributions to the new constellation. It is not clear to me, however, that this analysis helps resolve critics' concerns that caring may not only fail to resist existing forms of gendered oppression, but that it may even perpetuate it in particular circumstances. Recall for a moment the situation I described in Chapter 3, concerning the gender stereotyping reflected in the relative percentages of women who teach more often than they lead, and teach younger students more often than older ones. Recall Gutmann's (1987) conclusion that "the authority structure within schools serves as an additional lesson in the nature of 'normal' gender relations. Girls learn that it is normal for them to rule children, but abnormal for them to rule men. Boys learn the opposite lesson" (p. 114).

The difficulty this situation poses for Noddings lies in the fact that caring does not seem to give us much purchase on how to understand the institutional and social implications of such stereotyping, even (we might say especially) when caring relationships have been successfully established between teachers and students. It is not that Noddings' discussion of the differences that exist between teachers and students is descriptively wrong, or that such relationships are in themselves sources of oppression (although the more radical critique of caring as mere compliance with prevailing social norms might suggest this). Rather, the point is that Noddings' analysis seems distressingly mute on a key aspect of the dilemma women face in our patriarchal society, namely, that the meanings and practices associated with caring are currently constructed in ways that constrain the opportunities women possess in education, employment, and elsewhere. Without a broader or more structural account of how caring is practiced, and by whom, we are left vulnerable to the possibility that schools may unwittingly help perpetuate a system in which caring remains the work of women, and women remain constrained by their practice and identity as caregivers.

Ann Diller, an advocate of caring herself, shares a similar concern about the circumstances under which we remain faithful to our caring convictions. Recognizing that caring is the right thing to do, does not resolve the ambivalence associated with struggling to create caring relationships in a society that often turns this effort back against those for whom it is a primary responsibility.

Noddings ... seems to leave us precisely where the dangerous position would predict—with no recourse but to go on caring as well as we can under a set of antithetical conditions, while the larger structures remain beyond our power to change as long as we adhere to this morally admirable *and* politically powerless ethics of care. It is here that those of us whose work, responsibilities, and morality fits an ethics of care must face what Marilyn Frye (1983) has aptly termed the "fatal combination of responsibility and powerlessness: we are held responsible and we hold ourselves responsible for good outcomes for ... children in almost every respect though we have in almost no case power adequate to that project." (Diller, 1996a, p. 101, emphasis in original)

Although Diller, rightly I think, argues that Noddings would confront such powerlessness with "unrelenting persistence and insistence when it comes to conditions for caring," it nevertheless may be necessary to look beyond a theory of care for additional support. We must figure out how to create and sustain the circumstances under which caring is both possible *and* emancipatory.

I want to be clear about the conclusions one can draw from this argument. The kind of critical position I think is justified here suggests that caring, by itself, does not provide the tools necessary to explain the larger social structures associated with women's oppression, or the tools necessary to resist the oppressive consequences of these structures for women who engage in caring. This does *not*, however, give us grounds to reject or dismiss the kinds of relationships (in schools and elsewhere) that Noddings has described in terms of caring; my later recommendations run completely opposite to this conclusion. I do believe these arguments suggest a limit, however, in the contribution that caring can make to educational theory, beyond which it fails to be a useful guide for emancipatory practice. Without some additional or complementary understanding of caring as a social or institutional practice, we cannot be clear about how schools can best guide students' resistance to the social norms that oppress them.

A second limit to caring as an emancipatory educational theory follows from the worry that it may be less useful in describing moral reasoning and responsibility outside of a particularly local domain or, which amounts to the same thing, caring for the stranger or distant other. Noddings has noted that the suspicion she expressed in her earlier work, that we are unable to care for distant victims of famine because it is impossible to initiate or complete the caring relationship at such a distance, "upset many readers" because it seemed to follow from her analysis that we (in the affluent West) possessed no moral obligation to support relief efforts in famine-plagued nations around the globe. In *The Challenge to Care in Schools*, Noddings (1992) responds to this criticism, saying, "I still think this is an accurate descriptive account of a major difficulty in trying to care at a distance. I did not mean to suggest, however, that because we cannot really care in such situations, we are not obligated to do *anything*" (p. 110, emphasis in original).

In education, one of the most salient issues associated with caring for strangers involves the metaphorical "distance" that often exists, even within the same classroom, between students of different cultural or linguistic backgrounds, or between teachers and students who may also differ in this way. It would not be inappropriate to add other important aspects of social identity to this list, including gender, social class, sexual orientation, able-bodiedness, and religion, among others. The question this debate has raised for caring is whether it can guide educational practice in relation to such differences in social identity, and whether caring can provide the tools we need to resist systematic forms of intolerance such as racism, sexism, and homophobia. As above, it is quite possible that caring can provide an important, even essential, guide for emancipatory educational practice, without fully meeting the challenges that have been leveled against it as a moral theory.

In *The Challenge to Care in Schools*, Noddings (1992) rightly rejects the acquisition of "multicultural knowledge" as alone sufficient to "reduce misunderstanding, stereotyping, and the instinctive fear of strangers" (p. 113). Most research and writing in multicultural education has left behind the naive hope that simply teaching *about* one or another minority group (or eating their food, sampling their forms of dress, etc.) will contribute significantly to the understanding, tolerance, and respect shown by members of the majority culture to others (e.g., Banks, 1994; Nieto, 1996; Sleeter, 1991). It is the *relational* aspect of multicultural education that holds out the most promise for improving our understanding of living in a diverse society, according to Noddings (1992), and she notes that "students need motivation to undertake such studies energetically. A powerful source of motivation comes from living others" (p. 114). As we might expect, this is exactly the "domain" in which caring is most relevant and effective as an educational guide, and Noddings' suggestions about "preparing [students] to care" mark an important contribution to emancipatory educational theory.

What Noddings says about how schools might prepare students to care for strangers or (metaphorically) distant others falls into two general categories: self-reflection and active participation in community (especially through dialogue). Self-reflection is a necessary aspect of all forms of caring, although it seems a little surprising at first that Noddings would place so much emphasis on it in describing the relationships we might build with people who hold assumptions and values that are quite different from our own. We must remember, however, that we are dealing with a particularly problematic range of differences here, which are quite likely to involve deeply embedded antagonisms set firmly in place through history and stereotype.

Noddings' commitment to self-reflection follows from her belief that the first steps to be taken in dealing with the barriers that exist among us is to recognize their roots in the beliefs we have about ourselves and the communities these beliefs in part help to construct. She argues that "schools often ignore this level of questioning and reflection" and she (again) criticizes approaches to curriculum and instruction that focus on the "inert knowledge of others" (Noddings, 1992, p. 118).

> Schools should give far more attention to understanding ourselves and our various allegiances. . . . The problem is that most of the people outside our circles feel the same way we do. They, too, cherish caring relations and feel the need to protect themselves against external attack. When we understand why we draw circles and erect barriers, we can begin to explore the differences between belonging and encountering, between established relations and potential relations. (Noddings, 1992, p. 117)

Noddings' emphasis here and elsewhere is on understanding difference through the examination of what makes each of us who we are, and what makes each of us different (and the same) as others. By thinking about identity in this way, Noddings argues, we are also encouraged to think about the ties that might bind us with others whom we have not recognized or acknowledged, and the ways we might extend the boundaries of our communities to be more inclusive.

Noddings also argues strongly for the importance of open communication between communities, and for the importance of caring as a guide for the exploration of common bonds and shared projects. Noddings (1992) examines a number of challenges that caring must face in this regard, including the seeming paradox of separatist communities where exclusion may not be an "irrelevant criterion" (e.g., sex-segregated schools), organizations whose membership is based on "earned exclusivity" (e.g., the Cleveland Symphony Orchestra or the San Francisco Forty-Niners), and groups who are defined wholly by their "past performance" (e.g., Phi Beta Kappa) (p. 122). She explains that while such groups may be justified in limiting their membership in certain ways, each must be committed to some common goals such as "reach[ing] beyond itself to share what it does with interested members of the public" and creating "mutually beneficial connections with other morally thoughtful groups" (Noddings, 1992, p. 121).

As we might expect from such a strong and persistent advocate of caring, Noddings argues that we should err on the side of openness, even with (especially with) those whom we are most inclined to exclude from our communities. These may be enemies whom we misunderstand and vilify unfairly, and they share more with us than we are willing to admit. "It is imperative to keep the lines of communication open," Noddings (1992) emphasizes, so that we can "prevent this separation and provide [ourselves] with direct knowledge of the others whose behavior concerns us."

> The purpose of such discussion is not to fix blame, nor is it to reject one's own group and embrace another (more moral, more enlightened) group. It is to understand and perhaps to resist pressures that lead us as individuals and groups to perform outrageous acts. We need to press speakers to translate their recommendations into the language of living bodies, and then to ask whether we can participate in the proposed acts. If we are prepared to care, we must say: "Speak to me, if you must, in terms of dollars, of territory won and lost, of cities destroyed, of enemies overcome—but also speak to me in terms of shattered homes, crippled bodies, crazed minds, grieving mothers, and lost children. And ask me, make me think about, what *I* would do—with whom, to whom, why." This is the language of education for caring. (p. 118, emphasis in original)

Noddings' example of wartime decisions (e.g., to bomb civilian population centers during World War II), made by people who refused to confront the actual consequences ("on living bodies") of their exclusionary thinking is not inappropriate for what many consider to be the likely consequences of our continued inability to face the deep and widening divisions of race and class in this country (see, for example, Carl Rowan's book, *The Coming Race War in America: A Wake-Up Call*, 1996).

Consider, for example, as a complement to the preceding analysis of gender relations in schools, Derrick Bell's explanation of "the permanence of racism" in *Faces at the Bottom of the Well* (1992), a book whose title suggests a provocative image of race relations in this country. The importance of Bell's work for this analysis of caring lies in the form of the argument he offers about the roots of racism and the function it serves in society. Bell (1992) argues that, "the critically important stabilizing role that blacks play in this society constitutes a major barrier in the way of achieving racial equality," and he provides numerous examples to support his contention that Blacks have been used by White politicians as "scapegoats for failed economic or political policies" throughout history (p. 8).

Citing Toni Morrison in one of his dialogues with the fictional character Geneva Crenshaw, Bell argues that this scapegoating of Blacks has led "poor whites to identify with . . . well-to-do whites, particularly those who attribute social problems to blacks rather than to the policies that they, the upper-class policymakers, have designed and implemented" (p. 151). This process, as a structural feature of American society, "enables a bonding by whites across a vast socioeconomic divide" (p. 151).

The opposition between Blacks and Whites that lies at the heart of America's intransigence in dealing with issues of race, according to Bell, is only subtly accessible to our consideration of the everyday interactions between these groups. As Bell (1992) notes, the antagonism between Blacks and Whites is often expressed in terms of the "preferences" that Whites hold in dealing with Blacks, the cumulative meaning of which is revealed as racial discrimination only through our awareness of the pattern (or we might say, structure) they create.

> Careful examination reveals a pattern to these seemingly arbitrary racial actions. When whites perceive that it will be profitable or at least cost-free to serve, hire, admit, or otherwise deal with blacks on a nondiscriminatory basis, they do so. When they fear—accurately or not—that there may be a loss, inconvenience, or upset to themselves or other whites, discriminatory conduct usually follows. Selections and rejections reflect preference as much as prejudice. . . . Racial policy is the culmination of thousands of these individual practices. (p. 7)

Bell argues that no one has been able (or willing) to confront the way that white people are actually served by racism, and the social and economic roots of this relationship. All the more reason, one might argue, to make it part of the open dialogue that Noddings supports based on a sound educational program aimed at preparing students to care. I agree with this response, but will caring be enough?

Caring, when we consider its broad rejection of principled normative argument, may actually make it more difficult for us to pursue the connection between the personal and the political in our social relations. Even if we believe that the basis for all social change lies in the work of individuals, which is a hope that Bell holds firmly, although often with more passion than optimism, we still need the proper tools to describe and resist the powerful ways that structural forms of oppression like racism shape the meanings we make in our attempts to care. Just as Gutmann's argument about the way schools support and reproduce gender stereotypes undermines the capacity of caring to avoid becoming a dangerous ethic, arguments like Bell's suggest that too much of a conceptual focus on individual behavior may leave us without the tools necessary for describing and resisting the social and economic roots of oppression.

In neither case (Gutmann's or Bell's), however, should we conclude that caring is a bad idea, or that it should be restricted rather than vigorously pursued in our schools. As in my analysis of caring within the inner circle, I believe Noddings' work says a great deal that is important for emancipatory education, about the nature of school communities and how they might help students understand the reasons and costs associated with exclusionary social practices. Caring also has its limits, however, especially when we ask it to account for the educational reforms necessary in a society built upon deeply embedded structural inequalities. To the critics of caring, we may admit that we have not been able to resolve their worries about the potential for it to be both dangerous and limited in its application to a particular domain. In fact, we have some reason to support a certain kind of vigilance on both counts. But by now we should be accustomed to the conclusion that the emancipatory educational theories under consideration here are incomplete, and that this is an important part of the justification for trying to create a new constellation. What caring and postmodernism have to contribute to this effort, I describe below as an understanding of autonomy as authenticity.

AUTONOMY AS AUTHENTICITY

In the introduction to this chapter, I warned that particularist emancipatory perspectives would require a certain amount of reconstruction in order to find their proper place (and relationship) in the new constellation. Thus, a good deal of what I have written here concerns the limits of postmodernism and caring, and the recognition that each approach confronts certain obstacles that must be overcome. I see this critical work as constructive, however, in the larger context of the new constellation, as a way of promoting the kind of shared insights that will benefit all of the approaches considered here. Thus, it is not so much *in spite of these concerns* that we can learn from particularist perspectives, as it is consistent with the general strategy I take in this work to use such analysis as the basis for illuminating the significant contribution of each approach to emancipatory educational theory.

As a way of understanding how we are enmeshed in communities and relationships, postmodernism and caring refocus our attention, albeit in different ways, on the local context of our actions and the degree to which our immediate circumstances necessarily shape the capacity we have to create and pursue our life-plans. When individuals draw on these local resources in ways that expand the range and possibility of their choices, increase the potential of their choices to meet their needs, and encourage the development of new interests and talents, then these relationships and communities support a capacity for autonomy that is generally not explained, and in some cases not supported, by universalist theories alone.

Authenticity, suitably elaborated in relation to the concept of autonomy, is the quality that I believe best describes the powerful connection between postmodernism and caring in the new constellation. To describe authenticity as an aspect of autonomy, and of emancipatory theories generally, requires that we consider both the inward experience of our deliberation over possible choices and life-plans, and the outward experience of recognition we feel through the understanding and support that others express for our choices. These two aspects, one experienced self-reflectively, the other in our relations with others, are key aspects of authenticity.

Charles Taylor has described the way we experience authenticity as a recognition of our own originality and uniqueness. This interpretation is central to understanding the capacity for authenticity as, in part, an awareness or articulation of self, an awareness that guides and integrates an individual's developing sense of identity by focusing on its source in each of us.

> There is a certain way of being human that is *my* way. I am called upon to live my life in this way, and not in imitation of anyone else's. . . . Being true to myself means being true to my own originality, and that is something only I can articulate and discover. In articulating it, I am also defining myself. I am realizing a potentiality that is properly my own. (Taylor, 1991, pp. 28–29, emphasis in original)

It is important to see in Taylor's comments here an emphasis on the active *construction* of self, rather than the revelation or expression of some eternal essence. Authenticity of the kind I am describing does not require that our choices or life-plans conform to some preordained pattern or model of human development, or move in the direction of some common human ideal. Postmodernists, among others, have given us good reason to reject such essentialist views. Instead, the definition of authenticity that I propose for the new constellation involves a commitment to self-reflection and exploration consistent with the view that identity is constructed rather than given, and that this process of construction takes place in a complex landscape of historical contingency.

This understanding of authenticity demands that we pay particular attention to the circumstances in which people deliberate over alternative goals and plans of action (i.e., the exercise of autonomy), and the barriers they encounter in this process. The new constellation gives an important place, in this respect, to postmodern theories that are concerned with school policies and practices that constrain individual efforts to deliberate over questions of identity by "silencing" attempts at self-expression and marginalizing those who try to follow or create emancipatory alternatives (e.g., Ellsworth, 1992; Lather, 1991). Other postmodern educational theorists (e.g., Giroux, 1992; Giroux & McLaren, 1994) have used the geographical metaphor of the "border" to define dissident (Taylor's "original") voices that come from outside the dominant culture or institutions of society, and to explain the role these voices might play in the construction of alternative social identities. In these accounts, schools are institutions that frequently constrain students' efforts at self-expression and produce an "other" (i.e., identities outside of the mainstream, or at the margins of society) through practices that "colonize" and distort. The capacity for authenticity is constrained in such circumstances by students' inability to find a voice in which to express their own originality or realize their potential through efforts at self-definition.

In addition to this inward-looking or self-reflective component, the capacity for authenticity also depends on qualities associated with participation in community, and the degree to which relationships with others enable or constrain efforts to explore and pursue a variety of life-plans. Taylor (1991) also explores this aspect of authenticity as a way of articulating the significant contribution our social relationships play in the process of forming and transforming our conception of self.

> On the intimate level, we can see how much an original identity needs and is vulnerable to the recognition given or withheld by significant others. It is not surprising that in the culture of authenticity, relationships are seen as the key loci of self-discovery and self-confirmation. Love relationships are not important just because of the general emphasis in modern culture on the fulfillments of ordinary life. They are also crucial because they are the crucibles of inwardly generated identity. On the social plane the understanding that identities are formed in open dialogue, unshaped by a predefined social script has made the politics of equal recognition more central and stressful. It has, in fact, considerably raised its stakes. Equal recognition is not just the appropriate mode for a healthy democratic society. Its refusal can inflict damage on those who are denied it, according to a widespread modern view. The projecting of an inferior or demeaning image on another can actually distort and oppress, to the extent that it is interiorized. (pp. 49–50)

Authenticity, as a capacity for making decisions about goals and life-plans, requires a local context that recognizes and supports such efforts. Instead of treating freedom from constraint as a normative ideal for community, Taylor argues for recognizing the mutual dependence that characterizes our experience and urges us to assess our individual actions and social institutions accordingly.

Noddings' (1984) promotion of "caring apprenticeships" for students (p. 188) and Diller's (1996b) elaboration of caring in diverse communities as involving "co-exploring" and "co-enjoyment" (pp. 163, 166) are recommendations that draw on the richness of our community relationships without sentimentalizing or underestimating the potential for conflict and disagreement. As my analysis of Noddings' work suggests, the ethic of care has much to say about how we can help create and sustain circumstances that support authenticity in the context of community, and how schooling can help students grow in their relations with others. This growth increases students' capacity to see their mutual dependence on (and even their conflicts with) others as a basis for making informed and healthy decisions about their own life-plans, as well as their ability to make a similar contribution to this process of growth in others. A diminished capacity for authenticity in schools is marked by some degree of isolation or alienation, and fewer opportunities for self-realization.

The central insights of postmodernism and caring revolve around the meaning and embeddedness of choice in the local context of community and in our relations with those to whom we are closest. Both approaches give us good reasons to focus on the local circumstances in which emancipatory educational practice must be undertaken to support or enlarge the capacity for autonomy as authenticity. This, I have argued, is key to the exploration of issues associated with identity, self-expression, and the realization of human potential.

5

Emancipatory Theories of Education in the New Constellation

In Chapters 3 and 4, I focused on making connections *within* universalist and particularist perspectives. I argued that critical consciousness and authenticity can bring together some of the most important insights offered by these two general approaches. Now I want to focus more pointedly on developing the new constellation in terms of the conceptual gap that currently exists *between* universalist and particularist perspectives. The strategy I pursue here extends the preceding analysis by elaborating the complementary role that critical consciousness and authenticity play *with respect to each other* in the new constellation.

MAKING CONNECTIONS IN THE NEW CONSTELLATION

The following two sections are organized and related in a way that draws explicitly on the spatial metaphor of navigating within a new constellation of ideas. In each section, I propose a journey that starts on one "side" of the new constellation (i.e., with a universalist or particularist perspective). Then, by considering specific examples of emancipatory theories at work, I show how each analysis, regardless of its staring point, pulls us toward the increasingly complementary insights of the perspective (again, universalist or particularist) that was previously considered to be both critic and competitor. By doing this twice, that is, beginning from starting points on either side of the new constellation, I press an argument for this new framework on behalf of all four emancipatory traditions, looking for common goals, shared insights, and mutually reinforcing strategies for social change.

From Universalist to Particularist Theories

I have suggested that universalist theories are most attractive in terms of the powerful principles and explanatory frameworks they offer for understanding and assessing the general structure of society, as well as the actions of individuals, across differences in time and culture. This approach is particularly persuasive because of the conceptual tools it provides for understanding social contexts in which power and status create hierarchical relationships among individuals and groups. We also saw in Chapter 3, however, that universalist theories are not without their critics. These critics argue that universal principles and the elaborate conceptual frameworks that support them are not sufficiently embedded in our actual experience of the world or our relationships with others to be effective guides for moral assessment.

Universalist theorists have attempted to answer these critics through various concessions and accommodations. Contemporary liberal theorists (whom I will call simply "liberals" from now on, unless some specific contrast is required), for instance, emphasize the role played by the context of choice in shaping individual decisions and the capacity of individuals to participate in meaningful ways to determine the kind of opportunities available to them in society (Howe, 1997; Kymlicka, 1991). Critical theorists, on the other hand, have advocated reaching beyond traditional Marxist views of social class in order to develop a pluralistic framework that addresses the different ways in which individuals can be oppressed, exploited, or marginalized in particular contexts (Apple, 1993; McCarthy & Apple, 1988).

Whether these responses have been successful (i.e., as defenses of liberalism or critical theory *per se*) is not an issue that is important to settle here. More important for this analysis is the fact that, by trying to incorporate or account for the circumstances under which issues of power and status play out in the lives of individuals, liberalism and critical theory have moved toward each other (through their common commitment to critical consciousness) *and* toward their particularist critics. Using the tools of the new constellation, and my analysis of autonomy as a central goal of emancipatory education, this growing *rapprochement* between universalist and particularist perspectives can be further elaborated and extended.

Given that universalist theories are to some (contested) extent vulnerable to the criticism that their descriptive and normative accounts are insufficiently grounded in the rich circumstances of individual experience, it is reasonable to question the adequacy of critical consciousness, by itself, as a guide for actions at the level of community or in close relationships with others. Even with a good understanding of how power and status are embedded in the organization and norms of social institutions, critical consciousness will be incomplete if it does not help individuals gain a rich understanding of the local communities in which their plans and projects are carried out. The new constellation helps show that efforts to build the capacity for critical consciousness depend for their success on some of the complementary qualities associated with authenticity.

Resistance, identity, and the culture of power: An example. As a way of pursuing the relationship between critical consciousness and authenticity, I want to consider several issues associated with the education of minority and immigrant students in the United States, and especially the current debate over the role that Standard English should play in public schooling. With respect to the literacy goals of our public schools, there is widespread agreement that we must provide all students with the fundamental tools necessary for social and economic success in "mainstream" American culture. Virtually all participants in the debate over literacy instruction acknowledge that, for good or ill, the possession of Standard English is necessary to reach this goal. Advocates of multicultural and linguistic tolerance recognize the role played by Standard English as a social and political reality (e.g., Delpit, 1995; Nieto, 1996), as do the neo-conservatives I quoted in Chapter 2 who, indeed, celebrate it as a central achievement of Western culture (e.g., Bennett, 1992; Hirsch, 1987a). The positions maintained by these two groups can hardly be described as similar, however, since their views on whether there is anything wrong with this situation, and what follows from it for schools' treatment of students' nonstandard dialects or first languages, differ in obvious and important ways. The landscape of this debate is important for the way we think about emancipatory educational theories in the new constellation.

Hirsch and other neo-conservatives rely on an uncritical characterization of cultural assimilation as an appropriate social and educational goal for minority students. This is no less true in the consideration neo-conservatives give to Standard English, which more or less begins with the assumption that Standard English is *the* (or certainly the most effective) means by which knowledge is organized and communicated in society. Hirsch's (1987a) work provides a reasonable representation of this perspective, and likewise of the way it characteristically obscures the role of culture and power in defining linguistic standards behind what otherwise appears to be historical happenstance.

> Although standard written English has no intrinsic superiority to other languages and dialects, its stable written forms have now standardized the oral forms of the language spoken by educated Americans. The chief function of literacy is to make us masters of this standard instrument of knowledge and communication, thereby enabling us to give and receive complex information orally and in writing over time and space. (p. 3)

The general view of assimilation held by neo-conservatives ignores many significant issues associated with acquiring the behaviors and attributes characteristic of the dominant culture, and this is especially true when we consider issues of language and literacy. To begin with the assumption that the linguistic tools held by a particular group in society provide the only appropriate or acceptable marker for identifying "educated Americans" or those who possess the "standard instrument of knowledge," already frames the education of minority students in compensatory terms and treats the distance between dominant and minority cultures as a deficit to be remediated in schools.

Lisa Delpit (1995) and other advocates of linguistic pluralism have offered views of literacy instruction that take into account the social and political context in which Standard English has come to assume its current status. Delpit describes the dissonance or conflict that many minority students experience in school as in part a question about social identity outside "the culture of power." She assesses different forms of literacy instruction in relation to their capacity to achieve two sorts of goals. First, literacy instruction should support the efforts of minority students to be successful in the dominant culture by developing the capacity of these students to use Standard English in situations where not to do so would exact a high social or economic cost. Even in these cases, however, the explicit rationale for using Standard English is largely and transparently instrumental.

The second claim made by Delpit and other advocates of linguistic pluralism is that schools must explicitly support and sustain the "home" language/culture of each minority student, as individually *and* socially legitimate forms of knowledge and communication. Indeed, it is quite likely that teachers of minority students will need to locate their efforts explicitly within a larger instructional context that confronts the inequities of a society in which cultural norms often masquerade as objective measures of linguistic or educational competence (or superiority). Delpit's treatment of linguistic and cultural differences (among African American and Athabaskan students, for example) depends for its effectiveness on demystifying the social and political context in which language is a powerful component of social status, and schools serve a clear gatekeeping, sorting, and stratifying role.

The ongoing debate about language and literacy in the public schools is a good example of how emancipatory educators have recognized the need to develop and nurture the capacity for critical consciousness in students. An awareness of the social and political embeddedness of cultural attributes like language is crucial for recovering, maintaining, and bolstering self-respect and a sense of self-efficacy for minority students who do not possess the skills and knowledge required to "pass" (in *both* senses of this word) in the culture of power. Lisa Delpit and others have problematized the debate over reading and language instruction by illuminating the social and political consequences of conflicts that were previously understood as "professional" (i.e., technical) disagreements over alternative teaching methodologies or individual pedagogical preferences (e.g., the skills/process debate).

This analysis of the need for critical consciousness gets more complicated (and problematic), however, when we consider the role and consequences of cultural attributes that represent loyalty to a sense of shared identity developed in explicit opposition to the dominant culture. We can, in one sense, see the creation and persistence of oppositional cultural characteristics in minority communities as evidence of resistance to oppression, a form of resistance marked by the outward representation (enactment) of an identity that does not conform to the one presented (demanded) by the dominant class in society. Creating and maintaining this common identity, which we can say results, in part, from the exercise of critical consciousness, can have quite paradoxical results with respect to autonomy, however. By appealing to the work John Ogbu and Signithia Fordham, who offer a more complex sociohistorical understanding of the relation between community and identity, we can better understand how these circumstances illuminate the limitations of critical consciousness.

Ogbu (e.g., 1988) has written widely about the experience of African Americans in relation to their collective social identity as a "caste-like minority." This status is a result, according to Ogbu's analysis, of African Americans having first entered American society (in large numbers, anyway) through "forced incorporation" or as "involuntary immigrants." Ogbu argues that the cultural and historical legacy of slavery has led African Americans to develop an oppositional social identity, or a "Black folk system and cultural frame of reference," in order to survive in a society built upon such fundamental and institutionalized racist foundations. In the context of this oppositional frame of reference, the possession of qualities identified with the dominant culture (working hard and being successful in school, in this case) is understood as a betrayal of cultural membership and an acquiescence to the oppressor group, motivated (perhaps) by the false hope that through compliance one might win material advantage.

Signithia Fordham and John Ogbu (1986) have described how this dynamic plays out in schools as the "burden of acting white," and they have traced out its negative consequences for adolescent educational achievement among minority students. African American students who participated in Fordham and Ogbu's study reported a variety of conflicts between school norms and their own perceptions of peer identity. For some, this realization was relatively explicit, and they talked openly with researchers about the educational trade-offs they saw themselves making. Following the comments of one participant, Shelvy, Fordham and Ogbu (1986) write:

> Shelvy's analysis of the dilemma of the brainiac clearly suggests that the academically successful black student's life is fraught with conflicts and ambivalence. The fear of being differentiated and labeled as a brainiac often leads to social isolation and a social self which is hurt by negative perceptions. . . . Shelvy is more aware than many of her peers concerning why she is not performing as well academically as she could and perhaps should. As she explains it, she is keenly aware of her peers' concurrent "embracement and rejection" of school norms and behaviors. In that sense she realizes that seeking school success at Capital High is immersed in boundary-maintaining devices. (p. 191)

Students like Shelvy consciously try to negotiate the cultural conflict between school success and membership in their cultural peer group. They are, nonetheless, often compelled by these circumstances to make decisions that lead predictably to diminished levels of school achievement and impoverished adult opportunities. For other students, these decisions are less conscious and therefore, in some ways, even more dangerous. In this case, oppositional (and self-destructive) norms persist as unreflected-upon background assumptions, further constraining the capacity for autonomy and obscuring the trade-off students are forced to make between solidarity and success.

Looking at this situation through the lens of emancipatory educational theory, we might draw two very different conclusions. On the one hand, the development of an oppositional culture among minority youth (as well as members of the larger society) might be understood as a positive political and educational achievement, supported by efforts to build the capacity for critical consciousness. One might support this claim by arguing that the existence of an oppositional cultural frame demonstrates how African Americans "penetrate" (Willis, 1977) the meritocratic facade of public schooling and thus reject the false promise of exchanging classroom compliance for deferred social or economic rewards that, in fact, never come. The resistance of African American students to schools' complicity in their oppression is expressed through withdrawal and through the active subversion of "appropriate" school activities.

But we are faced with a troubling irony in defending this position. While the capacity for critical consciousness among African American youth may help them understand the institutionalized nature of racism in schools, it has not prevented these insights from being transformed into oppositional cultural norms that are immediately unproductive in terms of educational attainment and that, over the long run, help to reproduce some of the very differences on which the "acceptability" of racial stereotypes are based (e.g., disruptive behavior in class, the elevation of athletic success over academic success, diminished aspirations for higher education, etc.). While critical consciousness enables insights concerning the false meritocracy associated with schooling in our society, it does not seem to provide sufficient guidance for individual or collective action aimed at disrupting these stereotypes and their perpetuation in the culture of power. This situation leaves critical consciousness saddled with a troubling paradox regarding its capacity to support emancipatory growth under such circumstances.

In response to this observation about the limits of critical consciousness, we might argue that this conclusion is simply evidence that the capacity for critical consciousness needs to be developed *even further,* that additional insights are necessary to reveal and transform the counterproductive consequences of *current* forms of resistance. While I believe the capacity for critical consciousness indeed needs to be extended in this way, it will still likely be inadequate to capture fully the complex ways that oppositional cultures develop and the need for oppressed or marginalized groups to engage in a process of reflection and reconstruction *within* their communities. This need is better expressed, and more likely to be met, through efforts to build the capacity for authenticity.

Building the capacity for authenticity supports the efforts of oppressed or marginalized groups to assess the cultural norms that exist within their communities and the extent to which these norms support the growth and development of their individual members. Understanding that existing norms have grown out of (or in opposition to) circumstances that are disposed against the success or well-being of oppressed groups suggests that we must wait and see what emerges from this process as an account of the needs and interests of these groups. While critical consciousness does not provide answers for these questions, it opens the way or creates a space for the kind of self-reflection and dialogue that the capacity for authenticity is meant to describe.

Fordham and Ogbu (1986) point out the need for building the capacity for critical consciousness and authenticity *together* when they suggest that their analysis has implications at "different levels" of social and educational reform (p. 202). The first level they identify, consistent with the way I have characterized the insights of critical consciousness, acknowledges that "important change must occur in the existing opportunity structure" of American society "through an elimination of the job ceiling and related barriers" (p. 202). These social reforms follow from students' and others' awareness of the hollow promise that schools hold out for graduates who enter a world in which their skin color often means more than the grades on their transcript or the words on their diploma. These students understand the constraints of living in a racist society and the opposition it justifies within institutions like schools that are identified with the dominant class.

What is "particularly important," according to Fordham and Ogbu (1986, p. 203), however, is the role that African American communities themselves must play in reconstructing the meaning and values associated with education as a cultural practice that promotes positive growth and development. The primary purpose of this reconstruction is to create circumstances under which members of the African American community can find a legitimate sense of shared purpose in education, one that avoids the counterproductive opposition that has had such a negative impact on the achievement (and life chances) of African American adolescents. Fordham and Ogbu (1986) write:

> The black community has an important part to play in changing the situation. The community should develop programs to teach black children that academic pursuit is not synonymous with one-way acculturation into a white cultural frame of reference or acting white. To do this effectively, however, the black community must reexamine its own perceptions and interpretation of school learning. Apparently, black children's general perception that academic pursuit is "acting white" is learned in the black community. The ideology of the community in regard to the cultural meaning of schooling is, therefore, implicated and needs to be reexamined. (p. 203)

Indeed, there is a considerable amount of work being done among African American scholars and social activists that represents just such a commitment to the conscious reconstruction of community norms and leadership. These efforts have helped to create a new context for constructive dialogue and a renewed commitment to questions about how communities enable and sustain the growth of their members, especially in the face of a society that constantly threatens to turn this solidarity back against its source (for a consideration of related issues see West, 1993, especially pp. 9–20 and 33–46; for interesting collections on controversial issues within the African American community, see Morrison, 1992, on the Anita Hill–Clarence Thomas hearing, and Morrison & Brodsky-Lacour, 1997, on the O. J. Simpson trial).

It is crucial, in considering the recommendations made by Fordham,

Ogbu, and others who have pursued this line of argument, to resist absolutely any interpretation that "blames the victim" or suggests that African American communities are somehow culturally deficient or pathological. On the contrary, this work demonstrates that the oppositional culture of African American communities has been a source of enduring strength among people whose recent past includes surviving legally sanctioned slavery and who still confront its racist legacy throughout American society. Despite all efforts to resist and reconstruct these racist structures (and the degree to which we have actually pursued this goal is a topic open to vigorous debate), it remains the case that, for African American students, the rejection of norms associated with the dominant culture in this society is based on an accurate perception of the constraints on meaningful choice and diminished chances for social success that these students face.

The complementarity of universalist and particularist approaches. Having considered this example of the complementary relationship between critical consciousness and authenticity, it is now appropriate to ask what it can tell us about the broader relationship between universalist and particularist theories. Instead of criticizing or rejecting universalist theories as inadequate because of their (over)dependence on generalizable normative principles in assessing constraints on individual autonomy, the new constellation gives us a way of incorporating the local circumstances of choice and decision making into this analysis. Recall that authenticity, as a sense of originality or uniqueness, draws its power from the insights of particularist theories that focus our attention on the local context of individual action and decision making, and the specific historical processes that constitute a group's or community's identity. It reflects a concern for the circumstances in which questions about the growth and flourishing of individuals in a community are negotiated. These circumstances are essential for understanding what it means for a choice to be meaningful, and for understanding how the choices that individuals make contribute to their growth and development.

As I have suggested, liberal theorists have already begun to move away from interpretations of justice that are rooted in the belief that abstract and principled reasoning over the distribution of social resources is sufficient in itself to describe the foundation of a just society or to guide the creation of emancipatory schools. I discussed the work of Ken Howe as a liberal educational theorist who believes that concepts like justice and equality can evolve in a way that provides a more persuasive account of the relationship between principled normative reasoning and local context, or between the generalizability of moral claims (about equality of opportunity, for instance) and their relation to individual experience.

Howe and others adopt a more participatory view of what constitutes a meaningful choice and therefore the requirements of social institutions in democratic societies.

The development of this new interpretation of liberal theory turns on two claims that are closely tied to the role I have described for authenticity in the new constellation: first, that inquiring into the local context of choice is necessary for understanding the full implications of any educational practice that we describe or advocate as emancipatory; second, that we cannot take the local context of choice as given in trying to identify the needs and wants of particular communities, since what excluded or marginalized people need or want will only emerge from a process of reflection, dialogue, and negotiation. As Howe (1997) notes:

> Liberal-egalitarianism has historically been associated with a compensatory interpretation of equality of educational opportunity. Such an interpretation acknowledges the interactive nature of contexts of choice and seeks to remove disadvantages. But it is inadequate in many circumstances because it preempts debate about what is to be deemed educationally worthwhile by wrongly accepting as satisfactory the standards and practices associated with the status quo, in terms of which the marginalized and excluded should be compensated. In response, liberal-egalitarianism has moved toward participatory interpretations that seek to avoid the inadequacies of both compensatory and formal interpretations by including in the articulation of equal educational opportunity the need to question and negotiate what the educational standards and practices worth wanting should be. (p. 33)

Participants in this process of dialogue and negotiation need to be able to identify their own needs and interests, while seeing how these needs and interests are informed and conditioned by their relations with others in their communities. To move back and forth between this inward search for "originality" and the outward experience of recognition and mutual understanding that we receive from others is just what the capacity for authenticity supports. Emancipatory schools that are guided by this new interpretation of liberal theory should strongly support policies and practices that build the capacity for authenticity in their students.

Critical theorists have also acknowledged the need to attend more carefully to the multiplicity and social construction of categories that help to explain individual experience, especially the experience of oppression and exploitation in relation to a dominant group. This development is, in part, a response to postmodern critics who have accused critical theorists of ignoring the important differences that fracture traditional interpretations of social class into complex patterns of mutually reinforcing or contradictory social identities, based on the intersection of class with race, gender, sexual orientation, religion, able-bodiedness, and so on (e.g., Ellsworth, 1992). A more sympathetic, but no less motivating, version of this critique has come from socialist feminists, who have for some time pointed out the limitations of social class as sufficient for explanations of the oppression experienced by women (e.g., Jaggar, 1983, p. 379).

Critical theorists in education are wrestling with these issues and, as the sweeping dismissals issued by particularists have faded (somewhat, anyway), a more constructive dialogue has slowly emerged. Michael Apple (e.g., 1979), who has long supported the cultural dimension of neo-Marxist educational analysis, has suggested that critical theorists might deal with these issues by looking even more closely at the connection between theory and practice in emancipatory social movements. In language that would not offend many postmodernists, Apple suggests that critical theorists have a lot to learn from the conflicts and contradictions that emerge within these movements. Without admitting that the conceptual apparatus of critical theory is in any way ill-prepared to meet the challenge, he argues that critical theory should become more responsive to the ambivalences and contradictions embedded in our social experience and that emancipatory social practice should be understood in a way that acknowledges and takes into account the complexity of individual identity. Apple (1993) argues that:

> Critical work needs to be done in an "organic" way. It needs to be connected to and participate in those progressive social movements and groups that continue to challenge the multiple relations of exploitation and domination that exist. . . . I realize that this is a very complicated issue, both theoretically and politically, in itself. We should not assume that there aren't contradictions here. Some challenges to dominant relations may have contradictory effects. After all, an important and expanding literature has effectively argued against essentializing uses of such concepts as "progressive," class, race, gender, and so on, as if all people of color, or women, or working-class groups think alike. Not only are there tensions within and among these groups, but individuals themselves are internally contradictory. (p. 7)

Like many contemporary liberals, critical theorists have begun to change the way they look at the needs and interests of individuals, and the processes by which these are defined in the concrete (and often contradictory) circumstances of individual experience. This is just the kind of reflection and inquiry that building the capacity for authenticity supports as a part of emancipatory educational theory. Authenticity gives a kind of experiential authority to members of oppressed or marginalized communities to describe the nature of their experience and the normative prescriptions that might follow from it. Without giving up broad (structural) notions of what constitutes oppression or exploitation, and what these concepts entail for assessing emancipatory social institutions in different contexts, critical theorists can appeal to authenticity as a means of incorporating some of the most important insights of approaches that emphasize the particular.

From Particularist to Universalist Theories

My goal in this section, as it was in the last, is to show how we can begin on one side of the new constellation, this time with particularist approaches and the concept of authenticity, and find our way back across to universalist theories and the need for critical consciousness. As the preceding analysis suggests, the strength of particularist theories rests in their ability to engage the local circumstances in which social relations are negotiated and carried out. The focus on voice and discourse in postmodernism, and on attentiveness and engrossment in theories of care, emphasizes the rich and complex texture of individual experience, taking into account the nuances of language, the implicit and unexamined assumptions that regulate behavior, and the moral implications of our intimate relationships with others. The "fine-grained" nature of these accounts helps us understand the dilemmas people actually face in the choices they make and in the relationships they maintain (or don't) with others.

Particularist approaches are also limited in important ways, however, especially when it comes to providing an adequate account of the structural qualities associated with oppression and exploitation. Critics point to the resistance (sometimes antipathy) expressed by advocates of particularist approaches to principled and generalizable forms of moral reasoning, as a basis for arguing that these approaches may fail to prevent—indeed some worry they may even help to perpetuate—just the kinds of entrenched privilege and patterns of domination that make emancipatory schools necessary in the first place. This irony has a certain epistemological flavor in critiques of postmodernism, one that might be described in terms of the tension between hyperskepticism and demystification, while care theories face a similar set of normative challenges, based on the effort to distinguish between behavior and dispositions we ought to oppose, because they are implicated in women's traditional work/oppression, and those we ought to valorize, for the good they might do all of us.

Science, single-sex schooling, and patriarchy: An example. To see how elaborating the complementary relationship between authenticity and critical consciousness might help to address this pattern of strengths and weaknesses (i.e., preserving the strengths and finding ways to accommodate the weaknesses), it is helpful to again consider gender issues in schooling and, in particular, educational practices designed to meet the distinctive needs that girls and women bring to the classroom. I return to an issue raised earlier, namely, the disproportionate absence of girls and women in advanced science classes and thus their underrepresentation in jobs that utilize these forms of knowledge and skill. In my current treatment of this issue, I am especially interested in the recommendation that women should be taught science, at least during pivotal periods of their educational development, in sex-segregated classrooms or schools.

Justifications for sex-segregated schooling emphasize the effort to build the capacity for authenticity by creating a context that recognizes and values the distinctive qualities girls and women bring to their education, and by reducing the fear that they will encounter androcentric norms that exclude or invalidate their experience. In comparison to coeducational environments, sex-segregated schools or classrooms are thought to make possible an instructional milieu characterized by less competition, more collaboration, and work that has a clearer connection to the quality of life people experience in society. These characteristics have been associated with "women's ways of knowing" (Belenky, Clinchy, Goldberger, & Tarule, 1986) and together suggest the foundation for a school environment that would be more "female friendly." In summarizing the desired outcomes of single-sex education and their cumulative effect over time, Sadker and Sadker (1994) conclude: "Girls in single-sex schools have higher self-esteem, are more interested in nontraditional subjects such as science and math, and are less likely to stereotype jobs and careers" (p. 233).

But to describe the motivation for sex-segregated education in this way does not yet commit us to any particular view of what it means within these classrooms to become a scientist or what goals will be served by increasing the number of girls and women who learn science or enter science-related careers. I entertain three potential answers to these questions here, each of which suggests a crucial role for critical consciousness. In fact, without building the capacity of critical consciousness among girls and women, we set out on a course that may, at best, have little effect on women's experience in science or, at worst, actually increase the likelihood that women will continue to be excluded from and injured by androcentric scientific research. The following analysis owes much to work by Sandra Harding on feminism and science (1991, especially pp. 51–76).

One way of explaining the rationale behind encouraging girls and women in science is to say that such efforts aim at achieving sex-equity in relation to standard measures of school achievement (i.e., grades and test scores) and/or in relation to the pattern of careers that women select. On this account, sex-segregated schooling aims at equally educating women and men with the same scientific knowledge, skills, and degree of preparation for future careers, albeit through different instructional means. This rationale for altering the conditions under which girls and women learn (the same) science is "minimally" compensatory, because it suggests that there are no significant differences in the skills, knowledge, or future responsibilities we expect women to obtain relative to what men (and some women) now possess.

But as much progress as this conception of sex-equity in science education might entail, especially for women who have been denied the most basic opportunities for an adequate education in science, it is nonetheless based on the problematic assumption that the practice of science is itself gender-neutral. This is problematic for reasons similar to the ones that led us to consider sex-segregated instruction in the first place, namely, that social relations in a patriarchal society are frequently organized around and regulated by norms that marginalize girls and women. This same reasoning makes suspect any approach to learning science that ignores the larger social context in which girls and women have experienced or been subjected to the norms and social practice of science as a hostile or constraining force. As Sandra Harding (1991) points out, this "conventional perspective" on the gender neutrality of science is hard to defend today, given what feminist critiques have shown us about the various ways that scientific research has been constructed around (i.e., distorted by) the needs and interests of men.

> Feminist researchers in biology and the social sciences have shown in convincing detail the sexist and androcentric results of research that does not carefully enough follow well-understood principles of method and theory. Basing generalizations about humans only on data about men violates obvious rules of method and theory. Failing to question why women's responses to moral dilemmas do not comfortably fit categories designed to receive men's responses should long since have been regarded as unreasonable. Research designs that legitimate having only men interview only men about either men's or women's beliefs and behaviors are bound to distort reality. Assumptions that women's reproductive systems normally function in immature or pathological ways lack grounding in principles of biology, not to mention in common sense. (p. 57)

To say that sex-segregated schooling should be directed primarily at obtaining better access to existing roles and practices ignores the substance of these critiques and what they imply for emancipatory educational practice. Learning science in a way that fails to address explicitly its misuse or abuse in society will fall considerably short in the degree to which it helps build the capacity for critical consciousness in students. Under these circumstances, sex-segregated schooling would continue to mystify the connection between gender and science in society, and would keep girls and women in the dark about the extent to which their own participation in science might contribute to the persistence of patriarchy.

The inadequacies of the conventional view lead us to a second perspective on the goals of improving science education for girls and women. This one aims at improving current forms of scientific inquiry by identifying and critiquing research that is plagued by the kinds of sexist norms, gender-biased assumptions, and exclusionary forms of inquiry described above. Harding (1991) calls advocates of this view "critics of bad science" (p. 53). According to the view held by critics of bad science, girls and women in science classrooms must be equipped first and foremost with a firm knowledge of sound methodological principles and a keen eye for biased or tendentious research. In order to be good critics of bad science, students also must learn about the specific ways that scientific inquiry has ignored or distorted the experience of women and other marginalized groups. (Particularly clear and compelling examples of this kind of analysis are available in the growing literature about the androcentric norms, explanations, and procedures associated with women's bodies in medicine, e.g., Martin, 1987.)

The view advocated by critics of bad science suggests a clear and important role for critical consciousness in the classroom. Building the capacity for critical consciousness is important because it helps girls and women identify instances in which their experience has been excluded or distorted in scientific research; indeed, it helps them see how such research has been used "against" girls and women, to control and regulate them (and their bodies). Teachers of would-be critics of bad science would make special efforts to encourage their students to be aware of, and concerned about, the misuse of science in society. They might do this by using examples that foreground the damaging consequences of gender-biased research and by giving students the opportunity to pursue projects that serve women's interests (just *including* women's interests would be a positive change in many fields). We need to keep in mind, however, that this critique adheres to existing methodological principles in its response to bad science and thus requires little in the way of fundamental revisions in current conceptions of (sound) scientific practice.

A third perspective on the rationale and potential benefits of reforming science education for girls and women takes a radical step beyond the critics of bad science; it holds the transformation of science itself as the most important goal for women entering the field. Advocates of this view believe that increasing the number and success of women in science fields will help disrupt the commonly assumed value neutrality of scientific knowledge and demonstrate that science is itself a social practice that reflects the needs and interests of particular groups in society (and, conversely, marginalizes and exploits others). These "critics of science-as-usual" (Harding, 1991, p. 58) reject the separation of science from social context and argue that scientific inquiry is irredeemably part of a world in which issues of power and status are played out according to rules that are often obscured by the facade of "objective" or "disinterested" scientific methodologies.

On this view, building the capacity for critical consciousness is necessary not only to tell good science from bad, but indeed to understand what "doing science" means at all. Freed by the recognition that scientific research is unavoidably entangled with issues of human need and interest, critics of science-as-usual argue that more female scientists will help us push beyond the work done by critics of bad science and begin the process of reconstructing scientific practice around explicit social values. According to this view:

> The problem is not that there are sexist and androcentric "misuses and abuses" of scientific technologies such that they could be ended and leave pure, gender-impartial sciences and technologies. Instead, it is inevitable that women will be victimized by the sciences and their technologies in a society such as ours where women have little power, where almost all scientific research is technology-driven, and where political issues are posed as requiring merely technological "solutions". . . . Because the social processes that eventuate in everyday life in the laboratories begin far away from the laboratories—in a sluggish economy, in the desire to win a war in Asia, in attempts to control African Americans in cities, in desires to limit population growth in Asia—firsthand expertise in the laboratories won't go far toward providing an explanation of laboratory life. (Harding, 1991, p. 73)

In order to understand what scientific practice is and should be, we must consider the broader social context within which scientific inquiry is conducted and its products are put to use. Critical consciousness provides an essential foundation for this effort to reconstruct scientific principles around socially explicit (e.g., emancipatory) values and commitments.

Let's return here to the proposal for sex-segregated schooling, based on appeals to authenticity, and consider the implications of the preceding analysis for my claim that critical consciousness is necessary to guide efforts to improve the achievement of girls and women in science. My analysis of the various rationales described above suggests that it would be futile, and on some accounts potentially even counterproductive, to involve girls and women in sex-segregated science instruction without creating circumstances in which they also can develop the capacity for critical consciousness. As Harding's critics of science-as-usual suggest, unless we can somehow disrupt the conventional practice and perhaps even the accepted methodologies of scientific inquiry, our efforts to increase the number and influence of women in science will contribute little to their emancipation generally and may even contribute to the reproduction of existing social hierarchies. Harding (1991) concludes:

> From this perspective, at best it makes no difference at all to women's situation in general if women are added to the social structure of a science that appears to be so thoroughly integrated with the misogynist, racist, and bourgeois aspects of the larger society. More likely it is a bad thing, since it diverts women's attention and energies from struggles against the *sources* of male domination and adds their energies to science's misogynist, racist, and bourgeois tendencies (whether or not these are intended by individual scientists). (p. 67, emphasis in original)

Even so, because the social practice of science is unlikely to change anytime soon, we will probably have to settle for aiming at educating more and better critics of bad science. The role of critical consciousness is still central in this perspective, as I have argued, as a way of framing the experience of learning science against the background of a broader society in which science is often used to marginalize and exploit women.

My use of this extended example illustrates how building the capacity for authenticity in schools is not, by itself, sufficient for emancipatory educational practice, even when these efforts are carefully directed at taking into account the needs and interests of a particular group. The possession of critical consciousness fosters an awareness of the broader social context and its role in shaping the meaning and consequences of our actions. In the end, critical consciousness goes hand in hand with authenticity to help define emancipatory educational goals and identify instructional practices that help teachers achieve them.

As in the preceding section, I conclude here by looking briefly back at the new constellation as a framework within which particularist and universalist approaches can be seen as more complementary than competitive, based on the interdependence of authenticity and critical consciousness. As I warned earlier, the potential rapprochement from the particularist side is nascent, and to some extent still mired in strident critiques and dismissive rhetoric. Nonetheless, there are some encouraging signs that scholars working in the particularist tradition are beginning to moderate their disavowal of universalist norms associated with concepts like equality and justice, and they have also offered views that are more compatible with the structural interpretations of power and difference we need to resist oppression. This work supports the development of the new constellation and is, in turn, supported by it.

The complementarity of particularist and universalist approaches. In *Postmodern Education* (1991), for example, Stanley Aronowitz and Henry Giroux offer a defense of postmodern educational theory that acknowledges some of its limitations and suggests appropriate accommodations to the modernist tradition. They promote a view of postmodernism that does not reject the usefulness of moral claims about justice and democracy, for instance, based on a position that sounds at least somewhat similar to the participatory view I discussed in relation to the work of Kymlicka and Howe. Aronowitz and Giroux (1991) urge advocates of postmodernism to take advantage of "the democratic claims of modernism" as well as concepts like "social justice and human freedom" (p. 81) to further articulate emancipatory educational practice.

While I found fault with postmodernists earlier for appropriating language that I did not believe their theoretical framework could sustain, Aronowitz and Giroux see their new approach to postmodern analysis as integrating "difference, power, and specificity" with "radical democracy," as a more powerful way of accounting for the nature of public life. They conclude:

> In the end, postmodernism is too suspicious of the modernist notion of public life, and of the struggle for equality and liberty that has been an essential aspect of liberal democratic discourse. If postmodernism is going to make a valuable contribution to the notion of schooling as a form of cultural politics, educators must combine its most important theoretical insights with those strategic modernist elements that contribute to a politics of radical democracy. In this way, the project of radical democracy can be deepened by expanding its sphere of applicability to increasingly wider social relations and practices; encompassing individuals and groups who have been excluded by virtue of their class, gender, race, age, or ethnic origin. . . . When linked with the modernist language of public life, the notions of difference, power, and specificity can be understood as part of a public philosophy that broadens and deepens individual liberties and rights *through rather than against* a radical notion of democracy. (Aronowitz & Giroux, 1991, p. 81, emphasis in original)

What Aronowitz and Giroux propose are just the kind of common bonds that critical consciousness and authenticity might be used to explore. The new constellation provides a foundation for locating postmodern analyses of subjectivity within a broader normative account of social context; this is a crucial step forward in developing the mutually reinforcing insights of particularist and universalist approaches.

Care theorists like Nel Noddings have also enlarged the boundaries of particularist perspectives by giving more attention to issues of social context. As we saw in Chapter 4, Noddings' use of care as a guide for schooling expanded the range of things that might count as "objects" of caring. Her "centers of care" support and extend the idea that caring is exercised in a variety of ways, and in a variety of "domains," not all of which can be described in terms of relationships between individuals. These developments in Noddings' (1992) educational theory help situate it in a social context where differences in group identity (which are easily related, as we have seen, to differences in power and status) make a difference in the practice and expression of caring.

> Care, as we have seen, can be developed in a variety of domains and take many objects. We want to consider care for self, care for intimate others, care for associates and distant others, for nonhuman life, for the human-made environment of objects and instruments, and for ideas. As we consider how education might be organized around domains or centers of caring, we have to recognize that people take different perspectives on each of these domains not only because of individual interests, but also because they belong to different races, nations, sexes, classes, and religions. All of these group associations affect our interpretations of what it means to care in each domain and which domains should have top priority. Therefore we must add a set of "basic affiliations" to our analytic framework. (p. 47)

Creating and sustaining these "basic affiliations" in diverse communities requires an education that builds the capacity for authenticity and critical consciousness. Authenticity supports the need for recognition and reciprocity among community members as a foundation for caring relationships. Critical consciousness is required to understand these relations in connection to the broader structures of society, as a way of protecting and enlarging the potential for individuals to pursue their life-plans.

In the analysis of the previous two sections, I have tried to draw a firm (if not always straight) line between critical consciousness and authenticity, the two brightest stars in the new constellation. To summarize and conclude this analysis, I rephrase a common philosophical dictum: Critical consciousness without authenticity is empty, frustrating, and cynical. Authenticity without critical consciousness is blind, potentially self-defeating, and vulnerable to manipulation.

THEORY BUILDING IN THE NEW CONSTELLATION

In this section, I give two examples of how work might proceed within the new constellation by exploring its implications for concepts that are central to the development of emancipatory educational theory. My purposes in looking at social structure and community here include modeling the kind of theoretical work that might be done in the new constellation and providing further support for the complementary relationship emerging between universalist and particularist theories. Critical consciousness and authenticity again figure prominently as capacities that allow us to put these insights into practice in emancipatory schools. Of course, much more can (and needs to) be said about each of these topics; the analysis presented here is only a start.

Social Structure(s)

All emancipatory educational theories are concerned with the way schooling affects individuals' conceptions of self and their understanding of the choices and possibilities available to them in society (i.e., their potential life-plans). I have indicated my general support for structuralist interpretations of social hierarchy that place special emphasis on the systematic way that particular aspects of identity (associated with gender, social class, race, etc.) become the foundation for oppression and exploitation in society. In order to further elaborate connections in the new constellation, it would be helpful to say more about the nature of these social structures, as constraints on autonomy, and how emancipatory schooling might disrupt and help to reconstruct them.

The new constellation supports an understanding of social structures that treats them as a fundamental feature of everyday life and the background against which choices and decisions take on their shared meaning. This is a relatively common starting point, however, and many perspectives on the nature of social structures are consistent with this view. It is much too big a job to survey the various alternatives here and, fortunately, such a task is unnecessary for the purpose of identifying some preliminary insights that might help guide emancipatory schooling. Contemporary sociologists, for example, have offered a number of insights about the nature and general features of social structures that are well suited to development within the new constellation and promising in their application to educational practice. Interestingly, some of this work has been directed at trying to resolve the so-called structure/agency dilemma, a problem that shares some important similarities with my effort to reconstruct the relationship between universalist and particularist theories.

An understanding of social structure that is consistent with the goal of promoting autonomy through emancipatory schooling could not treat these structures as static or deterministic in relation to the lives and choices of individuals in society; this would make the question of autonomy moot. Nor does it make much sense to treat social structures as merely ideas that individuals hold in their heads about social identity or about the roles that individuals take in society. Instead, we might find it more profitable to begin with the idea that, as sociologists like Derek Layder (1990), Anthony Giddens (1979), and Jeffrey Alexander (1988) have argued, social structures are both the product of, and a constraint on, the ongoing activities of individual members of society.

This account begins with a recognition of the constructed or context-dependent nature of human actions, without abandoning the idea that there are limits and constraints on what individuals can think or do, such that their actions are meaningful or intelligible to others. This approach bridges traditional distinctions between agents and social structures in a way that parallels my reconstruction of the relation between universalist and particularist educational theories; it recognizes the power of social structures without diminishing or disregarding the significance of individuals' actions at the local level of community or in the relationships they have with others.

Three propositions about the nature of social structures are particularly relevant for the new constellation. First, social structures are both enabling and constraining in their effects on individual action. On this account, social structures constitute part of the very foundation for meaningful behavior by providing the resources on which individuals draw to make their thoughts and actions intelligible to others. Social structures are *enabling* insofar as they present various clusters of beliefs, attitudes, and values that make up the building blocks of self-expression and identity. These same structures are *constraining* insofar as they constitute boundaries beyond which it is difficult or impossible for individuals to act or express themselves in ways that are coherent, intelligible, or acceptable to others (Layder, 1990). As my educational examples in Chapter 6 demonstrate, some of the most powerful constraints on identity and action are those that frame the meaning of our plans and projects in relation to the beliefs and assumptions of others.

Second, while social structures are not constituted by the particular behavior of any individual or group (dominant or oppressed), they are nonetheless the product of the conjoined activities (intentional and unintentional) of many individual actors and groups over time. This is a complex claim about the ontology of social structures that requires a fuller account than I can provide here. The heart of this proposition, however, is that social structures are created or constructed from the patterns of behavior and shared practices that evolve over time within any group or society. On this view, there exists, at any given time and place, a variety of social structures that constitute the values, meanings, forms of identity, and patterns of interaction for that society. These structures are "real" in the sense that they exist outside the beliefs, desires, and actions of any particular individual. They are constantly "created" in the sense that they result from the collective beliefs, desires, and actions of all members of society, coalescing into various forms and arrangements over time.

Social structures are, in this sense, "relatively independent" of the intentions and behavior of socially situated actors and therefore have an ontological status that depends on mutual or collective construction. Thus, while the nature of social structures can be understood in general or theoretical terms, their actual content will always be profoundly historical and contingent upon a great many empirical features of society. We can treat John Ogbu's (1988) account of the "Black folk system and cultural frame of reference" (p. 174) as an explanation of how the meaning of African American experience in this country has been constructed within the social structures that mediate race and racial identity. In a similar way, we might find it helpful to see caregiving as an explanation of the meaning of women's experience (in the family, school, and a variety of vocations) that has been constructed over time within the social structures that mediate gender and gender identity.

Finally, and partly as a result of the two previous claims, social structures are a source of emancipation as well as oppression. By thinking about social structures in a constructivist, historically contingent manner, emancipatory theorists grasp a powerful tool for assessing the choices available to socially situated individuals, as a function of the enabling and constraining effects of social structures on autonomy. This conception of social structure helps us understand the collective nature of constraints on identity and points us in the direction of leverage points that we can use to change society (i.e., reconstruct the social structures on which it is based). Lynne Arnault, a feminist moral philosopher, argues similarly that the importance of autonomy can be expressed in terms of the degree to which members of social groups exercise control over the resources necessary for self-definition. She writes, "Having moral autonomy . . . is being a member of a group that has sufficient collective control over the socio-cultural forms of discourse that one is able to express one's point of view in a nondistorted, nonrepressed way without having it marginalized or discounted" (Arnault, 1989, p. 202).

Throughout this analysis, I have used examples that demonstrate how race, gender, and social class operate as structures that enable and constrain the autonomy of individuals. Social structures have a constraining effect on autonomy when they construct meanings that distort experience to serve the interests of a dominant class or group. The oppositional culture of African American adolescents, for example, which is based in part on an accurate perception of the barriers they face in employment and elsewhere in the adult world, is only too readily constructed in a racist society as evidence of academic incompetence, disrespect for social convention, and genetic inferiority. The constraints of gender as a social structure can likewise be understood in relation to caregiving as a normalized limit on (and way of exploiting) the roles, abilities, and life-plans available to women.

The masking or mystification of these oppressive social structures is extremely difficult to dislodge, in part because of the extent to which they are embedded in our day-to-day experience and the unreflective assumptions that guide our actions. An awareness of these structures, based on the capacity for critical consciousness, encourages individuals to define themselves and their projects in ways that support autonomy, and expand the range of opportunities and life-plans available to them. Critical consciousness helps African American students see how the false educational meritocracy in which they participate mystifies pressures for cultural assimilation at the same time that it reproduces social inequality. Similarly, feminists have utilized critical consciousness to expose the androcentric norms that have oppressed women and exploited their work as caregivers. Promoting critical consciousness is essential for self-understanding as well as for the reconstruction of social institutions and norms of interaction that expand rather than constrain autonomy.

Authenticity also plays an important role in this account of how social structures work. Given the historical contingency of social structures, and the sense in which they are always "under construction," understanding autonomy as authenticity focuses our attention on the "local" effects of relationships that can reinforce and reproduce existing structures, or resist and reconstruct them. One of the ways we can disrupt the power and adverse consequences of oppressive social structures is through reciprocal relationships that promote the recognition of all members of our communities, establishing a foundation for a dialogue that amplifies rather than restricts the possibilities of pursuing new plans and projects (together). Building the capacity for authenticity requires that we pay particular attention to how institutions like schools can create conditions that support constructive dialogue over the meanings (associated with self and other) that are mediated by oppressive social structures. If emancipatory schools can accomplish these things, they will help students build the kind of constructive relationships that can transform oppressive social structures by disrupting and resisting the circumstances that once created and now sustain them.

Community

Throughout this analysis, I have used the concept of community, sometimes quite loosely, to describe the local circumstances in which relations between individuals are negotiated and carried out. I have also used community to describe the kind of context that might be provided in schools to develop and sustain collaborative relationships among all participants (students, teachers, parents, etc.). Notwithstanding its multiple meanings, embedded assumptions, and contentiousness among philosophers of various sorts (e.g., in political philosophy, see Young, 1990, and in educational philosophy, see Stone, 1993), community is an important concept to elaborate in the new constellation. In part, this is because community plays an important role in all of the emancipatory theories considered here; it is fundamental to the way individuals interact in a healthy and productive school environment, regardless of the approach used to describe its other features. Even more to the point for this analysis, however, is that community plays an essential role in the pedagogical strategies I present in Chapter 6, as examples of what might be included in an education for autonomy.

Although offering a full account (or even defense) of community lies beyond the scope of this work, it still makes sense to describe the importance of community in the new constellation and confront some of the strongest objections that have been offered to it as a basis for emancipatory educational practice. I summarize two critiques of community below and show that, while the general thrust of each critique represents a reasonable concern about the adverse consequences of communities built around exclusive or oppressive social relations, critical consciousness and authenticity go a fair distance in resolving these worries. As in the preceding analysis of social structure, this consideration of community takes us across the boundaries that separate universalist and particularist approaches, based on the fuller conception of autonomy as critical consciousness and authenticity.

The first argument against the emancipatory potential of community that I want to consider here is similar in form to one of the concerns I raised about caring in Chapter 4. There I worried that valorizing attributes associated with caregiving in specific communities like schools might inadvertently legitimize and reproduce relationships that were oppressive and exploitative for women in the larger society. Recall that this ambivalence has been expressed by feminist critics of caring for some time, as a concern about the trustworthiness of normative conclusions derived from the roles of women in patriarchal societies. Critics of care theories have argued that we must, at the very least, critically assess existing forms of activity associated with women's roles in order to determine whether they actually constitute a more viable foundation for moral communities, or whether they belie this promise and instead further reinforce the oppressive relations that currently exist between women and men.

Marilyn Friedman's (1989) analysis of community in feminist thought is a good starting point for looking at the role autonomy might play in providing an answer to this concern. In her essay, "Feminism and Modern Friendship: Dislocating the Community," Friedman draws a distinction between "found" communities and those we choose in a "critically reflexive" manner. This contrast is useful because it distinguishes between communities built around the common and unreflective norms of society (that we know are frequently oppressive) and communities created in a more self-conscious manner by their members. Friedman (1989) encourages the right kind of skepticism about found communities, while leaving open the possibility that individuals might find the "resources and skills" necessary to create alternative identities and life-plans somewhere else.

> The commitments and loyalties of our found communities, our communities of origin, may harbor ambiguities, ambivalences, contradictions, and oppressions which complicate as well as constitute identity and which have to be sorted out, critically scrutinized. And since the resources for such scrutiny may not be found in all "found" communities, our theories of community should recognize that resources and skills derived from communities which are not merely found or discovered may equally well contribute to the constitution of identity. (p. 285)

According to Friedman (1989), "Communities and relationships of 'choice' . . . point toward a notion of community more congenial to feminist aspirations" (p. 285). This approach is more congenial, in part, because women need to find sources of self-definition that are not oppressive or limiting. Members of voluntary communities may draw on the resources of their found communities, but these resources are used in new ways, to promote the conscious reconstruction of identity. Friedman (1989) concludes:

> Perhaps it is more illuminating to say that communities of choice foster not so much the constitution of subjects but their reconstitution. They may be sought out as contexts in which people relocate the various constituents of their identities.... The modern self may seek new communities whose norms and relationships stimulate and develop her identity and self-understanding more adequately than her unchosen community of origin, her original community of place. (p. 289)

We can use this same kind of distinction to explain the difference between communities (and the norms associated with them) that diminish the capacity for autonomy among particular groups, and those that might be (re)constructed, based on the qualities of critical consciousness and authenticity. We need these two aspects of autonomy, and an account of how they are related, to understand how actions undertaken in voluntary communities are related to the larger social context in which these actions may either reinforce or resist oppressive social relations. To pursue this line of argument, we must appeal to the account of social structures developed in the previous section.

I argued above that social structures enable and constrain the efforts of individuals to define themselves in relation to their own plans and projects. In pursuing these plans and projects, and thus a sense of self-identity, individuals draw selectively on the symbolic and other resources made available to them in society. Such efforts are individual insofar as they involve a personal choice among existing alternatives. They are also necessarily collective, however, in the sense not only that one's choices affect and are affected by others, but that all of these choices, over time, can serve either to reinforce existing patterns of social relation or to contest and reconstitute them. Given this, we can characterize the praiseworthy community (including the praiseworthy school community) in terms of the extent to which relations within it tend to increase the capacity of members to choose and pursue a variety of potential life-plans as members of the larger society.

This emphasis on the reciprocal relation between community and society turns on the capacity individuals possess for authenticity and critical consciousness. Good communities are places where individuals can explore their "original" life-plans (i.e., life-plans that originate in the undistorted needs and interests of the individual), and where such efforts receive the recognition and support of others. These aspects of authenticity are essential features of emancipatory communities and they "attach" to these communities at the local level of individual relationships. Critical consciousness helps members of communities determine the potential of their actions at this local context to reinforce or reproduce social structures that limit rather than expand the opportunities individuals possess in society (to construct a variety of identities or pursue a variety of life-plans). To exercise critical consciousness in this respect is to explore the relationship that exists between the norms of a community and the social structures that influence the distribution of power and status in society. Taken together, critical consciousness and authenticity can guide our efforts to (re)construct community relationships in the new constellation, based on the idea that the communities we need are both rich in the resources they offer to individuals for the pursuit of their plans and projects, and socially progressive or emancipatory in relation to the larger society.

A second objection to treating community as fundamental to emancipatory social movements holds that affirming qualities such as recognition and reciprocity may actually encourage groups to adopt exclusionary attitudes or practices toward others, instead of nurturing the diverse identities and relationships on which emancipatory communities ought to be based. Iris Marion Young, for instance, rejects a *strong* version of the "ideal of community" because of its propensity to define membership, at least in part, negatively; that is, the parameters of community define who *lacks* the necessary (and valued) qualities as powerfully as they identify those who possess them. While I do not defend the strong ideal of community Young (1990) has in mind (in fact, my own view is closer to Young's than first examination suggests), her critique is still relevant to the position described here.

> For most people, insofar as they consider themselves members of communities at all, a community is a group that shares a specific heritage, a common self-identification, a common culture and set of norms . . . self-identification as a member of such a community also often occurs as an oppositional differentiation from other groups, who are feared, despised, or at best devalued. Persons feel a sense of mutual identification only with some persons, feel in community only with those, and fear the difference others confront them with because they identify with a different culture, history, and point of view on the world. The ideal of community, I suggest, validates and reinforces the fear and aversion some social groups exhibit toward others. If community is a positive norm, that is, if existing together with others in relations of mutual understanding and reciprocity is the goal, then it is understandable that we exclude and avoid those with whom we do not or cannot identify. (pp. 234–235)

In fact, Nel Noddings (1992), who is a strong proponent of communities based on qualities like recognition and reciprocity, worries about the same thing.

The problem is that communities often act like bloated individuals. Just as an individual may have a personal rival or enemy, so may a community or group. But now the situation is more dangerous because we feel safer acting as a group. So long as we are in a positive relation with *some* people, we need not be so concerned about our relations with others. To make matters worse, our relations with an in-group sometimes require us to treat others badly, and we are rewarded for doing things to outsiders that would bring recrimination and punishment if done inside the group. (p. 118, emphasis in original)

Both Noddings and Young offer responses to these critiques of community, although, as one might expect, they differ significantly. As we saw in Chapter 4, Noddings (1992) recommends that people (especially students) be encouraged to reflect more deeply and personally on the choices and circumstances of others, thereby increasing their sensitivity to members of more "distant" communities (p. 110). Young (1990), on the other hand, rejects "the ideal of community" more decisively, in favor of "city life as a normative ideal" (p. 236).

While I quite agree that intolerance between communities undermines the goals of emancipatory education (and politics), the power of this indictment depends on recognition and reciprocity being the only (or primary) qualities that constitute community. Given the kind of community that critical consciousness and authenticity support, we are not forced to choose between comfortable, but exclusionary, communities and "the being together of strangers" (Young, 1990, p. 237). A balanced or integrated view of critical consciousness and authenticity provides a foundation for understanding communities that is quite different. Such communities would likely be fluid, overlapping, and difficult to define precisely, as many urban communities are today, and as Young argues they ought to be. But members could nonetheless make deliberate efforts to create a sense of mutual respect and regard through qualities like recognition and reciprocity, without becoming oppressive or intolerant. To demonstrate how this might be so requires another version of the argument I have offered for the complementary relationship of critical consciousness and authenticity.

Critical consciousness provides individuals with a way to see past the mystifying barriers that are constructed within *and between* communities, and it establishes a context within which the qualities associated with authenticity can be a basis for seeking diversity rather than fleeing from it. As I have argued, these barriers often result from an array of disguised or mystified social hierarchies, which persist in part because of their capacity to turn marginalized groups against one another. Such scapegoating is crucial to the dominance of social, political, and economic elites. Examples of how autonomy is constrained and deformed in this way, by racist, sexist, heterosexist, and classist social structures of meaning, are easy to locate in contemporary discourse: Violent, drug-addicted, Black, inner-city youth make metropolitan areas into war zones; lazy, scheming, welfare-mothers drain federal coffers of funds reserved for the "legitimately needy"; radical, man-hating, lesbian feminists make it impossible for "normal" women to stay home and raise healthy children. As I suggested above, these stereotypes and distortions are especially damaging when they are exchanged by groups who do not realize they share a marginalized social position and a sense of alienation born of diminished expectations of social success. (Indeed, I believe this helps explain much of the popular support for neo-conservative educational policies, as Michael Apple suggests in the work I quote in Chapter 3.)

What critical consciousness promotes in a society plagued by these forms of intolerance is not more walls, within which narrow and exclusionary views of self-identity and group identity are pursued, but rather more openness and increased access to the building blocks of self-identity and self-expression. Because membership in communities is multiple, crosscutting, and often unstable, critical consciousness can expand the capacity of individuals to find authenticity beyond the boundaries of their current affiliations. The authenticity achieved through dialogue among diverse communities thus is enabled by critical consciousness, especially (again) where these connections are made between oppressed or marginalized groups.

Treating autonomy as an important educational goal requires that the capacity for self-understanding and self-expression be shared among all groups in society, and doing so promotes understanding between, as well as within, these groups. Communities that support critical consciousness and authenticity will create strong, supportive relationships among individuals who seek diversity as a valuable resource. Thus, communities based on these emancipatory values will be better equipped to resist intolerance within and outside of their boundaries.

This chapter has offered a preliminary map of the new constellation, one that I hope describes (and blurs) some important boundaries, and one that reveals something about the kind of collaborative work that might grow within this emerging landscape. As I have maintained from the start, this analysis is intended to be explicitly formative, laying the groundwork for future dialogue among emancipatory theorists that will extend, elaborate, and refine the kinds of solutions offered to the pressing problems that exist in schools. My interest in the next chapter is to confront these problems more directly and explore some specific instructional elements that are part of an education for autonomy.

6

Emancipatory Educational Practice
in the New Constellation

My analysis of the connection between critical consciousness and authenticity has important implications for schooling. Finding a common basis on which to proceed with the development of emancipatory educational approaches gives us a better chance of overcoming differences that have inspired more polemic than productive dialogue in the past, refocusing our attention on changes that will make a real difference in schools. The final step in elaborating this new framework brings us to issues associated with application and implementation. In this chapter, I revisit the need for emancipatory schools by looking at some of the ways that students' autonomy is limited or constrained by the circumstances they face in school. I then look at three examples of emancipatory pedagogy that could move schools toward a conception of teaching and learning that supports the development of autonomy in students. In both cases, I demonstrate how the neo-conservative agenda fails to address these constraints; indeed, it often exacerbates their negative consequences.

REVISITING THE NEED FOR EMANCIPATORY SCHOOLS

We have traveled a considerable distance from my initial characterization of the neo-conservative agenda in Chapter 2. Throughout this journey, the need to explain and justify emancipatory schools in relation to the view promoted (quite successfully) by neo-conservatives has remained a central motivation. I have argued that emancipatory theories of education give us a persuasive vision of what schools should be about, and good reasons for opposing the neo-conservative educational agenda. These theories focus our attention on the social context in which students grow and develop through the decisions they make and the life-plans they pursue. Based on their commitment to autonomy, emancipatory schools help students understand how choice is influenced by structures of power and privilege, and how relations among individuals (in school and elsewhere) are influenced by this larger social context. Emancipatory schools give students the tools they need to understand society by exploring its norms, assumptions, and stereotypes. These tools are critical and self-reflexive; they help students understand themselves and the way their conceptions of self are embedded in a particular set of social relations.

As a way of elaborating the connection between schooling and autonomy, I have found Sandra Lee Bartky's (1990) analysis of women's oppression very helpful. Bartky begins her essay, "On Psychological Oppression," by drawing an analogy between women's experience in patriarchal societies and Frantz Fanon's "anguished and eloquent description of the psychological effects of colonialism on the colonized" (Bartky, 1990, p. 22). The point of her comparison is to show how oppressed people can be blocked from drawing on the cultural resources necessary to explore alternative conceptions of self and self-identity. This results when dominant groups appropriate the means of self-definition and create social hierarchies that exclude and diminish others.

> The creation of culture is a distinctly human function, perhaps the most human function. In its cultural life, a group is able to affirm its values and to grasp its identity in acts of self-reflection. Frequently, oppressed persons, cut off from the cultural apparatus, are denied the exercise of this function entirely. To the extent that we are able to catch sight of ourselves in the dominant culture at all, the images we see are distorted or demeaning. (Bartky, 1990, p. 30)

This account of the psychological effects of oppression demonstrates how a structural relation of inequality between two groups in society can affect the individual members of each, in terms of how they think about themselves and how they think about others. While many of the *effects* of this relation can be thought of psychologically or individually, their *causes* are social or structural, and this helps explain why the consequences of oppressive social structures (like the reasons to promote autonomy) are necessarily shared. Bartky (1990) recognizes that this position is consistent with the view defended by Marxists; she draws an explicit parallel between the effects of psychological oppression and the kinds of alienation from self that I discussed in Chapter 3.

> In many ways, psychic alienation and the alienation of labor are profoundly alike. Both involve a splitting off of human functions from the human person, a forbidding of activities thought to be essential to a fully human existence. Both subject the individual to fragmentation and impoverishment. Alienation is not a condition into which someone might stumble by accident; it has come both to the victim of psychological oppression and to the alienated worker from without, as a usurpation by someone else of what is, by

rights, *not his to usurp.* Alienation occurs in each case when activities which not only belong to the domain of the self but define, in large measure, the proper functioning of this self, fall under the control of others. To be a victim of alienation is to have a part of one's being stolen by another. (p. 32, emphasis in original)

The importance of this characterization for schools lies in understanding how the plans and projects of individuals are affected by social structures that promote constrained and distorted views of identity and thus limited conceptions of self. Bartky's analysis shows us what to look for in social relations that constrain the capacity of students to exercise autonomy in the decisions they make about themselves and their futures. Schools are clearly examples of institutions where judgments about self-worth and identity are routinely made (implicitly and explicitly), by teachers and peers. While schools often are thought to be involved in cultivating individual talents, it is clear that large groups of students are not nurtured or encouraged in this way.

To understand how autonomy can be limited or constrained in an educational context, consider the following narrative from a collection of life histories published by undergraduates at the University of Michigan. *Inside Separate Worlds* (Schoem, 1991) includes the autobiographical narrative of John B. Diamond, an African American student who describes his experience sitting for the SAT exam as a senior in high school.

> I was a bit nervous, not only because of the importance of the test but because I was going to take it in unfamiliar surroundings. I walked into the test room and was glad to see another student from Lansing Sexton. I believe his name was Jim. He was a tall, brown-haired white kid: a typical student in my high school. We were what I considered friends—not close, but we knew each other. I walked over and sat down next to him.
>
> "What's up?" I tried to hide my concern about the test.
>
> "Hey, John, how are you?" he responded.
>
> "Pretty good, just not enough sleep last night." High school students have this desire to present themselves as party animals who never study but somehow manage to get good grades. And for this reason no one in his right mind would admit that he had slept from 11:00–7:00 a.m.
>
> "Yeah, I know . . . seems like I never get enough sleep."
>
> "Well . . . how do you feel about the test?" I said, after a brief hesitation. I was wondering if he was as worked up as I was.
>
> "It shouldn't be too bad," he responded, smiling falsely, as if he were unconcerned. He then gave me a curious look and asked me an ignorant question. "Are *you* smart?"
>
> I was shocked. Why the hell would I be taking the test if I weren't smart? Who was he to ask me something like that? Who the hell did he think

he was, anyway? Any of these responses would have been appropriate, but I chose none of them. Instead, in a sarcastic tone, I simply smiled and said, "No, I'm not."

For that brief instant I thought, Maybe I *don't* belong here. I was able to catch myself and realize that, if anyone belonged, it was me. But at the same time I began to wonder how others would have responded under the same circumstances. Maybe for them it wasn't so easy to overcome that initial doubt? Maybe they really believed they didn't belong? I looked around the room and saw only a few Black faces, and then I thought about my response to his question. I thought about how I had understated my abilities. I started to tell him how I really felt about him having the audacity to ask me something like that, but, as I began to open my mouth, I was given my test and told not to speak. (pp. 196–197)

This narrative helps illuminate the connection between social structures, self-identity, and Bartky's idea of psychological oppression. In it, John shows that he understands that the expectations placed on him by his White "friend" are part of a larger pattern of racist imagery associated with intelligence. Nonetheless, he experiences the self-doubt and potential complicity this form of oppression can inspire. John entertains the notion, if only briefly, that *he* has misunderstood something, and that perhaps he does not "belong" in the group taking the test.

Instead of being blinded by racist images that reflect a limited and distorted view of his abilities, however, John begins to consider the source and potential effects of these views and assumptions. He reflects, for instance, on whether these commonly held beliefs might be causing other African Americans at the test site to doubt their own abilities or the legitimacy of their presence. John exercises his capacity for critical consciousness in this situation insofar as he comes to understand the constraining effects of racist views held by others and their connection to the broader society in which he lives.

If John had not developed this capacity for critical consciousness, however (which did not happen at school, as we will see in a moment), the initial interaction with Jim could well have affected his ability to succeed on the test, and to reach a point later in his life and education where he could reflect on this event and understand it for what it was: an example of the subtle gatekeeping and marginalizing practices that occur all too often in our schools and, almost as often, go unexamined. Indeed, we are left, like John, with the question of how many people never even registered for the test for the same kinds of reasons that Jim (who, unfortunately, could just as easily have been a teacher, counselor, principal, or neighbor) helped to provide. Bartky (1990) notes how judgments of this kind are based on powerful stereotypes that resonate socially and psychologically with the structures that (in this case) support and sustain racism.

> Stereotyping is morally reprehensible as well as psychologically oppressive on two counts, at least. First, it can hardly be expected that those who hold a set of stereotyped beliefs about the sort of person I am will understand my needs or even respect my rights. Second, suppose that I, the object of some stereotype, believe in it myself—for why should I not believe what everyone else believes? I may then find it difficult to achieve what existential-ists call an authentic choice of self, or what some psychologists have re-garded as a state of self-actualization. (p. 24)

John's actions also reflect the aspect of autonomy I have associated with authenticity. By participating in a writing group that focused on the experience of "separateness" in society, John was able to better under-stand and articulate how experiences in his family and community pre-pared him for such racist encounters. These relationships helped John to see himself as successful and to see that this success resulted in large part from being able to find support for his sense of identity outside the "white power structure." John's support came from a family that never questioned his abilities and that gave him the "inner strength to define himself." The final statement in his autobiographical account appears un-der the heading, "It Takes a Nation of Millions to Hold Us Back."

> I have led a good life as an African-American man in this country. The white power structure, through its school system, tried to track me in the wrong direction, but I was lucky. I was able to muster the strength to tell an *entire society* that it was wrong about me. I was able to form my own Black identity. I was able to shake off the white man's guilt and place it back where it be-longed. But, for every person like myself who was lucky enough to be born with a supportive family network, an actual opportunity to "get ahead," and the inner strength to define himself, there are millions who are not so lucky. (Schoem, 1991, p. 202, emphasis in original)

John did not receive support for his efforts to "get ahead" from school. In fact, John came to understand how schools had tried to enforce the same vision of his future that Jim tacitly assumed (and then explicitly articulated). John accuses schools of being a part of the racist system that tried to "track me in the wrong direction." The question for emancipatory schools is how to resist this legacy and help students like John *and* Jim further develop their capacity for (and commitment to) autonomy.

Neo-conservative educational policies fail to provide an adequate basis for addressing examples like this because they place little value on the kind of school experiences that John needed most in order to envision the constraints that were in fact operating in his life. The commitment shared by neo-conservatives to a canonical core curriculum, and the transmission-oriented pedagogies associated with it, fail to encourage, and may actually block (because of the resistance to schooling they often inspire), the insights necessary to connect individual experiences like John's with the broader social structures that frame and mediate them. The neo-conservative approach to curriculum and pedagogy also deflects the kinds of exploration that might have helped John recognize earlier that he shared his circumstances with others who occupy a similar social position (with respect to race, in this case) and who are thus similarly vulnerable to the effects of racist stereotyping on their future life-chances.

Bartky explores a second dimension of psychological oppression that is also useful in elaborating the need to develop autonomy in emancipatory schools; she calls this one "cultural domination." Her analysis of this point reinforces the account I have given of how social structures work to constrain the meaningful choices that are available to oppressed or marginalized groups in society. For Bartky, cultural domination is a form of oppression characterized by the pervasive institutionalization of social practices and ways of understanding the world that subordinate a particular group. Patriarchy is a good example of cultural domination.

> To claim that women are victims of cultural domination is to claim that all the items in the general life of our people—our language, our institutions, our art and literature, our popular culture—are sexist; that all, to a greater or lesser degree, manifest male supremacy. (Bartky, 1990, p. 25)

While this explanation returns us to a broader and more abstract view of oppressive social relations, it can be rather directly applied to the classroom as a guide for emancipatory school practice.

Here I consider two examples from recent educational research concerned with the experience of students of color in schools that are dominated by Anglo- or Eurocentric perspectives: The first is from Michelle Fine's (1992) analysis of classroom practices that "silence" students' critical insights into issues associated with race, gender, and social class; the second is a case study from Sonia Nieto (1996), in which she describes an example of "coercive acculturation." In both cases, oppression results from the promulgation of demeaning images of self, and from constraining the capacity of students to envision alternatives to the world presented to them in school.

Michelle Fine (1992) set out to study "what's not said in schools," a practice of silencing that "signifies a terror of words, a fear of talk" (p.

115). What she found, based on her ethnographic research in a comprehensive high school in New York City, was that, while silencing took a variety of forms, its results were almost always the same: to forestall the pursuit of personal accounts of institutionalized racism and sexism, and to discourage the elaboration of a personal position that in any way stepped out of the preordained categories permitted by the teacher or lesson. In one briefly recounted case, for example, a student told Fine that abortion was a topic that could not be discussed in class. Fine (1992) recalls, "When I asked a school district administrator about this policy, she qualified: 'It's not that they can't *talk* about it. If the topic is raised by a student, the teacher can define abortion, just not discuss it beyond that'" (p. 124, emphasis in original).

Fine's analysis presents several situations where students try to clarify difficult or complex positions in ways that reflect a struggle with important personal/political issues. In one such case, an African American student named Deidre works to understand her ambivalent views regarding vigilantism and the level of violence in her neighborhood.

> In early spring, a social studies teacher structured an in-class debate on Bernard Goetz—New York City's "subway vigilante." She invited "those students who agree with Goetz to sit on one side of the room and those who think he was wrong to sit on the other side." To the large residual group who remained mid-room, the teacher remarked, "Don't be lazy. You have to make a decision. Like at work, you can't be passive." A few wandered over to the "pro-Goetz" side. About six remained in the center. Somewhat angry, the teacher continued: "OK, first we'll hear the pro-Goetz side and then the anti-Goetz side. Those of you who have no opinions, who haven't even thought about the issue, you won't get to talk unless we have time."
>
> Deidre, an African-American senior, bright and always quick to raise contradictions otherwise obscured, advocated the legitimacy of the middle group. "It's not that I have no opinions. I don't like Goetz shootin' up people who look like my brother, but I don't like feelin' unsafe in the projects or in my neighborhood either. I got lots of opinions. I ain't bein' quiet cause I can't decide if he's right or wrong. I'm talkin'." (Fine, 1992, p. 128)

In this example, Deidre tries to express her capacity for critical consciousness by drawing out the complex threads that will help her make up her mind on the topic of the Goetz shootings. Deidre's response is based on her awareness of the conflicting reactions the teacher's question has elicited in her. In this situation, she tries to balance or integrate her understanding of racism in the community with her (similarly firsthand) knowledge of how dangerous it can be to live there. It seems clear, however, that her response has no place in the teacher's understanding of the activity, nor does it fit within the teacher's broader pedagogical approach to these students.

The effect of this quite literal silencing is to constrain Deidre's capacity for critical consciousness; it limits her efforts to reflect on her own beliefs and experiences, and diminishes her ability to take a justifiable position on the topic being discussed. Fine describes this pedagogy in a way that is consistent with my critique of neo-conservatives, not only in the way they ignore or discount the importance of social context in understanding students' interaction with (i.e., their role in helping to construct) the curriculum, but also in the way that the teacher is given final authority to dictate the terms of all questions, answers, conflicts, and dilemmas in the classroom. In addition to her own work, Fine (1992) cites research by Linda McNeil (1981) and concludes:

> If "lived talk" was actively expelled on the basis of content, contradictory talk was basically rendered impossible. Social contradictions were folded into dichotomous choices. What does this obscure, and whom does this accommodate? The creation of such dichotomies and the reification of single truths may bolster educators' authority, reinforcing the distance between those who *know* and those who *don't*, often discrediting those who think in complexity. (p. 128, emphasis in original)

The teacher's actions in this example also undercut Deidre's attempts to exercise and develop the capacity for authenticity, insofar as she is constrained from exploring experiences she shares with a variety of people in and outside of her community. In addition to the obvious sense in which Deidre is excluded from the community of the classroom (recall that she is literally forbidden to speak after other students have taken their sides), she is prevented from exploring her relation to key participants in the event under discussion: Goetz, the armed White subway rider who feared enough for his physical safety to carry a gun; the African American adolescents who were shot and who "looked like" Deidre's brothers; and, finally, Deidre's relation to other inhabitants of the projects who, like her, fear the violent and dangerous circumstances they face each day. This result radically diminishes the capacity for authenticity in the classroom, not only for Deidre, but for others who missed the opportunity to join her in creating a community (in and outside of the school) that might understand and take action on these issues.

The silencing of voices like Deidre's not only presents a barrier to self-reflection and self-worth, it also diminishes the possibility of creating solidarity within and between groups that experience oppression. As Fine (1992) argues, it "establish[es] impenetrable barriers between the worlds of school and community life" (p. 119). These obstacles to solidarity, which result in part from mystifying the causes of oppression, are among the most significant challenges to efforts aimed at creating emancipatory schools that make a difference in their communities. Consider "Black-on-Black" crime and the virulent misogyny reflected in many rap music lyrics. These are issues that many African American activists and intellectuals have wrestled with in their efforts to organize movements against racism (hooks, 1994a, 1994b; Wallace, 1990; West, 1993). Emancipatory schools should be a part of this effort.

Another important (and unfortunately common) way that students experience cultural domination is through the institutionalization of derogatory and exclusionary forms of curriculum. This form of oppression concerns the way that views and experiences expressed by students who are not members of the majority culture are received in the classroom, especially in those cases where cultural values and assumptions come into explicit conflict. Such conflicts over culture and identity, and how they can be suppressed in classroom interactions, are powerfully represented in the story of Fern Sherman, a Native American (Turtle Mountain Chippewa and Northern Ponca) eighth-grade student whose experiences are recounted in Sonia Nieto's *Affirming Diversity* (1996).

> [My teachers don't understand my culture.] Like if I say, "This isn't done in my culture. This isn't the way it's done. . . ." Like talking about abortion in history or something. For Native Americans, abortion is just . . . like you should really put the mother in jail for it. Because . . . the baby is alive, just like we are. And that's the way I feel. And when they sit there and say, "It's the mother's right to do it," well, I don't think, really, it's the mother's right because it's not the baby's fault the mother doesn't want it. And so, when I try to tell them, they just, "Oh, well, we're out of time." They cut me off, and we've still got half an hour! And so that kinda makes me mad.
>
> If there's something in the history book that's wrong, my dad always taught me that if it's wrong, I should tell them that it is wrong. And the only time I ever do is if I know it's *exactly* wrong. Like we were reading about Native Americans and scalping. Well, the French are really the ones that made them do it so they could get money. And my teacher would not believe me. I finally just shut up because he just would not believe me . . . Just my arguments with them, they just cut it off. (p. 129, emphasis and paraphrase in original)

Like Deidre, Fern experiences a kind of silencing here that removes her from the discussion as a worthy and knowledgeable participant, and it denies the legitimacy of the cultural critique she tries to offer. In this case, the classroom becomes a context for cultural domination rather than exploration; Fern is denied a space where her self-identity and culture can find reasonable expression, and her capacity to act autonomously is thereby diminished.

As in John Diamond's case, Fern's awareness of the constraints placed on her at school is accompanied by the recognition that this experience is an important issue for others in her community and, indeed, for all Native Americans. Fern reflects on the role that cultural difference plays for her and other Native American students at school, and on whether this is ultimately an important factor in the decision that many Native American students make to drop out.

> We do have different values. . . . We do have different needs and we do have different wants. . . . I don't know why . . . other Native Americans have dropped out of Springdale schools. Maybe it's because I just haven't been in high school yet. But I remember one time, my sister came home and she was just mad. They said that . . . "Geronimo was a stupid chief riding that stupid horse" and my sister got mad! (Nieto, 1996, pp. 129–130)

Native Americans and other students of color face educational circumstances that are often distrustful of, if not openly hostile to, the expression of cultural difference in the classroom. This result follows from the belief, widely promoted by neo-conservatives, that issues associated with cultural identity are tangential to the core body of knowledge that all students must possess, and that a focus on diversity reflects an illegitimate politicization of the curriculum (i.e., the result of lobbying by special interest groups). Failing to join in the (implicit or explicit) process of assimilation, as the preceding examples suggest, increases the chances that a student will drop out, be unemployed, and/or experience a number of other debilitating results (drug and alcohol abuse not least among them). Ironically, the cost of successful assimilation may be almost as high, when we consider its "psychic costs," as Signithia Fordham and John Ogbu (1986), Richard Rodriguez (1982), and Ki-Taek Chun (1995), among others, have suggested.

Autonomy, understood in terms of critical consciousness and authenticity, supports the efforts of individuals to demystify, resist, and reconstruct the illegitimate constraints that result from oppressive social structures. Neo-conservatives, as I have argued throughout this work, deny that such efforts are necessary (given the assumption that we live in a functioning meritocracy), and reject the values on which they are based as guides for educational practice. If we follow the current neo-conservative agenda in education, the consequences of our actions will be to reinforce and reproduce a system of inequality that privileges a few at the expense

of many. Without significant reforms, large numbers of students will continue to be marginalized in this process and their predictable failure will
continue to be used against them as evidence of their cognitive (or even
genetic) deficits, their disengagement from learning, and, ultimately,
their ineducability.

PEDAGOGY AND EMANCIPATORY EDUCATION

In this section, I present three forms of pedagogy that could help us create and sustain emancipatory schools. An important goal of this analysis
is to support forms of instruction that promote critical consciousness and
authenticity by showing how they can be brought together in a coherent
approach to educational practice. It is also important to recognize, however, that because these pedagogies are sensitive to the students and communities they serve, each can be pursued in a variety of ways and in a
variety of educational contexts; there is no single model for emancipatory
schooling that is "right" for all circumstances.

Reconstructing Subject Matter in the Social Context of Experience

Challenging both the pedagogical primacy and moral authority of subject
matter in the school curriculum is essential to the development of emancipatory educational theory. An overwhelming emphasis on subject matter
in defining curriculum cuts against critical consciousness and authenticity by relegating the most pressing questions about identity and community to instrumental concerns about how to disseminate information most
efficiently. Our current focus on the academic disciplines as a foundation
for curriculum is one of the most important obstacles to creating conditions that support and develop the capacity for autonomy in students.

A powerful critique of disciplinary definitions of curriculum can be
found in Jane Roland Martin's essay, "Two Dogmas of Curriculum" (1994).
In this essay, Martin reveals the misleading logic and false assumptions
that underlie the "Dogma of God-Given Subjects" and the "Dogma of the
Immutable Basics." Her goal is to make explicit the choices we face in
creating the school curriculum.

> The prospects of constructing an adequate theory of curriculum are dim so
> long as the dogmas to be discussed here remain intact, and so are the pros-
> pects for true curricular reform. Reform which goes beyond mere tinkering
> with existing curricula requires that proposals for new subjects be taken
> seriously and that the present hierarchy of subjects be challenged. These

dogmas of curriculum serve as barriers to such change. An adequate theory of curriculum must illuminate clearly the choices confronting those who develop curriculum. To do this it must adopt a generous conception of subjects and acknowledge the fact that our subjects are complex human constructions to which we ourselves attach value. So long as these dogmas of curriculum are allowed to go unexamined, theoretical illumination will continue to elude us. (Martin, 1994, pp. 187–188)

Martin disrupts the unquestioned validity and givenness of traditional subject areas and places them squarely in the debate described in Chapter 2, recalling William Bennett's (1992) pronouncement that "at the end of the day, somebody's values will prevail" (p. 258). The key to Martin's argument is that existing definitions and structures of curriculum are the product of human choice and, further, that these decisions always represent (implicitly or explicitly) the values of the choosers.

With respect to the "Dogma of God-Given Subjects," Martin (1994) summarizes her argument simply enough: "Anything can be a subject because subjects are made, not found" (p. 188). The series of arguments she gives for this claim supports the view that curriculum is always embedded in experience, whether we recognize it or not, and therefore that judgments about curriculum must be open to dispute based on the goals and commitments of a particular community. I summarize Martin's argument briefly here, as I am more interested in its implications for emancipatory educational theory than the elaborate task of deconstructing the disciplines themselves.

In essence, Martin argues that there is no coherent or defensible means of defining subjects in a way that distinguishes the worth or validity of one from another, *in principle.* Martin (1994) draws a useful distinction between "subject," the name that we give to what we study, and "subject-entity," the "something 'out there' in the world" (p. 189) into which we actually inquire. Martin, for instance, compares physics and chairs, as subject and subject-entity, respectively. She notes that while a scientist may study physics, this description of the physicist's work takes nothing away from the furniture maker who may just as well and just as profitably inquire into the construction of chairs (p. 188). The importance of the distinction lies in her attempt to show that virtually anything can be a subject-entity and that the elevation of *subject-entities* to *subjects* depends on social convention. Her examples of *subject-entities* include objects like chairs and hamburgers; people like Humphrey Bogart; activities like writing, cooking, or sewing; fields of study like physics; or even "small things" like the phrase of a Chopin waltz. *Subjects,* like physics and geography, on the other hand, depend on complex social and historical conventions for their status, as well as a practical connection to human needs. Subjects are the result of a process that is distinctively human and value-laden (Martin, 1994, p. 189).

The point of this argument for emancipatory educational theory is not to suggest that all subject-entities are equally worthy of study (as subjects) or that compelling reasons cannot be given regarding what students should learn in school. Rather, the point is to show that the "Dogma of God-Given Subjects" confuses what *can* be a subject with what *ought* to be one, thereby mystifying the construction of knowledge within the social context of schooling. When we encounter the traditional school day, as neo-conservatives would have it, divided into classes of English, math, social studies, science, and so on, we are prone to think of these as "the" (i.e., the given) subjects of study in school. And further, we may suppose that these subjects have existed throughout history (i.e., that they are immutable) and thus represent some kind of objective epistemological structure that should not be tampered with. Finally, based on these arguments, we are left to conclude that neither the disciplines themselves, nor the school day that has been built upon them, are open to reasonable question or debate.

But these assumptions are misguided and oppressive. The subjects we teach today and use to organize our schools have emerged from human experience over time and in ways that are, in large part, complex enough to be well beyond our everyday awareness. Some evidence of the constructed nature of academic subjects, as Martin points out, is remarkably close at hand, however. She notes that examples of contestation periodically occur, and have again recently, in debates over "new subjects" like women's and Black studies, and even in "well-established subjects" like social studies. But the real question for Martin, and for my conception of emancipatory education, concerns what role students themselves should play in defining the nature of the curriculum. Critical consciousness and authenticity support the notion that school communities should be built around a more self-reflective and participatory process of curriculum construction, and that collaborative relationships among students are essential to learning and growth.

Martin offers an alternative way of envisioning the nature of curriculum that embodies both aspects of autonomy. For her, the question of how schools should be organized is rooted in a concern for what makes a life worth living and a community worth living in. Radical proposals to reform education like Martin's go beyond proposing alternative instructional strategies. She argues that, to be truly emancipatory, schools must open up the very process by which they define the processes of teaching and learning.

> To change curriculum radically it is not enough to introduce new ways of learning old subjects as open education did. The old subjects must be abandoned or else made to cede some of the curriculum space they now occupy to new subjects. When true curricular reform is wanted, simply extending the range of learning activities and materials, important as this may be, is not sufficient. Nor is it sufficient simply to give students the freedom to make their own curriculum, as some radical school reformers tended to assume. New subjects must be seen to be chosen and they must be created in order to be seen. Unless the eyes of students are opened to a wide range of alternative subjects, there is no reason at all to suppose that they will see, let alone choose, new ones. (Martin, 1994, p. 194)

Martin argues that to determine what ought to be taught in school requires first that this question be made explicit in the community and that students and teachers pursue a range of possible answers *together*. The answers that members of the community come up with will still be historically contingent and not immutable (this is just the point, after all), but if the process is open and inclusive, it should embody and reflect (in a variety of different ways, no doubt) the undistorted needs and interests of all participants.

But it would be just as big a mistake to throw out existing disciplinary structures altogether as it would be to persist in holding the curricular dogmas of god-givenness and immutability. The question before us now—and, as we will see, it is hardly a new one in education—concerns how we should think about the relationship between subject matter (as an expression of disciplinary knowledge) and experience (as an expression of individual needs and interests). As early as the turn of the twentieth century, John Dewey considered this same question, and his argument that the opposition between subject matter and experience is based on a profound misunderstanding of both, remains central to the foundation of emancipatory educational theory. Understanding the general terms of this argument is key to reconstructing subject matter in the social context of experience, and it is worth turning briefly to Dewey's short and well-known work, *The Child and the Curriculum* (1956/1902), for the insights it provides and for the sense it gives us (after almost 100 years) of just how obdurate this conflict has remained.

In *The Child and the Curriculum* Dewey considers the dilemma of whether instruction should be organized around the developing experience of the child or the disciplinary distinctions that define knowledge in the adult world of the teacher. Dewey (1956/1902) marks the question as a serious challenge in education, first because the terms of the dilemma appear in such stark opposition to each other.

First, the narrow but personal world of the child against the impersonal but infinitely extended world of space and time; second, the unity, the single wholeheartedness of the child's life, and the specializations and divisions of the curriculum; third, an abstract principle of logical classification and arrangement, and the practical and emotional bonds of the child's life. (p. 7)

Dewey (1956/1902) also notes the seriousness of the dilemma in light of the tendency for entrenched advocates on either side to maintain their respective positions, no matter what the countervailing facts or arguments (which should, by now, sound quite familiar).

Any significant problem involves conditions that for the moment contradict each other. Solution comes only by getting away from the meaning of terms that is already fixed upon and coming to see the conditions from another point of view, and hence in a fresh light. But this reconstruction means travail of thought. Easier than thinking with surrender of already formed ideas and detachment from facts already learned is just to stick by what is already said, looking about for something with which to buttress it against attack. (pp. 3–4)

In contrast, Dewey approaches the dilemma presented by the child and the curriculum using the signature strategy of American pragmatism: by turning a troubling contradiction inside out to reveal an opposition based on misleading interpretations of key concepts. In this case, he argues that the opposition between the child and the curriculum cannot be resolved without altering our customary understanding of both terms.

According to Dewey (1956/1902), to resolve the dilemma of the child and curriculum, we must "get rid of the prejudicial notion that there is some gap in kind (as distinct from degree) between the child's experience and the various forms of subject-matter that make up the course of study" (p. 11). He argues that we must "abandon the notion of subject-matter as something fixed and ready-made in itself, outside the child's experience; cease thinking of the child's experience as also something hard and fast; see it as something fluent, embryonic, vital; and we realize that the child and the curriculum are simply two limits which define a single process" (p. 11). Dewey's subsequent discussion of teaching using the metaphors of map and guide, and his understanding of learning as growth from educative experiences, still provide us with some of our best arguments for why teachers should act as guides, mentors, or coaches, rather than "bankers" of knowledge, and why the motivation for learning in the classroom must be drawn from students' experiences, rather than imposed externally by rote, reward, or the avoidance of punishment. Where neo-conservatives have gone wrong in this regard, drastically wrong, is in their assumption that the only alternative to imposition in schooling is a kind of vacuous or narcissistic permissiveness. The extent to which neo-conservatives like Finn, Bennett, and Bloom have fallen into (indeed, have worked hard to reinforce) the kind of false distinctions Dewey describes, is as striking in the similarity of its historical visage as it is damaging in its contemporary practice. As Dewey (1956/1902) notes, "There are those who see no alternative between forcing the child from without, or leaving him entirely alone. Seeing no alternative, some choose one mode, some another. Both fall into the same fundamental error" (p. 17).

Re-establishing the role and significance of experience in the classroom will not be an easy task, and it is crucial to guard against any interpretation of this effort that suggests it is directed at *replacing* the current emphasis on traditional subject matter with an *exclusive* focus on individual experience. Indeed, despite Dewey's clarity on this point and his prescience regarding perennial disputes over curriculum orientations, his legacy is dogged by the misinterpretation that he was a supporter of "child-centered" education (where this position is defined by one end of the continuum Dewey himself described in *The Child and the Curriculum*). It would be well to say here that the reforms suggested by an education for autonomy treat individual experience as a framework and foundation for meaningful curriculum content; they do not reject or exclude it. Of course, what counts as "meaningful" is the crux of the matter here, especially given the neo-conservative view that this body of knowledge can (and should) be specified both in detail and in advance.

The commitment of neo-conservatives to the primacy of disciplinary knowledge and their belief in the general (often profound) irrelevance of individual experience to matters of curriculum construction are evident in many of the works associated with this perspective, including E. D. Hirsch's co-edited reference volume, *The Dictionary of Cultural Literacy* (Hirsch, Kett, Trefil, & Hirsch, 1993); his "core knowledge" series, beginning with *What Your First-Grader Needs to Know: Fundamentals of a Good First-Grade Education* (1993) and continuing through each of the next five grade levels; and works like *Books to Build on: A Grade-by-Grade Resource Guide for Parents and Teachers* (Hirsch & Holdren, 1996). These texts clearly reflect the predictable and codifiable content of curriculum at each grade level and give support to calls for a national framework of content objectives and a common battery of standardized tests to assess students' acquisition of this knowledge.

Opposition to this perspective does not require that emancipatory educators reject curriculum content or the idea that teachers possess authority in the classroom based on their expertise in traditional subject areas. As Ira Shor (1992) notes:

Affirming student culture does not mean that students know all they need to know or that teachers don't know anything special. In fact, what teachers know is crucial to the transformative process. Pedagogical skills and academic knowledge are required for critical teaching. The question is how to use expert knowledge to facilitate rather than hinder student learning. (pp. 202–203)

Emancipatory schools integrate traditional subject matter into student experience, based on an understanding of who their students are and what they need. I have argued that this is an inherently political process, as it occurs in a social context where power and status play a key role in determining the outcome of deliberation. To educate students for autonomy is to prepare them to deliberate freely and critically over possible life-plans, without having their needs and interests distorted by others, in a community of individuals who share a similar project. What any member of a community needs, at any particular time, will depend on much that cannot be known in advance; our answers to questions of curriculum will always depend on the individuals and circumstances that surround our efforts.

Making students' experience a vital part of the classroom means overcoming a number of important barriers in our current schools. The following recommendations suggest some concrete starting points for this transition.

Integrating student experience into existing definitions of curriculum. As one might expect, based on my preceding comments, the first major barrier that needs to be addressed in this regard is the widely accepted definition of curriculum in terms of disciplinary content. While the relatively abstract nature of the critique I offered earlier does not immediately identify potential points of leverage, a number of possibilities exist. One is located among the many instrumental ways that schools use traditional subject areas to organize and divide their faculty, school day, assessment procedures, and instructional goals. Dislocating the dominance of disciplinary knowledge in many or all of these areas could open up a number of possibilities for emancipatory school practice. Current examples of such efforts include the development of interdisciplinary or project-based curriculum, faculty team teaching in block schedules, and alternative or performance assessment procedures that push students to exhibit their learning in more integrated and "real-world" settings (Meier, 1995; Sizer, 1984, 1992).

A second way of addressing the disconnection between subject matter and individual experience in public schools can be found in the teacher education programs offered by our colleges and universities. Despite their best efforts to promote reform-minded pedagogies among preservice teachers, most of the faculty and courses within schools of education continue to be defined and divided along disciplinary lines (e.g., subject-specific methods courses, practica, and student teaching placements). Developing emancipatory schools will require the support of teacher education programs that are themselves interdisciplinary and that give preservice teachers explicit opportunities to explore in greater detail the connection between experience and teaching (Knowles, Cole, & Presswood, 1994).

Finally, school reform efforts based on the establishment of a national core curriculum, created through federal legislation and enforced by national standardized assessments, should be opposed. Unless these guidelines are of the most general nature, which would call their usefulness into question in the first place, it is difficult to see how their implementation could be anything but an obstacle to developing emancipatory practices that integrate student experience into the school curriculum. Instead of trying to develop and enforce such standards, it would be wiser to invest in the kind of organizational reforms and professional development activities that would help create communities based on more collaborative and egalitarian models (Apple & Beane, 1995; Bastian et al., 1986; Howe, 1994).

Changing the relationship between teachers and students. A second barrier to reconstructing subject matter in the social context of experience lies in the relationship that often exists between teachers and students in the traditional classroom. As long as subject-matter definitions of curriculum persist, teachers will, with few exceptions, always possess the most valuable knowledge and skills. The relationships of authority and dependence that result from this imbalance provide little room for legitimate student involvement. Based on these assumptions, students are likely to spend most of their time answering questions in teacher-led discussions, reporting on information that can be found in textbooks that teachers have assigned, or filling in tests created by teachers. Under these circumstances, the appeal to experience, as Dewey points out, is more often used as a way of ascertaining what is missing or insufficiently developed in students than as a basis for discerning the unique contribution that a student might make.

Giving greater attention to student experience requires us to admit that there is at least one essential thing that teachers cannot firmly know before entering the classroom, that they cannot be experts on by virtue of their advanced education, and that they cannot divine from workshops provided by outside consultants. Knowing students' experience requires knowing the students themselves, and that means moving away from the front of the room, taking up less space in class discussions, and giving students a more significant role in creating both the form and content of the curriculum. These changes would almost certainly alter the balance of power and authority in most classrooms. We should expect resistance, as current reform efforts have shown, from teachers and students alike (Meier, 1995; Shor, 1992; Sizer, 1992). But the resulting changes have convinced many that this risk is worth taking.

It is worth pointing out that these kinds of changes in the nature of authority in the classroom can also have a salutary effect on the role that parents and the community might play in schools. Opening the door to students' experience may lead teachers and school administrators to throw it open even further, to others in the community who may also be able to make a meaningful contribution to students' (and teachers') education. The wealth of expertise, special knowledge, and concern for students that exists in the community can be an expansive addition to the curriculum of an emancipatory school. But this also requires that the teacher take a fundamentally different role, at least some of the time. In addition to being a guide or coach for students, teachers must sometimes give up the role of expert or authority in order to free students to find new resources outside the context of ordinary instruction. This may include other people who have skills or experiences that the teacher does not possess and it may also require that teachers grant students a good deal more independence and responsibility than is customary in our schools.

Making schools democratic communities of learning. Pursuing the connection between experience and education also leads us toward a fuller consideration of democratic values and their implications for how emancipatory schools ought to work. Facing this challenge requires that we confront a system that has discouraged virtually all of its participants, including teachers, from taking an active role in constructing institutional goals or reflecting on individual practice. In the language of emancipatory educational reform, we might ask how schools can become places in which teachers and students engage in activities that promote collaboration and communication, and that contribute to building the capacity for autonomy among all community members. To move in this direction, students would need to become active participants in their own education, and it would not be surprising if this had a kind of ripple effect through relationships in peer groups, families, and local communities.

To engage in this process of democratization will require teachers to be constantly involved in finding out where their students come from, what experiences and interests they possess, and what they plan to do when they leave school. It will require that teachers reflect on their practice in terms of the general goals that they hold for students and the judgments they make each day about how to help students move in that direction. Such a pedagogy would force us to adopt the unwieldy responsibility of parents who want the best for their children, without always knowing what the future will look like, or what skills and knowledge will be needed to achieve a sufficient measure of success and happiness in society. This is the challenge of creating schools whose curricular and other responsibilities are no longer safely defined by the limits of subject matter (see Beyer, 1996, for a collection of essays by teachers who are taking on these challenges).

The effort to fundamentally revise the school curriculum requires us, as Jane Roland Martin argued, to ask what kind of life is worth living, and what kind of society is worth living in. Emancipatory schools serve students by giving them the power and opportunity to grow through the decisions they make and the life-plans they pursue. The questions students ask and the projects they pursue will help them frame their choices and understand the consequences of their decisions. This is why a pedagogy that makes student experience inseparable from subject matter in the school curriculum is crucial for emancipatory education and for building the capacity of students to act autonomously.

Creating a Culturally Relevant Pedagogy

One of the most articulate descriptions of pedagogical practice aimed at meeting the needs of African American students is Gloria Ladson-Billings' (1994) work on culturally relevant teaching. Ladson-Billings' work (along with that of other scholars on multicultural issues) adds significantly to our understanding of emancipatory school practice and gives us good examples of how teachers and students have implemented these ideas in their classrooms. It is important to remember, however, that any particular understanding of what culturally relevant pedagogy looks like in a school must be rooted in a careful understanding of the particular students for whom it is intended. This is certainly true of the instructional practices and relationships that characterized the teachers and students in Ladson-Billings' study.

I consider culturally relevant pedagogy in some detail here because it is an approach to emancipatory education that strongly supports the development of critical consciousness and authenticity among students who are often the most marginalized and disenfranchised in our schools. Consistent with the goal of educating for autonomy, culturally relevant pedagogy supports emancipatory school practices in two ways: first, by developing an awareness among teachers and students of the larger social context within which identity is constructed; and second, through the creation of a school community that supports and sustains the efforts of individuals to see themselves as an integral part of a collective endeavor.

Given the goal of integrating emancipatory educational practices, my treatment of culturally relevant pedagogy will sometimes overlap with the recommendations I made above, concerning the importance of including student experience in definitions of curriculum, as well as those that I make later, on the pedagogical potential of narrative. This overlap is not something to be avoided, however. On the contrary, it helps us to see better how these pedagogies are mutually reinforcing and gives us better reasons to be optimistic about the potential for emancipatory educational reforms.

Culture, identity, and the curriculum. A culturally relevant pedagogy requires that teachers recognize difference as a starting point for education, rather than an obstacle to achieving it. Where critics of multicultural education see an American culture in which ethnic identity should be subsumed or even eliminated, culturally relevant teaching begins with the recognition that ethnicity lies at the very heart of how we understand and define ourselves. Given this, culturally relevant pedagogy insists that students of color understand not only who they are, but also who they are in relation to the dominant culture in society. It is important, therefore, for students of color (and other frequently marginalized students, including girls and women) to understand the ways in which the mainstream of American culture has excluded and distorted their experience in the past. The starting point of a culturally relevant pedagogy lies in developing an awareness of the connection between self and society, and how schools play a crucial role in mediating the construction of identity.

Ladson-Billings points out that the effort to develop a critical perspective on race and ethnicity in society brings us immediately up against the tradition of assimilationism in education. According to Ladson-Billings, one of the most important problems posed by assimilationist pedagogies is their dependence on and promulgation of negative stereotypes about African American and other children of color. Consistent with the analysis of social structure that I offered earlier, Ladson-Billings (1994) argues:

> One perspective on these low expectations and negative beliefs about African American students comes from mainstream society's invalidation of African American culture. This invalidation of African American culture is compounded by a notion of assimilationist teaching, a teaching style that operates without regard to the students' particular cultural characteristics.

According to the assimilationist perspective, the teacher's role is to ensure that students fit into society. And if the teacher has low expectations, the place that the teacher believes the students "fit into" is on society's lower rungs. (p. 22)

Included among the harms of assimilationist teaching are alienation from one's own cultural values and the psychic cost exacted by social success when it is achieved on the terms of the dominant culture (Fordham & Ogbu, 1986; Ladson-Billings, 1994; Ogbu, 1988; Rodriguez, 1982).

Culturally relevant pedagogy provides a perspective on the meaning and significance of an American identity that is distinctly different from the one that neo-conservatives have promulgated. If the dominant culture holds out only demeaning or constraining identities for minorities, women, and others, then assimilation becomes an act of submission or degradation, not self-improvement. Neo-conservatives who champion assimilationist school policies, even in what they think of as a pluralist society, miss the point of arguments made by people of color. For those who fall outside the mainstream definition of American culture, education may present the potential for deeply personal loss (of one's sense of self), rather than a "golden opportunity." As Sonia Nieto (1996) has pointed out, "*Americanization* in the past has always implied *Angloization*" (p. 346, emphasis in original). This might help resolve some of the confusion that neo-conservatives express over the intensity of discussions about self-esteem among the supporters of multicultural education.

As a guide for considering issues of racial or ethnic (or some other form of) identity in the classroom, culturally relevant pedagogy holds out a number of implications that support emancipatory educational practice. Most important perhaps is that teachers must recognize how differences in culture (or gender, class, sexual orientation, etc.) mediate communication and interaction, and thus why they are important factors in the conduct of instruction. I can think of no better story of a teacher's growing awareness of the role played by race in a teacher's conception of herself in the classroom than Vivian Gussin Paley's autobiographical narrative, *White Teacher* (1979). Paley is relentlessly honest and inquisitive in reflecting on how her views about race have developed and how these developing views have changed her teaching. Concerned about issues of equity and civil rights throughout her life, Paley (1979) nonetheless realizes that her assumptions have led her to exclude or ignore race from her decisions in the classroom; early in her career, color blindness had seemed to her to be the "essence" of fairness.

When Valerie told Fred she wanted a white partner I was silent. I did not know what needed to be said to help both of them. If she had told Fred his painting was scribble-scrabble I might have said, "Fred, Valerie thinks you're painting scribble-scrabble. Is that what you're doing?" Then Fred could have told us how he felt. But I could not transfer this matter-of-fact, nonjudgmental description of what was being said when race or color was involved. When Denise became annoyed with Valerie and told her not to sit next to her because this was not a "brown" chair, I responded with equal annoyance. "Valerie may sit wherever she wishes, Denise. Please don't tell people where to sit." I saw I was purposely avoiding the part about the *brown* chair. It was clear to me that I was unable to mention color in the classroom. When I was little we never referred to the color of the cleaning lady's skin. Of course we would not say "nigger." But, in her presence, we would never say colored, black, brown, skin, hair, maid, or Negro. In other words, we showed respect by completely ignoring black people as black people. Color blindness was the essence of the creed. (pp. 8–9, emphasis in original)

By reflecting on these events, Paley comes to understand the salience of social categories like race. She thinks more about the language she uses in the classroom, the assumptions other teachers make when they discuss her "difficult" students, and the relationship she develops with an African American student teacher. Paley's recognition of the importance of cultural difference represents an essential step toward developing a pedagogy that acknowledges students' identities (cultural and otherwise) and pays careful attention to them in the planning and practice of instruction.

A second important implication of culturally relevant pedagogy for classroom instruction lies in the connections that teachers must help students make between their conceptions of self and important aspects of the larger social context. The teachers Ladson-Billings studied provided a number of examples of how they encouraged students to expand their thinking from very local concerns and experiences, to more global or sociopolitically charged topics. In one of the narratives Ladson-Billings quotes at length, a teacher engages her students in a discussion of why their community should be concerned about the Gulf War. This topic initially came up because so many of the newspaper articles students had (voluntarily) chosen to bring to class involved the U.S. military operation in Iraq and Kuwait. After a brief worry that this issue might be important because bombs actually could be dropped on them, the class went on to consider one student's statement that the Gulf War was important to them because poor people were more likely to volunteer for the army and thus more likely to be represented later in the casualty figures. This was significant, the student suggested, because of the amount of poverty and unemployment that characterized their community.

A number of students verbally concur, while others nod in assent. As the discussion continues, students talk about the impact of having young males in particular leave their community. Given the fact that the numbers of African American and Latino males in this community are decreasing due to incarceration and other institutionalization, the prospect of losing even more men to war does not seem appealing. By the end of the lesson, students are working in cooperative groups and creating "casualty charts" where they list a number of current events and their possible impacts on their community. (Ladson-Billings, 1994, p. 51)

This example goes well beyond the venerable social studies tradition of bringing "current events" into the classroom. Culturally relevant pedagogy underscores the need to examine critically issues that affect the future lives of students, especially those who do not often find themselves the focus of "positive" public representations. While these topics sometimes may be gleaned from the day's newspaper or television news report, they may just as readily come from a student's fictional narrative or art project. The ultimate power of any particular example lies in the connections that teachers and students together make to the real world of their own needs, experiences, and aspirations.

The politics of knowledge. In a sense, the advocates of a culturally relevant pedagogy do not disagree with the neo-conservative claim that their view of knowledge and schooling is inherently political. Where there would be significant disagreement, however, is on the question of whether this is something new in education, and whether it should be feared or embraced. Implicit in the views of most neo-conservatives, as I argued earlier, is the idea that school knowledge can be defined unproblematically through the wisdom of disciplinary experts or the "most literate" among us. Such panels or boards would be responsible for presenting a "true" rather than a "politicized" curriculum, based on accepted knowledge in their particular fields.

But educational scholars have questioned this assumption from a number of perspectives and have challenged the objectivity or value neutrality of any school curriculum. The question of whose knowledge schools value has been a central issue for critical theorists in education (Apple, 1993), feminists (Luke & Gore, 1992), and researchers on race and ethnicity (McCarthy & Crichlow, 1993), to name a few. Ladson-Billings (1994) argues not only that knowledge is constructed in the sociocultural context of the classroom, but that giving students access to this process as "coconstructors" is a central goal of culturally relevant pedagogy.

Culturally relevant teaching involves students in the knowledge-construction process, so that they can ask significant questions about the nature of the curriculum. The ultimate goal is to ensure that they have a sense of ownership of their knowledge—a sense that it is empowering and liberating. As coconstructors in the knowledge-building process, they are less alienated from it and begin to understand that learning is an important cultural activity. (p. 77)

Bringing about this complex form of collaboration is difficult, however, and it has not been made easier by the enforced passivity that has characterized school culture for so long. The hierarchical structure of most schools and classrooms leaves students with very few meaningful questions that are really theirs to ask or answer, and few meaningful choices that are really theirs to make. The question for us is, where should this effort begin?

Sonia Nieto (1996) describes the long journey through "tolerance," "acceptance," and "respect" that she believes will finally lay the foundation for genuinely "accepting the culture and language of students and their families as legitimate and embracing them as valid vehicles for learning" (p. 355). The challenges posed by this process have far-reaching implications for school practice. There are many kinds of cultural difference, from language and dress to interaction patterns and family structures, that teachers from the majority culture may not understand or may misinterpret in the classroom. Teachers may find some of these characteristics puzzling, threatening, or even insulting. Shirley Brice Heath's *Ways with Words* (1983), for example, is a powerful analysis of how differences in language patterns (e.g., questioning, storytelling, etc.) and forms of interaction (e.g., asking questions about family members) can dramatically affect the understanding teachers develop about their students.

The point of this analysis for most of our schools, however, is less about difference than it is about deficit. Cultural differences in students of color are often translated into deficits and then used to justify stereotypical images that represent the students as ineffective, unmotivated, or ill-prepared for school by their upbringing. These images, in turn, reinforce the low expectations that some teachers hold already, and they perpetuate remedial pedagogical prescriptions that are even less likely to meet the needs of students of color. Culturally relevant pedagogy demands that cultural differences not be treated as deficits and that they play an immediate and public role in the life of the classroom and school.

Advocates of a culturally relevant pedagogy cannot stop at simply recognizing or even valuing these differences, however. For culturally relevant pedagogy to be truly emancipatory, students and teachers must critically reflect on the nature of cultural differences and how they attach to status and privilege in society. As my treatment of Lisa Delpit's work in the previous chapter suggests, the "culture of power" must be made explicit in the process of instruction and treated as an object of study in itself. At the same time, however, schools must acknowledge and nurture the marginalized cultural attributes that students of color bring to school. As a matter of classroom practice, Ladson-Billings (1994) argues that culturally relevant pedagogy requires "bridges" and "scaffolding" that help students use the skills and experiences they possess to become more capable of sustaining their own participation in the process of knowledge construction.

> By building bridges or a scaffolding that meets students where they are (intellectually and functionally), culturally relevant teaching helps them to be where they need to be to participate fully and meaningfully in the construction of knowledge. In contrast, assimilationist teaching assumes that students come to class with certain skills and suggests that it is impossible to teach those who are not at a certain level. (p. 96)

Finally, a culturally relevant pedagogy should help students see the connection between knowledge construction and empowerment. Schools have never been very good at convincing students who are outside of society's mainstream that the possession of school knowledge (represented by high academic achievement) will lead to social or economic success. Notwithstanding the experience of public figures like Supreme Court Justice Clarence Thomas and other prominent African Americans, whose success is often used as evidence of the good things that come to those who persist in the face of adversity, the research of John Ogbu and Signithia Fordham (Ogbu, 1988; Fordham & Ogbu, 1986) suggests that much of the resistance expressed by African American students comes from their rejection of schooling as a means of becoming successful adults. Because racism has persisted and even grown of late in our society, in spite of civil rights legislation and other powerful liberation movements, possessing the knowledge valued most by the dominant culture not only appears to be of little use to many young African Americans, but even threatens them with the accusation of "acting White."

Instead of trying to convince students that the traditional curriculum will serve them, if only they can finally master it, a culturally relevant pedagogy offers students an active role in questioning the knowledge they encounter in school and attempts to give students a place to engage in their own critical reconstructions. This kind of discussion might begin with something as seemingly trivial as an article from the newspaper or an ethnocentric quotation from an outdated textbook. What each example might become, however, is an opportunity for critically assessing what was once passively accepted (or simply ignored) in the classroom as a given fact. Ladson-Billings (1994) charges teachers who want to develop a culturally relevant pedagogy to open up their classrooms to discussions about the nature of curriculum itself.

> The ability to examine critically and challenge knowledge is not a mere classroom exercise. By drawing on the work of ethical theorists, culturally relevant teaching attempts to make knowledge problematic. Students are challenged to view education (and knowledge) as a vehicle for emancipation, to understand the significance of their cultures, and to recognize the power of language. As a matter of course, culturally relevant teaching makes a link between classroom experiences and the students' everyday lives. These connections are made in spirited discussions and classroom interactions. Teachers are not afraid to assume oppositional viewpoints to foster the students' confidence in challenging what may be inaccurate or problematic. (p. 94)

Emancipatory schooling must develop this capacity in all students, but Ladson-Billings helps us see how utterly crucial it is for those who are being least well served by today's schools.

Learning communities and communities learning. In response to neo-conservative concerns about divisiveness and separatism, advocates of culturally relevant pedagogy have good reason to argue that what they stand for is perhaps our best hope of avoiding the worst kind of social unrest. It is no doubt true that awakening a capacity for critical consciousness and authenticity in students who have been unfairly constrained in the pursuit of their life-plans and exploited for the benefit of others is likely to result in vigorous efforts to transform society. And it's true, feelings of bitterness and anger may well accompany this growing capacity for autonomy. But to resist these changes in the belief that modest reforms in the present system can meet the needs of society's most disadvantaged, or that meaningful reforms are being undertaken now that will significantly improve the future of impoverished and marginalized students, is a strategy that rests on false hope (or, worse, duplicity).

A culturally relevant pedagogy attempts to build in the classroom what we so desperately lack in American society, namely, a commitment to thinking and acting as if we truly believed that our own success as individuals depended on the success of our community. The teachers in Ladson-Billings' study believed strongly in the power of community and in the extended sense of "family" they tried to create in their classrooms. They were motivated in their everyday decisions about teaching by concern for the local community in which their school was situated, and they encouraged students to recognize and respond to the needs and demands of others outside of the classroom.

> The kind of teaching advocated by these teachers seeks to help students see community-building as a lifelong practice that extends beyond the classroom. Living in a community ravaged by drugs, unemployment, underemployment, high drop-out rates, high crime, and poverty spawns an innate pessimism in the children. They fail to see how they can succeed unless it is at the expense of others. Thus the teachers have to work hard to help them see beyond the decimation caused by federal, state, and county neglect to the real strengths of their community. (Ladson-Billings, 1994, p. 73)

A number of changes in the classroom might facilitate this process of community building. First, the norms of competition and compliance need to be replaced with values that support shared concern and cooperation. Ladson-Billings points out, for example, how the issue of community norms has become especially important among African American teachers and students who see schools as dominated by a cultural model that values individual achievement and effort above all else. She cites research (Nobles, 1973) that describes important differences between Western conceptions of the self as independent and self-sufficient, and African cultural norms that promote a view of self that depends on a shared sense of community for its meaning. The argument for a collaborative environment in the classroom does not depend solely on the kind of historical or sociological differences that Ladson-Billings describes here, however. Emancipatory educational theory suggests that truly cooperative learning strategies are essential for everyone, and that helping students see that the success of each individual is connected to the success of others who are similarly situated is essential for building the capacity for autonomy.

Second, the relationship between teachers and students needs to change from a strictly hierarchical one based on authority and control, to a collaborative arrangement based on mutual concern and a shared commitment to exploring and understanding difference. Nieto (1996) refers to this relationship as "mutual accommodation" (p. 334). She notes that this approach requires not only that teachers recognize the unique histories of each of their students, but that teachers themselves strive to grow in ways that encompass these new experiences within their pedagogies. This will challenge many teachers to push beyond the limits of their current instructional practices, since, as Nieto (1996) notes, "using students' language, culture, and experiences as the basis for their teaching might mean that teachers have to expand their own repertoires" (p. 335).

Finally, the school and its students need to be seen as effective participants (and agents of change, if necessary) in their local communities. It is unproductive and unwise to think that schools can be self-sufficient entities, without ties to the families on which they depend and to the local areas in which they are situated. Even under the most desperate circumstances, where students find school a refuge from physical threats and insecurity, teachers who practice a culturally relevant pedagogy will find their work enriched by the connections they make between what students do in the classroom and concrete efforts to make the local community a better place. This integration of classroom and community is essential for helping students to recognize the power and responsibility they hold for initiating or sustaining the process of social change. The following summary of a discussion in the classroom of one of the teachers Ladson-Billings (1994) studied exemplifies this aspect of culturally relevant pedagogy:

> In Ann Lewis's class, a student remarked, "I hate this community. I can't wait till I grow up and move away from it." Lewis calmly asked, "Do you hate your parents? Do you hate the church you attend? Do you hate the friends you play with each day? Do you hate me?" To each of these questions the student replied no. Lewis explained to him (and, of course, to the rest of the class) that all of these things she mentioned made up the *real* community. The drugs and the crime had invaded the community and if the students did not learn how to build it up, they would overrun it. Rather than suggest to the students that their education should take them away from their community, Lewis was reinforcing the idea that it would give them the power to make their community what they wanted it to be. (p. 73, emphasis in original)

Culturally relevant pedagogy provides a powerful instructional and curricular foundation for developing students' capacity for critical consciousness and authenticity. In terms of empowering students to critically assess their place in the larger society, and in terms of the support for a community of learners and co-constructors of knowledge within each classroom, the fit between a culturally relevant pedagogy and these two aspects of autonomy is quite strong. Culturally relevant pedagogy also constitutes a powerful answer to the neo-conservative critics of multicultural education; in its light their assimilationist arguments are unpersuasive and even counterproductive. To implement a culturally relevant pedagogy in our schools is one of the best hopes we have for genuinely making education an emancipatory experience for all students.

The Pedagogical Potential of Narrative

A third element of instructional practice that holds great potential for emancipatory educators involves the use of narrative in the classroom. Research on narrative and personal history writing has expanded significantly recently, including scholars from a number of fields (e.g., in education: Casey, 1993; Middleton, 1993; Witherell & Noddings, 1991; in psychology: Josselson & Lieblich, 1993; in sociology and social work: Riessman, 1993). These sources also represent a fair diversity in terms of the uses to which narrative might be put, from the pedagogical to the therapeutic. I draw primarily on the literature in education here to describe some of the ways that narrative might be used in emancipatory schools. As a way of raising issues concerning self-identity and pursuing them in collaboration with others, personal narratives provide an excellent opportunity for students to engage in a process that supports the development of critical consciousness and authenticity.

It may be worth noting that this section differs somewhat from the previous two in the sense that the issues I raise here have not, generally speaking, been engaged by neo-conservatives. That does not mean, however, that the following ideas would be warmly accepted by them. In fact, the form of pedagogy I describe here would almost certainly be dismissed by neo-conservatives as only so much more fluff in an already "watered down" curriculum (Bennett, 1992, p. 52). Worse, these ideas might be strongly opposed by neo-conservatives who are committed to excluding any consideration of "values" from the classroom and who see this approach as an illicit means for teachers to learn more about the "personal" lives of their students. As the preceding analysis suggests, these reactions are consistent with neo-conservatives' opposition to individual experience as an important aspect of curriculum and their commitment to teaching as essentially a process of transmission.

Narrative and the construction of meaning. The use of narrative in schools is very much in keeping with all that I have said above about the construction and negotiation of knowledge. Personal writing of many kinds, including autobiographies, journals, diaries, stories, and essays, open up the opportunity for students to reflect openly on how they have "created" themselves. This kind of writing illuminates not only the sense in which identity is an ongoing process of construction, but also the power that students have to develop, alter, or change the course of events in their own lives. Teachers who adopt a pedagogy of empowerment or emancipation can use narrative as the foundation for a wide range of innovations, from new ways of approaching traditional disciplinary material, to the process of reconstructing the curriculum itself.

One reason that teachers have adopted narrative techniques is to show students that learning can be an active process that engages them as individuals, rather than empty vessels to be filled by a text or lecture. Andra Makler (1991), for instance, helped students overcome the belief that "history is dead certainty and/or [a] meaningless lists of names, places, and dates," by giving them the opportunity to write through the persona of a fictionalized historical character. Rather than an instructional gimmick or simple writing prompt, we can see in this assignment a chance for students to think of themselves as actors in a complex web of historical cause and effect.

> Developing these narratives (entries in diaries, letters, expository essays) was a means for students quite literally to write themselves into the historical record. As textbooks are manifestations of the relationship between publishers and markets, female students, minority students, and students from "ordinary" homes often do not see themselves in the text; thus, the historical project we fashioned was the project of creating ourselves—of seeing ourselves as agents, acting upon and in the world, as we moved through the years from the fifteenth century to the present. (p. 30)

The goal of these efforts is to provide a context within which narrative can become a common meeting ground for student experience and a powerful connection to people and events outside the classroom. In writing their own narratives, students become active participants in a world they help to create. Traditional textbooks and mass-marketed curricula serve best (if they are appropriate at all) as a scaffold for the new understandings of self that students are developing.

Other ways of using narratives in the classroom focus even more directly on the telling of personal stories. In diaries and journals, for instance, the curriculum is constructed, at least in part, from the actual life experiences of the writer her- or himself. Instead of mediating external curricular material, as Makler's earlier example suggests, this form of personal narrative allows students to tell their own stories, understanding that the act is purposeful and creative, and it has consequences. Journaling is a good example of personal narrative writing, and many teachers have used it to help students make conscious decisions about the meanings they create out of their own experience. Joanne Cooper (1991) describes her use of journals as illuminating not only the construction of a life's meaning, but also its future and purpose.

Writing a diary or journal is a powerful form of narrative in which we tell our own stories, allowing us to rethink our past, our present, and our future selves. It is a kind of journey, a journey from one moment to the next, from one entry to the next. We literally write our own stories, simultaneously incorporating our own future, as we reconstruct our past. . . . It is through telling our own stories that we learn who we are and what we need. Journal writers, through describing the reality of their daily lives, discover their own voices and simultaneously witness to future generations. (pp. 98–99)

The emancipatory power of this writing lies in its recognition of the capacity of every individual to be an author in the deepest sense of (re)creating his or her own identity and sense of purpose. To say that such concerns are outside the bounds (the "scope and sequence") of the school curriculum does not eliminate them; it merely covers them up and makes it more difficult for students and teachers alike to find the common ground of their pursuit.

Creating the self in relation to others. Just as personal narratives can be used to explore issues of self-identity and self-expression, they may also be used to illuminate relationships between individuals. These relationships can be between peers, between teachers and students, between children and parents, or in virtually any shared context that calls for mutual awareness and understanding. Writing personal narratives can help individuals communicate with others about complex issues and help them find shared concerns in unfamiliar or stressful circumstances.

After using fictional historical figures to inspire the narratives described above, Andra Makler (1991) had her students "confront their own realities—to research the history by which members of their own families (or family of their choice) had come to the United States and to the particular place they found themselves today" (p. 30). In making this request, Makler tried to help her students begin to see the web of historical connections that actually exist in their own lives; it helped them see the connections they had with others and the ways that these experiences overlapped and contrasted. Just as significantly, it also confirmed for Makler (1991) that students and teachers benefited from joining together in this process; through it she recognized that the relationship between teachers and students should be one of "interdependent knowers."

Students found this project interesting; they entered into dialogue with parents at home and telephoned and wrote to other relatives in distant states and foreign countries. They brought their stories to class and discussed their findings among themselves; they explored differences and similarities between their real family's history and that of friends. . . . I was surprised by the power of this curriculum, by the level of interest it generated among students and their families, by the change it provoked in the atmosphere of my classroom. It confirmed my suspicion that teachers and students are indeed interdependent knowers, learning to construct relationships to each other as much as to the subjects they study. (pp. 30–31)

Along with the recognition that narrative provides a way for teachers to develop deeper and more collaborative relationships with their students has come the realization that personal narratives written by teachers also have great potential for supporting constructive dialogue among their peers. As teachers have written more about their own practice in the classroom, these narratives have provided rich opportunities for learning from each other (Schubert & Ayers, 1992) and for initiating and guiding school reform efforts (Gitlin et al., 1992). Even the voices of preservice teachers have emerged in narratives about the nature of teaching and becoming a teacher (Clandinin, Davies, Hogan, & Kennard, 1993; Knowles, Cole, & Presswood, 1994). In all of these cases, teachers, like their students, were empowered through the act of self-representation; personal narratives provided a context in which to explore the important connection between self-identity and professional practice.

The importance of helping us to see ourselves and our projects in relation to others cannot be underestimated, especially during a time in this nation's history when competitive individualism is reinforced on so many cultural, political, and economic levels. Emancipatory educational practice should give students the opportunity to explore how these values and assumptions have come to prominence in our society and how collective action can change them. This shared sense of responsibility and power is essential to communicate in an emancipatory school. Thus, students must be able to find within their schools the kind of activities and sense of community (i.e., the circumstances) that support an education for autonomy.

The politics of the narrative. While my description of the role played by narrative began with the personal, it moved quickly to reflect the necessity of shared constructions of knowledge and meaning. Such constructions, as we saw in the case of culturally relevant pedagogy, are inherently political; they always connect to the outside community or society in some way. I want to make even more explicit here, however, the political dimension of a pedagogy that includes or emphasizes a narrative component. The main point of this argument is consistent with the very foundation of emancipatory educational theory, namely, that the act of meaning making in a community will always take place in relation to existing structures of power and status. The new forms of knowledge that narratives represent can give existing social structures greater weight, or they can contest these constructions and offer new, perhaps more emancipatory, alternatives.

Students build the capacity for autonomy when they are given the opportunity to make connections between their own narratives and the socially constructed and sanctioned meanings that they see written across the pages of their textbooks and that they hear on the evening news. We have considered Lisa Delpit's persuasive arguments for the need to make the culture of power explicit in classrooms, especially for those students who have been excluded from it. Delpit's work testifies to the fact that our understanding and use of narrative must itself confront political questions of power and social change. While all narratives have their own inherent dignity and worth regardless of their valuation by other cultural groups, students (and teachers of students) outside of the culture of power ignore these judgments at their own peril. Advocating the use of narrative in emancipatory schools, for students who do not arrive with the trappings of the culture of power, means walking a fine line between pride and knowledge of self on the one hand, and an awareness of and facility with the tools of an oppressor culture on the other.

Delpit gives a number of examples of how the teachers with whom she worked were able to walk this difficult line, by acknowledging the power of the personal and the necessity of the political. One of the most explicit and interesting examples of this kind of emancipatory pedagogy is from a teacher named Martha Demientieff, who works with her students to understand the differences between, and the different purposes of, their own "Heritage [or Village] English" and the "Formal English" that is required under certain specific circumstances (Delpit, 1988, p. 293). Demientieff reinforces the strength and beauty of her students' Heritage English, while giving them explicit opportunities (and support) for using Formal English in a way that prepares them to interact with others from outside of their local community.

The connections between self-expression and social change are also relevant for teacher narratives. Kathleen Casey (1993) conducted a study in which she looked at the language used by Catholic, secular Jewish, and African American women teachers in describing their conscious efforts to promote social change through classroom practice. As Casey (1993) argues, understanding the teachers' actions through their own narratives was essential for seeing the political dimension of their work.

> I have drawn attention to the ways in which "language is a site of political activity" (Newton and Rosenfelt, 1985: xxi). . . . The discursive contribution of ordinary teachers working for social change cannot be dismissed as merely individual or simply subjective, for these women theorize in active

and reciprocal relationships, as members of an interpretive community, and as part of a living tradition. . . . The particular understandings of the world which these women express in their discourses has been conceived in political practice. Not only do these women (re)create distinctive concepts and metaphors; they (re)produce particular forms of social relations, and they (re)construct specific dimensions of the social environment; they change their own lives and the lives of those with whom they work. New social languages for valuing education are presented in these narratives; and new worldviews, grounded in innovative educational and political projects, are revealed. As they tell the story of their own lives, these women are meaning-makers; they are authors of whole new volumes of social text. It is in all these senses that the women in this study have become "authors"—in the creation and recreation of social meaning through their educational, political, and narrative practices. (p. 165)

The teachers in Casey's study dealt with a wide range of social and institutional constraints, from religious doctrine to racism. What they held in common, according to Casey, was a "positive progressive political passion," which she saw as something both constructed by and expressed through their personal narratives.

Using narratives in the classroom, as well as among teachers, is a powerful tool for developing the capacity for autonomy. Narratives provide a context for writing, speaking, and thinking about the self in a way that illuminates not only the process by which meaning is constructed, but how its social significance is constructed as well. While the use of narrative may at first appear to focus primarily on the individual, this view is ultimately inadequate as an account of its potential contribution to emancipatory schooling. The production, interpretation, and implications of narratives are necessarily shared and, ultimately, can have important and lasting effects in the larger society.

The most important work to be done within the new constellation revolves around schools and what happens to students when they go there. A central aim in developing this framework has been to support the elaboration of instructional practices and changes in the organization of schooling that promote an education for autonomy. As the work represented in this chapter demonstrates, emancipatory educators have long devoted themselves to teaching in ways that build the capacity for critical consciousness and authenticity in their students. In the final chapter of this work, I offer a quick snapshot of the long and rather complex path we have traveled, as a way of summarizing this effort and leaving behind a map that others might use to continue such explorations.

7

Conclusion

Below I summarize the general line of argument advanced in the preceeding six chapters. This summary recapitulates the major steps of the analysis and thus provides an overview of the construction of the new constellation.

AUTONOMY, EMANCIPATORY EDUCATIONAL THEORY, AND THE NEO-CONSERVATIVE AGENDA

My consideration of the role played by autonomy in emancipatory educational theory is motivated by a concern for the way schools affect the choices and projects through which students construct a sense of self. I argue that there are two key dimensions to autonomy: critical consciousness and authenticity. Elaborating these two aspects of autonomy moves us from a narrow and simplistic interpretation of autonomy as noninterference, to a richer and more complex understanding of the way various aspects of social experience condition the capacity of individuals to make choices and pursue particular life-plans. Emancipatory theories of education require that we consider the powerful effects of social structures like gender, race, class, and sexual orientation as part of the background against which we assess the capacity of students to make free and informed decisions about their futures.

Emancipatory theories also require us to look carefully at the relationships that develop between individuals, and the communities that develop within and around schools, to understand how the environment of a school can encourage or inhibit the development of autonomy. Within these relationships and communities, students can find the recognition they need to pursue their diverse life-plans, and enter into the reciprocal relationships with others that this entails, or they can be marginalized in this process and have their capacity for autonomy limited or diminished. Emancipatory theories promote careful consideration of these issues as central to our understanding of educational practice and as necessary for any meaningful assessment of the quality of schooling that an individual or group receives.

The policies and programs supported by neo-conservatives limit the opportunities students have to develop and exercise autonomy, by emphasizing a narrow range of curricular content and instructional methods. Admission to the society that neo-conservatives describe requires a very particular set of qualifications, which, they argue, is most effectively obtained through a transmission-oriented pedagogy. Neo-conservative recommendations virtually ignore or explicitly reject student experience as an important component of the curriculum and place a high value on the capacity of students to accumulate the kind of knowledge or information that has been identified by cultural leaders as having high social status.

This approach makes it unlikely that educators will find much value in the kind of open-ended dialogue or classroom activities that begin with student experience, and unlikely that curricular issues will often be framed in any complex or critical way in relation to the distinctive identities students bring to school. This turning away from social context, based on the appeal to clearly and culturally delineated content, is highly problematic. It leads neo-conservatives, for example, to ignore or avoid questions about what it means for minority students to experience the "common" curriculum and adopt its meanings and values. Under these circumstances, difference turns all too easily into deficit, and assimilationist educational norms undercut the integrity and value of minority social identities. The approach advocated by neo-conservatives is least likely to educate students for autonomy and strongly favors the reproduction of existing social hierarchies.

UNIVERSALIST EMANCIPATORY THEORIES AND CRITICAL CONSCIOUSNESS

I identify universalist approaches in this analysis, based on their common commitment to generalizable moral principles and abstract accounts of human conduct, as the primary foundation upon which to understand social relations and institutions. The power of universalist theories turns largely on their generalizability. Consequently, there is an emphasis in them on constructing principles that are sufficiently abstract to guide our understanding of social relations under widely varying circumstances (i.e., independent of the particular persons or relationships concerned), and on using hypothetical models of human conduct to illuminate moral decision making. Critics of universalist theories dispute the adequacy of these models because of their abstraction from the local contexts and relationships in which our lives are actually lived.

In response to these criticisms, liberal and critical theorists have pushed the roots of universalist approaches deeper into the local circumstances in which our identity and relationships are constructed. Liberal and critical theorists have recognized the importance of describing oppression and exploitation in terms of the distinctive circumstances of a given time and place, and the multiplicity of factors that condition our social relations. For liberals (e.g., Howe, 1997; Kymlicka, 1991), this development has involved a more careful consideration of the "context of choice" and the way this context influences the meaning of opportunities that are available to individuals in society. For critical theorists (e.g., Apple, 1993, 1996), who already possess a more socially contextualized view, this line of development involves reaching beyond the analysis of class to understand other features of social experience as a basis for particular forms of oppression (e.g., by gender, race, sexual orientation, etc.).

Based on this analysis, and as a first step in building the new constellation, I argue for critical consciousness as an aspect of autonomy that helps illuminate the shared insights of liberal and critical theories, while also providing them with a way to extend their analyses in the direction of the local or particular. On this account, critical consciousness can be understood as a capacity that allows individuals to reflect on their construction of identity and pursuit of a life-plan in relation to the broad social structures of meaning that enable and constrain these efforts. Critical consciousness involves more than *self*-reflection, however. It also includes, indeed emphasizes, an awareness of the connections that exist between one's own sense of identity and the relative position of others in society who share a similar position with respect to, for instance, their race, gender, or class. Critical consciousness thus supports individual insights about the construction of identity and the pursuit of diverse life-plans, as well as showing how these insights might bring individuals together in emancipatory communities.

PARTICULARIST THEORIES AND AUTHENTICITY

Particularist theories resist the appeal of generalizability in an effort to confront the world in all of its local and inescapably rich detail. Notwithstanding the hyperskepticism critics have accused it of promoting (a charge with which I express some sympathy), postmodernism contributes to emancipatory educational theory by focusing its attention on the local in a way that helps us better understand how institutions constrain the autonomy of individuals through various forms of self-regulation and through the tacit internalization of social norms (e.g., Ellsworth, 1992; Popkewitz, 1991). Postmodern analyses of the relationship between power and knowledge aim at exposing oppressive "regimes of truth" through a kind of critical unveiling or demystification. Despite the similarity between this language and that of critical theory, postmodernists reject metanarratives like Marxism as "terroristic," and they ground their activism in the local, fragmented world of multiple perspectives and unstable identities.

Caring, on the other hand, directs our attention to the particular or local by exploring the qualities associated with our most significant relationships with specific others. Care theorists focus on our commitment to particular persons (lovers, friends, students) and give us a way to describe communities in which caring can be practiced and sustained. The construction of self-identity through the plans and projects that individuals pursue depends on what others do to acknowledge and support these efforts. Caring helps us understand the complexity of the dialogical or collaborative relations between individuals, and gives us good reason to look at emancipatory social institutions in terms of their capacity to build relations based on recognition and reciprocity. Thus, like postmodernism, theories of care describe a quality of local association that supports the efforts of individuals to pursue diverse life-plans under circumstances that acknowledge and extend their choices. These circumstances build the capacity for authenticity, the aspect of autonomy I use to illuminate the shared insights of particularist approaches.

Authenticity is a capacity that helps us understand ourselves, our sense of self-identity, as something original and unique (Taylor, 1991). It includes an awareness that the sense of originality or uniqueness we experience both shapes our life-plan and is, in turn, shaped by our pursuit of this plan in a local context or community where others acknowledge us for who we are and participate constructively in our projects. Foregrounding authenticity is a way of recognizing the key role played by our relationships with others and, in particular, the kinds of dialogical relationships that are rooted in the circumstances of a particular time and place. Authenticity depends on conditions (including institutions) that support and sustain communities in which individuals share a common commitment to recognition and reciprocity. Because the local circumstances of our deliberation over possible choices have such a dramatic effect on our capacity to envision and carry out alternative plans, it is especially important to create schools that build the capacity for authenticity among students who have been excluded or marginalized by the current norms of cultural membership and success.

CRITICAL CONSCIOUSNESS AND AUTHENTICITY
IN THE NEW CONSTELLATION

Having appealed to critical consciousness as a way of describing the shared insights of universalist theories, and using authenticity in a similar way with respect to particularist theories, I then consider the relationship between these two general approaches. The strategy I develop here is rooted in the complementary strengths and weaknesses of critical consciousness and authenticity. I focus on the relationship between these two aspects of autonomy, showing how each is incomplete without the support of the other. Using the metaphor of the new constellation as a map for navigating among emancipatory theories, I argue that no matter where we begin (with a universalist or particularist approach), we are pulled back in the direction of the other perspective and the complementary aspect of autonomy.

In the case of universalist theories, I argue that critical consciousness requires the complementary capacity of authenticity in order to assess and (if necessary) reconstruct communities around the insights generated by critical consciousness. Considering the education of minority students, for example, I argue that critical consciousness without authenticity leads to a self-defeating form of resistance that also has the unintended result of reinforcing the same stereotypes that support current explanations of low school performance among minority students as evidence of their deficiencies (of intellectual ability, character, quality of home life, etc.). Building the capacity for authenticity justifies and enables the explicit reconsideration of community norms (especially as they relate to group identity in this case) and the relation of these norms to autonomy. My treatment of this example begins by appealing to a universalist line of argument, based on critical consciousness, and then moves in the direction of a particularist perspective that emphasizes the importance of authenticity. In the end, *both* are required in order to address the issue adequately.

With respect to particularist theories, I argue that authenticity requires the complementary capacity for critical consciousness in order to determine whether actions and relations within communities are truly emancipatory when considered in relation to the social structures that characterize the broader society. As an example, I look at suggestions for sex-segregated science instruction as an educational reform rooted in a concern for authenticity. Inquiring into the goals of this proposal quickly delivers us to a consideration of the rationale for seeking to increase the number of women in science in the first place. My analysis of this question suggests that, without building the capacity for critical consciousness, sex-segregated science education is likely to have little effect on women's achievement in science or on the conduct of science generally in society. Furthermore, it is even possible that, without educating for autonomy in a way that includes critical consciousness, proposals for sex-segregated education may even reinforce existing social hierarchies and deflect future attempts at reform.

Based on this analysis, I argue that critical consciousness and authenticity constitute a powerful foundation for the new constellation. Rather than promoting a specific emancipatory theory itself, the new constellation provides a context in which diverse approaches can develop more satisfactory ways of dealing with their theoretical conflicts and more effective ways of implementing their combined insights in practice. As a way of showing how theoretical work might advance within the new constellation, I offer two examples of concepts that are important to emancipatory educational theory and that can be extended by the analysis I provide. Social structure and community are concepts that I argue both benefit from, and contribute to, my elaboration of critical consciousness and authenticity. I utilize both in my consideration of emancipatory schooling, and my description of alternative emancipatory approaches to curriculum and pedagogy.

EDUCATIONAL POLICY AND PRACTICE IN THE NEW CONSTELLATION

Emancipatory theories of education concern themselves with how schooling affects the relative status of groups that are oppressed or marginalized in society. The new constellation attempts to reconceptualize the parameters of these theories in a way that makes them better able to account for the experiences and perspectives of students who have been excluded from the process by which educational norms and opportunities are defined. It should also be clear, however, that I am proposing a general approach to education that *all* students deserve and that *all* students would benefit from receiving. Emancipatory educational reforms should be directed at supporting and sustaining the capacity for autonomy in all students, through the creation of circumstances in which critical consciousness and authenticity can be developed and practiced.

The obstacles to emancipatory educational reform are formidable, but not insurmountable. It is important to overcome the idea that emancipatory schools are a utopian dream that sacrifices pragmatic ideas about reform for theoretical purity. In response to the neo-conservatives, I offer a range of pedagogical strategies aimed at reconstructing subject matter in the social context of experience, giving serious attention to the role of culture in schooling, and calling on the voices and stories of students to be a central part of the curriculum.

The practices to which I appeal in this section are not, taken individually, new or original in the new constellation; in fact, the point of drawing them out of the current educational literature is to show that powerful examples of emancipatory pedagogy exist. What these practices lack, however, is a sufficiently flexible and powerful framework that that might bring them together and give them a common theoretical grounding. One of the most important achievements of the new constellation is its ability to provide this kind of consistent justification and, in doing so, provide new and better reasons for working to see that emancipatory practices are implemented (hopefully in concert) in our schools. Such reforms will depend on the courage and skill of teachers, of course, as they always have, which accounts for the focus on issues of curricular and pedagogical reform in Chapter 6. The new constellation will help improve education only if it can help bring theory(ies) and practice(s) together in a way that better supports educating all students for autonomy.

References

Alexander, J. C. (1988). *Action and its environments: Toward a new synthesis.* New York: Columbia University Press.

Anyon, J. (1980). Social class and the hidden curriculum of work. *Journal of Education, 162,* 67–92.

Apple, M. W. (1979). *Ideology and curriculum.* New York: Routledge & Kegan Paul.

Apple, M. W. (1993). *Official knowledge: Democratic education in a conservative age.* New York: Routledge.

Apple, M. W. (Ed.). (1996). *Cultural politics and education.* New York: Teachers College Press.

Apple, M. W., & Beane, J. A. (1995). *Democratic schools.* Alexandria, VA: Association for Supervision and Curriculum Development.

Apple, M. W., & Zenk, C. (1996). American realities: Poverty, economy, and education. In M. W. Apple (Ed.), *Cultural politics and education* (pp. 68–90). New York: Teachers College Press.

Arnault, L. S. (1989). The radical future of a classic moral theory. In A. M. Jaggar & S. Bordo (Eds.), *Gender/body/knowledge* (pp. 188–207). New Brunswick, NJ: Rutgers University Press.

Aronowitz, S., & Giroux, H. A. (1991). *Postmodern education: Politics, culture, and social criticism.* Minneapolis: University of Minnesota Press.

Ayers, W. (1993). *To teach: The journey of a teacher.* New York: Teachers College Press.

Baier, A. C. (1985). What do women want in a moral theory? *Nous, 19*(1), 53–63.

Baier, A. C. (1987). The need for more than justice. In M. Hanen & K. Nielsen (Eds.), *Science, morality, and feminist theory* (pp. 41–59). Calgary, Canada: University of Calgary Press.

Banks, J. A. (1994). *An introduction to multicultural education.* Needham Heights, MA: Allyn & Bacon.

Barber, B. R. (1992). *An aristocracy of everyone: The politics of education and the future of America.* Oxford, UK: Oxford University Press.

Bartky, S. L. (1990). *Femininity and domination: Studies in the phenomenology of oppression.* New York: Routledge.

Bastian, A., Fruchter, N., Gittell, M., Greer, C., & Haskins, K. (1986). *Choosing equality: The case for democratic schooling.* Philadelphia: Temple University Press.

Belenky, M. F., Clinchy, B. M., Goldberger, N. R., & Tarule, J. M. (1986). *Women's ways of knowing: The development of self, voice, and mind.* New York: Basic Books.

Bell, D. (1992). *Faces at the bottom of the well: The permanence of racism.* New York: Basic Books.

Bennett, W. J. (1987). *James Madison high school: A curriculum for American students.* Washington, DC: U.S. Department of Education.

Bennett, W. J. (1988, December). Moral literacy and the formation of character. *NASSP Bulletin, 72* (512), 29–34.

Bennett, W. J. (1992). *The de-valuing of America: The fight for our culture and our children.* New York: Summit Books.

Bernstein, R. J. (1992). *The new constellation: The ethical-political horizons of modernity/postmodernity.* Cambridge, MA: MIT Press.

Beyer, L. E. (1996). *Creating democratic classrooms: The struggle to integrate theory and practice.* New York: Teachers College Press.

Beyer, L. E., & Liston, D. P. (1996). *Curriculum in conflict: Social visions, educational agendas, and progressive school reform.* New York: Teachers College Press.

Bloom, A. (1987). *The closing of the American mind.* New York: Simon & Schuster.

Bordo, S. (1990). Feminism, postmodernism, and gender-scepticism. In L. J. Nicholson (Ed.), *Feminism/Postmodernism* (pp. 133–157). New York: Routledge.

Bowles, S., & Gintis, H. (1976). *Schooling in capitalist America: Educational reform and the contradictions of economic life.* New York: Basic Books.

Burbules, N. C. (1993). *Dialogue in teaching: Theory and practice.* New York: Teachers College Press.

Butler, J. (1990). *Gender trouble.* New York: Routledge, Chapman & Hall.

Carnoy, M., & Levin, H. (1985). *Schooling and work in the democratic state.* Stanford: Stanford University Press.

Casey, K. (1993). *I answer with my life: Life histories of women teachers working for social change.* New York: Routledge.

Cherryholmes, C. (1988). *Power and criticism: Poststructural investigations in education.* New York: Teachers College Press.

Chun, K. (1995). The myth of Asian American success and its educational ramifications. In D. T. Nakanishi & T. Y. Nishida (Eds.), *The Asian American educational experience* (pp. 95–113). New York: Routledge.

Clandinin, J., Davies, A., Hogan, P., & Kennard, B. (Eds.). (1993). *Learning to teach, teaching to learn: Stories of collaboration in teacher education.* New York: Teachers College Press.

Cooper, J. (1991). Telling our own stories: The reading and writing of journals or diaries. In C. Witherell & N. Noddings (Eds.), *Stories lives tell: Narrative and dialogue in education* (pp. 96–113). New York: Teachers College Press.

Delpit, L. D. (1986). Skills and other dilemmas of a progressive black educator. *Harvard Educational Review, 56*(4), 379–385.

Delpit, L. D. (1988). The silenced dialogue: Power and pedagogy in educating other people's children. *Harvard Educational Review, 58*(3), 280–298.

Delpit, L. D. (1995). *Other people's children: Cultural conflict in the classroom.* New York: New Press.

Dewey, J. (1956). *The child and the curriculum.* Chicago: University of Chicago Press. (Original work published 1902)

Dewey, J. (1980). *The public and its problems.* Athens, Ohio: Swallow Press. (Original work published 1927)

Diller, A. (1996a). The ethics of care and education: A new paradigm, its critics, and its educational significance. In A. Diller, B. Houston, K. P. Morgan, & M.

Ayim (Eds.), *The gender question in education: Theory, pedagogy, and politics* (pp. 89–105). Boulder, CO: Westview Press.

Diller, A. (1996b). An ethics of care takes on pluralism. In A. Diller, B. Houston, K. P. Morgan, & M. Ayim (Eds.), *The gender question in education: Theory, pedagogy, and politics* (pp. 161–170). Boulder, CO: Westview Press.

Ellsworth, E. (1992). Why doesn't this feel empowering? Working through the repressive myths of critical pedagogy. In C. Luke & J. Gore (Eds.), *Feminisms and critical pedagogy* (pp. 90–120). New York: Routledge.

Elster, J. (1985). *Making sense of Marx*. Cambridge: Cambridge University Press.

Faludi, S. (1991). *Backlash: The undeclared war against American women*. New York: Crown.

Fine, M. (1992). *Disruptive voices: The possibilities of feminist research*. Ann Arbor: University of Michigan Press.

Finn, C. E., Jr. (1991). *We must take charge: Our schools and our future*. New York: Free Press.

Fiol-Matta, L., & Chamberlain, M. K. (Eds.). (1994). *Women of color and the multicultural curriculum: Transforming the college curriculum*. New York: Feminist Press (CUNY).

Foley, D. E. (1990). *Learning capitalist culture: Deep in the heart of Tejas*. Philadelphia: University of Pennsylvania Press.

Fordham, S., & Ogbu, J. U. (1986). Black students' school success: Coping with the burden of "acting white." *The Urban Review, 18*(3), 176–206.

Foucault, M. (1972). *The archeology of knowledge*. New York: Pantheon Books.

Foucault, M. (1978). *The history of sexuality*, (Vol. 1). New York: Vintage Books.

Foucault, M. (1979). *Discipline and punish*. New York: Vintage Books.

Foucault, M. (1980). *Power/Knowledge*. New York: Pantheon Books.

Fraser, N., & Nicholson, L. J. (1990). Social criticism without philosophy: An encounter between feminism and postmodernism. In L. J. Nicholson (Ed.), *Feminism/Postmodernism* (pp. 19–39). New York: Routledge.

Freire, P. (1970). *Pedagogy of the oppressed*. New York: Continuum.

Freire, P. (1985). *The politics of education: Culture, power, and education*. Granby, MA: Bergin & Garvey.

Freire, P. (1992). *Education for critical consciousness*. New York: Continuum.

Friedman, M. (1989). Feminism and modern friendship: Dislocating the community. *Ethics, 99*, 275–290.

Friedman, M. (1991). The social self and the partiality debates. In C. Card (Ed.), *Feminist ethics* (pp. 161–180). Lawrence: University Press of Kansas.

Friedman, M. (1993). Beyond caring: The de-moralization of gender. In M. J. Larrabee (Ed.), *An ethic of care: Feminist and interdisciplinary perspectives* (pp. 258–275). New York: Routledge.

Giddens, A. (1979). *Central problems in social theory*. London: Macmillan.

Gilligan, C. (1982). *In a different voice*. Cambridge, MA: Harvard University Press.

Giroux, H. A. (1992). *Border crossings: Cultural workers and the politics of education*. New York: Routledge.

Giroux, H. A., & McLaren, P. (1994). *Between borders: Pedagogy and the politics of cultural studies*. New York: Routledge.

Gitlin, A., Bringhurst, K., Burns, M., Cooley, V., Myers, B., Price, K., Russell, R., &

Tiess, P. (1992). *Teachers' voices for school change: An introduction to educative research.* New York: Teachers College Press.

Gould, S. J. (1996). *The mismeasure of man.* New York: Norton.

Gutmann, A. (1987). *Democratic education.* Princeton, NJ: Princeton University Press.

Harding, S. (1991). *Whose science? Whose knowledge?* Ithaca, NY: Cornell University Press.

Hartsock, N. (1990). Foucault on power: A theory for women? In L. J. Nicholson (Ed.), *Feminism/Postmodernism* (pp. 157–176). New York: Routledge.

Heath, S. B. (1983). *Ways with words: Language, life, and work in communities and classrooms.* Cambridge, UK: Cambridge University Press.

Held, V. (1987). Non-contractual society. In M. Hanen & K. Nielsen (Eds.), *Science, morality, and feminist theory* (pp. 111–139). Calgary, Canada: University of Calgary Press.

Held, V. (1993). *Feminist morality: Transforming culture, society, and politics.* Chicago: University of Chicago Press.

Held, V. (Ed.). (1995). *Justice and care: Essential readings in feminist ethics.* Boulder, CO: Westview Press.

Herrnstein, R. J., & Murray, C. (1994). *The bell curve: Intelligence and class structure in American life.* New York: Free Press.

Hirsch, E. D., Jr. (1987a). *Cultural literacy: What every American needs to know.* Boston: Houghton Mifflin.

Hirsch, E. D., Jr. (1987b, December/January). Restoring cultural literacy in the early grades. *Educational Leadership,* pp. 63–70.

Hirsch, E. D., Jr. (1993). *What your first-grader needs to know: Fundamentals of a good first-grade education.* New York: Dell.

Hirsch, E. D., Jr. (1996). *The schools we need: Why we don't have them.* New York: Doubleday.

Hirsch, E. D., Jr. & Holdren, J. (1996). *Books to build on: A grade-by-grade resource guide for parents and teachers.* New York: Doubleday.

Hirsch, E. D., Jr. & Kett, J. F., Trefil, J., & Hirsch, E. D. (1993). *The dictionary of cultural literacy.* Boston: Houghton Mifflin.

Hoagland, S. L. (1991). Some thoughts about "caring." In C. Card (Ed.), *Feminist ethics* (pp. 246–265). Lawrence: University Press of Kansas.

Holland, D.C., & Eisenhart, M. A. (1990). *Educated in romance: Women, achievement, and college culture.* Chicago: University of Chicago Press.

hooks, b. (1994a). *Outlaw culture: Resisting representations.* New York: Routledge.

hooks, b. (1994b). *Teaching to transgress: Education as the practice of freedom.* New York: Routledge.

Houston, B. (1987). Rescuing womanly virtues: Some dangers of moral reclamation. In M. Hanen & K. Nielson (Eds.), *Science, morality, and feminist theory* (pp. 237–265). Calgary, Canada: University of Calgary Press.

Houston, B. (1996). Gender freedom and the subtleties of sexist education. In A. Diller, B. Houston, K. P. Morgan, & M. Ayim (Eds.), *The gender question in education: Theory, pedagogy, and politics* (pp. 50–64). Boulder, CO: Westview Press.

Howe, K. R. (1994). Standards, assessment, and equality of educational opportunity. *Educational Researcher, 23*(8), 27–33.

Howe, K. R. (1997). *Understanding equal educational opportunity: Social justice, democracy, and schooling.* New York: Teachers College Press.

Hoy, D. C. (Ed.) (1986). *Foucault: A critical reader.* Cambridge, MA: Basil Blackwell.

Jaggar, A. (1983). *Feminist politics and human nature.* Sussex, UK: Harvester Press.

Josselson, R., & Lieblich, A. (1993). *The narrative study of lives.* Newbury Park, CA: Sage.

Knowles, J. G., & Cole, A., with Presswood, C. (1994). *Through preservice teachers' eyes: Exploring field experiences through narrative and inquiry.* New York: Macmillan.

Kozol, J. (1991). *Savage inequalities: Children in America's schools.* New York: Crown.

Kymlicka, W. (1991). *Liberalism, community, and culture.* Oxford: Oxford University Press.

Kymlicka, W. (1995). *Multicultural citizenship.* Oxford: Oxford University Press.

Ladson-Billings, G. (1994). *The dreamkeepers: Successful teachers of African American students.* San Francisco: Jossey-Bass.

Larraine, J. (1983). *Marxism and ideology.* Atlantic Highlands, NJ: Humanities Press.

Lather, P. (1991). *Getting smart: Feminist research and pedagogy with/in the postmodern.* New York: Routledge.

Layder, D. (1990). *The realist image in social science.* New York: St. Martin's Press.

Liston, D., & Fletcher, S. (1992). Turning in(to) stories: A critique of the postmodern turn. *Review of Education, 14,* 215–222.

Luke, C., & Gore, J. (Eds). (1992). *Feminisms and critical pedagogy.* New York: Routledge.

Lyotard, J. (1979). *The postmodern condition: A report on knowledge* (G. Bennington & B. Massumi, Trans.). Minneapolis: University of Minnesota Press.

Maher, F. A., & Tetreault, M. K. T. (1994). *The feminist classroom.* New York: Basic Books.

Makler, A. (1991). Imagining history: A good story and a well-formed argument. In C. Witherell & N. Noddings (Eds.), *Stories lives tell: Narrative and dialogue in education* (pp. 29–48). New York: Teachers College Press.

Martin, E. (1987). *The woman in the body.* Boston: Beacon Press.

Martin, J. R. (1981). The ideal of the educated person. *Educational Theory, 31*(2), 97–109.

Martin, J. R. (1992). *The schoolhome.* Cambridge, MA: Harvard University Press.

Martin, J. R. (1994). Two dogmas of curriculum. In J. R. Martin (Ed.), *Changing the educational landscape: Philosophy, women, and curriculum* (pp. 187–199). New York: Routledge.

McCarthy, C., & Apple, M. W. (1988). Race, class, and gender in American educational research: Toward a nonsynchronous parallelist position. In L. Weis (Ed.), *Class, race, and gender in American education* (pp. 9–43). Albany: State University of New York Press.

McCarthy, C., & Crichlow, W. (Eds.). (1993). *Race, identity, and representation in education.* New York: Routledge.

McLaren, P. (1995). *Critical pedagogy and predatory culture: Oppositional politics in a postmodern era.* New York: Routledge.

McNeil, L. M. (1981). Negotiating classroom knowledge: Beyond achievement and socialization. *Curriculum Studies, 13,* 313–328.

McNeil, L. M. (1988). *Contradictions of control: School structure and school knowledge.* New York: Routledge.

McRobbie, A. (1991). *Feminism and youth culture: From Jackie to just seventeen.* Boston: Unwin Hyman.

Meier, D. (1995). *The power of their ideas: Lessons for America from a small school in Harlem.* Boston: Beacon Press.

Middleton, S. (1993). *Educating feminists: Life histories and pedagogy.* New York: Teachers College Press.

Morrison, T. (1992). *Race-ing, justice, en-gendering power: Essays on Anita Hill, Clarence Thomas, and the construction of social reality.* New York: Pantheon Books.

Morrison, T., & Brodsky-Lacour, C. (1997). *Birth of a nation'hood: Gaze, script, and spectacle in the O. J. Simpson case.* New York: Pantheon Books.

National Center for Education Statistics (1996). *Digest of education statistics 1996.* Washington, DC: Author. Available: http://nces.ed.gov

National Commission on Excellence in Education. (1983). *A nation at risk.* Washington, DC: U.S. Government Printing Office.

Neill, A. S. (1960). *Summerhill: A radical approach to child rearing.* New York: Simon & Schuster.

Newton, J., & Rosenfelt, D. (1985). Introduction: Towards a materialist-feminist criticism. In J. Newton & D. Rosenfelt (Eds.), *Feminist criticism and social change: Sex, class, and race in literature* (pp. i-xxxix). New York: Methuen.

Nieto, S. (1996). *Affirming diversity: The sociopolitical context of multicultural education* (rev. ed.). New York: Longman.

Nobles, W. (1973). Psychological research and the black self-concept: A critical review. *Journal of Social Issues, 29*(1), 11–31.

Noddings, N. (1984). *Caring: A feminine approach to ethics and moral education.* Berkeley: University of California Press.

Noddings, N. (1992). *The challenge to care in schools: An alternative approach to education.* New York: Teachers College Press.

Oakes, J. (1985). *Keeping track: How schools structure inequality.* New Haven, CT: Yale University Press.

Oakes, J. (1990). Opportunities, achievement, and choice: Women and minorities in science and mathematics. *Review of Research in Education, 16,* 153–222. Washington, DC: American Educational Research Association.

Oakes, J., Ormseth, T., Bell, R., & Camp, P. (1990). *Multiplying inequalities: The effects of race, social class and tracking on opportunities to learn mathematics and science.* Washington, DC: Rand Corporation.

Ogbu, J. U. (1988). Class stratification, racial stratification, and schooling. In L. Weis (Ed.), *Class, race, and gender in American education* (pp. 163–183). Albany: State University of New York Press.

Paley, V. G. (1979). *White teacher.* Cambridge, MA: Harvard University Press.

Palmer, B. D. (1990). *Descent into discourse: The reification of language and the writing of social history.* Philadelphia: Temple University Press.

Pateman, C. (1979). *The problem of political obligation: A critique of liberal theory.* Berkeley: University of California Press.

Peffer, R. G. (1990). *Marxism, morality, and social justice.* Princeton, NJ: Princeton University Press.

Popkewitz, T. S. (1991). *A political sociology of educational reform: Power/Knowledge in teaching, teacher education, and research.* New York: Teachers College Press.

Ravitch, D. (1990, Summer). Multiculturalism: E pluribes pluribes. *The American Scholar,* pp. 337–354.

Rawls, J. (1971). *A theory of justice.* Cambridge, MA: Harvard University Press.

Riessman, C. K. (1993). *Narrative analysis.* Newbury Park, CA: Sage.

Rodriguez, R. (1982). *Hunger of memory: The education of Richard Rodriguez.* New York: Bantam Books.

Rowan, C. T. (1996). *The coming race war in America: A wake-up call.* Boston: Little, Brown.

Ruddick, S. (1989). *Maternal thinking.* New York: Ballantine Books.

Sadker, M., & Sadker, D. (1994). *Failing at fairness: How America's schools cheat girls.* New York: Scribner's.

Schlesinger, A. M., Jr. (1992). *The disuniting of America: Reflections on a multicultural society.* New York: Norton.

Schoem, D. (Ed.). (1991). *Inside separate worlds: Life stories of young Blacks, Jews, and Latinos.* Ann Arbor: University of Michigan Press.

Schubert, W. H., & Ayers, W. C. (1992). *Teacher lore: Learning from our experience.* New York: Longman.

Schultze, C. L. (1996, October). Economic reality vs. campaign rhetoric (Brookings Institute Policy Brief No. 6). Available: http://www.brook.edu

Shklar, J. N. (1989). The liberalism of fear. In N. L. Rosenblum (Ed.), *Liberalism and the moral life* (pp. 21–39). Cambridge, MA: Harvard University Press.

Shor, I. (1986). *Culture wars: School and society in the conservative restoration 1969–1984.* New York: Routledge & Kegan Paul.

Shor, I. (1992). *Empowering education: Critical teaching for social change.* Chicago: University of Chicago Press.

Sizer, T. R. (1984). *Horace's compromise: The dilemma of the American high school.* Boston: Houghton Mifflin.

Sizer, T. R. (1992). *Horace's school: Redesigning the American high school.* Boston: Houghton Mifflin.

Sleeter, C. E. (1991). *Empowerment through multicultural education.* Albany: State University of New York Press.

Stone, L. (1993). Disavowing community. In H. A. Alexander (Ed.), *Philosophy of education 1992.* Urbana, IL: Philosophy of Education Society.

Strike, K. A. (1982). *Educational policy and the just society.* Urbana: University of Illinois Press.

Taylor, C. (1985). Foucault on freedom and truth. In *Philosophy and the human sci-*

ences: Philosophical papers 2 (pp. 152–184). Cambridge: Cambridge University Press.

Taylor, C. (1991). *Multiculturalism and "the politics of recognition."* Princeton, NJ: Princeton University Press.

Tronto, J. C. (1993). *Moral boundaries: A political argument for an ethic of care.* New York: Routledge.

Tyack, D., & Hansot, E. (1981). Conflict and consensus in American public education. *Daedalus, 110(3),* 1–25.

Wallace, M. (1990). *Invisibility blues: From pop to theory.* New York: Verso.

Weis, L. (1990). *Working class without work: High school students in a de-industrializing economy.* New York: Routledge.

West, C. (1993). *Race matters.* Boston: Beacon Press.

Willis, P. (1977). *Learning to labor: How working class kids get working class jobs.* New York: Columbia University Press.

Witherell, C., & Noddings, N. (1991). *Stories lives tell: Narrative and dialogue in education.* New York: Teachers College Press.

Young, I. M. (1990). *Justice and the politics of difference.* Princeton, NJ: Princeton University Press.

Index

About the Author

Scott Fletcher is Assistant Professor in the Department of Education at the University of New Hampshire. He teaches graduate and undergraduate courses in the philosophy of education, curriculum theory, and educational foundations. Fletcher also spends considerable time in the field, working with teaching interns at schools in New Hampshire and Maine. Fletcher has been a classroom teacher at the middle and high school levels, and has participated in a variety of local and national school reform efforts, including co-founding and co-directing a regional center for the Coalition of Essential Schools and working with the Annenberg Institute for School Reform.

2712
Gift